DEDICATION

∞∞∞∞∞∞∞∞∞∞∞∞∞∞∞∞∞∞∞∞∞∞∞∞∞∞

I

THIS BOOK IS LOVINGLY dedicated to Miss Katharine Taylor (1889-1960), the author's special education teacher from 1929 to 1936 at School No. Two in Paterson, New Jersey. Miss Taylor proved to be the very SIGNIFICANT teacher for whom Grace Donkersloot had been searching in School No. 15 in Clifton, New Jersey, but never found there. Grace wanted to learn but required the right teacher who could teach her to learn to read in order to read to learn. Miss Taylor ignited candles in the mind of this child who desperately needed a change agent in her young life, both at home and at school.

DEDICATION

II

THIS BOOK IS ALSO lovingly dedicated to nine Seeing Eye dog guides who filled more than sixty-seven years (1940-) with competent, trustworthy, and devoted service. They are:

Rachel, Circle, Esta, Vicki (German boxers)
Dola, Ruthie, Nannett (German shepherds)
Waffle, Esma (Labrador retrievers)

This is *our* story, not exclusively mine. Our story would be incomplete without inclusion of you extremely valuable ladies – with one of you at a time at one end of the leash in your harness and I at the other end of the leash.

PREFACE

WHAT SOME PERSONS VIEW as obstacles others regard as challenges or steppingstones to inviting opportunities. The truth is that human beings have no control over when, where, or in what condition life deposits them at birth. From then on, though, life provides a cafeteria of options from which we select or reject opportunities that may enable us to rise above what some other individuals view as insurmountable barriers or restrictions. It is as though life poses a question: Although your life be fraught with disadvantages and deprivations, what can you do with all the CHOICES available to rise above those circumstances?

Musicians have used the eighty-eight keys of the piano to compose limitless numbers of creations. Just so, our lives are compositions, determined by the rhythm, harmony, style, and melody chosen and waiting for the maestro's downbeat in order to be played and heard.

ONE

DURING THE EARLY DECADES of the twentieth century, school authorities cared little about students' absences, temporary or permanent. In fact, children often quit school well before entering high school in order to help contribute to their family's income by finding paying jobs or by helping their parents as unpaid employees. So was the situation with my father, Martin Donkersloot, who in 1905 at age eleven and after completing sixth grade began working fulltime for his father by delivering materials to construction sites with horse and wagon.

Similarly, my mother, Carrie Van Wageninge, quit school at fourteen to work in a woolen mill to help supplement her father's wages earned in another factory. As the oldest child in her family, she often missed school to help with a new sibling or a sick member of the family; hence, her formal education lacked even more than my father's.

When both of them were twenty-five, they married on May 26, 1920, she quitting the woolen mill to become a full-time housewife.

Their first home, a rental located less than one block from Daddy's parents, was extremely cold and uncomfortable during their first winter together. One evening, out of curiosity, they put a glass of water on the kitchen table. By morning, the water had changed to ice! This was especially difficult for Mamma, who by then was pregnant with my brother. She didn't want a baby to live in such a cold house the next winter. Shortly after my brother's birth in a hospital on May 31, 1921, Daddy, Mamma, and baby Martin moved into a second-floor rental directly across from Daddy's parents home in this Dutch ghetto. Within a short time, Mamma became pregnant again, this time with me. On June 29, 1922, I was born at home.

Mamma's parents lived within walking distance in Passaic, while Daddy's family resided in Clifton, New Jersey. In fact, Daddy had been born in The Netherlands and came to the United States as a babe-in-arms along accompanied by older siblings.

My grandfather, John Donkersloot, had been a supervisor on a farm in Holland; when the owner of the farm sold it, my grandfather was without employment. That fact prompted him to emigrate to seek a better life for his family.

Although Mamma and her parents had been born in the United States, they, too, were of Dutch descent. Thus, I came from very humble beginnings, in a close-knit extended family.

As soon as I started to walk, Mamma noticed that I appeared not to see objects in front of me but bumped into them. If I dropped a toy or tried to find a specific one, I could not see it. She discussed her concerns with Daddy. His first thought was to dismiss her fears because he knew she tended to worry excessively about countless matters. Nevertheless, to help calm Mamma, he improvised a few tests for me, such as having Mamma hold a cookie toward me without speaking. I didn't reach for it.

Now Daddy, too, was troubled. He suggested that they take me to an eye doctor. They did not know the difference between and among ophthalmologist, optometrist, or optician, but referred to all of them as "eye doctors." Perhaps whoever was the family doctor guided them to an ophthalmologist who, after examining me, explained to my parents that my choroids, that should be rich with blood vessels to nourish the eyes, were, instead pale because of insufficient supply of blood vessels. In short, I was blind though I could respond to light.

In addition, my eyes were strabismic. The ophthalmologist advised my parents not to seek surgery.

Mamma and I were immediately tested for syphilis. (Even though I was only two years old, I remember hearing the nurse or technician say "Wassermann," which is the name of the test for syphilis, though I did not know then what it meant.) Because the test results were negative, because I had not been born prematurely, because I had not experienced trauma or illness during my first two years of life, because I had no young, blind relatives, Dr. Glasgow, the ophthalmologist, concluded that I had been born with impaired vision as a birth defect. Because I reacted to light and had strabismus, he prescribed strong lenses, that I began wearing immediately.

To Mamma, this diagnosis was embarrassing and devastating. It was the same as condemning me to a life of helpless dependency upon her for the remainder of my life. Furthermore, as an uneducated person, she assumed that blindness coexisted with mental retardation. Happily for me, Daddy was more optimistic about my future, though lacking factual information. Unhappily for me, I was with Mamma more of the time than with Daddy because of his working away from the house.

Besides being unschooled, Mamma was superstitious and seemed to have only a superficial understanding of Christianity, while considering herself a Christian. Countless times, during our childhood, she referred to God as the One who was watching my brother and me and knew when we had been naughty, and He would punish us. I do not recall having heard that God or Jesus loved us.

Because she had that mindset, I assume that she viewed my blindness as punishment from God for some sin in her past or present life. When I was older but still a child, I heard her tell someone that she had not wanted to be pregnant with me. Then when she learned I was blind, she probably concluded that God was punishing her for not wanting the child He had sent. Burdened with that self-imposed guilt, she probably thought that persons who knew her even casually were also judging her to be a "bad" woman. Altogether, she was unequipped to serve as parent to a blind child. Innumerable times throughout my childhood, she referred to me as "naughty" or "bad" and blamed me for offenses I had not committed. I was a convenient scapegoat.

Daddy, by contrast, investigated before assigning blame or punishing anyone. Mamma did not encourage, commend, or show affection. Because she assumed that I was mentally retarded, she made little effort to teach me anything but reprimanded me when I did something wrong or failed to do the right thing.

From this moment on, I was no longer her darling little girl. Even at this early age, I sensed something was different about me that had caused my mother to change in her relationship with me.

At this juncture, something must be stated about young children's perceptions. Young children view themselves as totally acceptable, complete, normal (even when a part is impaired and that fact is yet unknown to themselves). Then when one or both parents draw away from these children with disabilities, these children assume that they must be bad or naughty children, and that's why Mamma or Daddy does not love them. They are too young to reason: *because I am blind (or deaf, cerebral palsied, ill, have only one normal arm), my parents are sad or distressed, or troubled.* The children cannot separate the parents' pain based on the disability from the pain based on the whole child. Therefore, the children turn the parents' negativity inward on themselves as total beings who are unlovable. Just when these children need demonstrations of parental love and acceptance, some parents are incapable of supporting them with evidence of affection and wholehearted love. Children then draw false conclusions and experience extreme sadness as outsiders, looking in at the family but feeling disconnected from it.

Mamma was pregnant at the time when she learned of my blindness. Over the next few months, she became increasingly tense and irritable. I was too young to comprehend that she feared the child within her might also be blind. Daddy did his best to comfort her, although I am sure he must have experienced many of the same apprehensions. After my sister, Ida, was born, also at home, on December 14, 1924, Mamma was extremely protective of Ida. She hovered over her and watched her every move for signs that would either confirm blindness or deny it. In reality, both Martin and Ida had normal vision.

Because of his growing family, Daddy felt the need to move again. Helped by his relatives, Daddy began building his first house as a new homeowner. We moved into this new house on Christmas Eve Day, 1925 at 535 Highland Avenue, Clifton. By evening the tree was up and trimmed. Mamma was unable to enjoy the excitement of moving day; Ida was very irritable on December 24, unwilling to go to any of the many relatives present, except Mamma, who tried to help move things or unpack even though limited to only one arm with which to work while carrying Ida in the other.

I have many fond memories of this house. It is the only house that I remember vividly as a child. Although it lacked many of the conveniences of that day and luxuries of 1925, I never felt deprived. We had an icebox instead of an electric refrigerator. Our gas stove stood on tall legs, contained limited storage space under the four burners, and held a broiler under the oven that was on the same level as the four burners. On the wall above the stove was a gas jet that was used for emergency illumination when electric power failed. Our living and dining rooms had rugs, not wall-to-wall carpeting. Our three bedrooms upstairs had linoleum floor covering with a throw rug beside each bed. Although the bedrooms had radiators, they were seldom turned on. The one in the bathroom was on all winter. The bathroom had a toilet, a sink with no vanity under it but a medicine cabinet and mirror above, and a bathtub on legs with no shower.

The attic was accessible via a door and two flights of stairs; it was hot in summer and cold in winter. Depending on its temperature, the attic sometimes provided a play area.

The front porch was open but with a roof and provided another play area for children or a sitting space for adults in pleasant weather.

Our entertainment equipment consisted of two separate items: a windup Victrola in my bedroom and a radio in the dining room. The first radio, an Atwater-Kent, had a speaker on top of the wine cabinet with the power source housed in an open metal case inside the wine cabinet. The second radio, modern in 1930, was a Philco, complete in its own cabinet that occupied space atop the wine cabinet, a piece of the dining room suite in which Daddy never stored wine. Seldom did we have wine in the house.

The radio provided much entertainment and information for the family. We children knew that from six forty-five to seven o'clock in the evening was Daddy's exclusive time to listen to Lowell Thomas present the news.

As children, we listened to dramas for youngsters, such as *Jack Armstrong* and programs about cowboys and Indians. Texas was always referred to by the actors as "way out west." In my mind, I had Texas against the Pacific Ocean until geography lessons later taught something different.

Our living room, besides having a rug, had a settee on tall legs and matching chairs, a rectangular library table in the middle of which was a metal Tiffany lamp operated by gas. Later, Daddy wired it for electricity. I still have that lamp today. The room had a few other table lamps and a floor lamp.

An archway between living room and dining room exhibited both rooms simultaneously. The dining room had an expandable table, six matching chairs, the aforementioned wine cabinet, a sideboard, and china hutch above which hung on the wall a windup clock that struck once on the half hour and the appropriate number of times on the hour. On the walls were plate racks where Mamma displayed her prettiest one-of-a-kind plates. In reality, the plate racks became dust-catchers.

At the back of the house behind the dining room was our sun parlor with five windows. In this room initially were Mamma's sewing machine, Daddy's desk and telephone, and sometimes our toys.

On Saturday afternoons, I tried to listen to the Metropolitan Opera House broadcasts from New York with the voice of Milton Cross, who described the opera before each act. Unhappily for me, my family jeered and pretended they could sing opera, louder than the radio. On Sundays, as soon as we returned home from church at noon, I rushed to the radio to tune in the Mormon Tabernacle Choir's broadcast. No one jeered then. On Easter morning, I left my bed early to slip downstairs to listen to sunrise services from Rome, Paris, London, and New York while the family slumbered on, not interrupting my pleasure.

The whole family sat in the dining room to listen to a variety of programs during our childhood years. The radio provided inexpensive entertainment and education; it also demonstrated excellent use of the English language, tragically absent today on radio and television. Parents then had no reason to worry about obscenity and vulgarity being broadcast into children's ears and minds, unlike the situation with TV and radio today. Furthermore, with only one radio and it located in the dining room, parents were aware of the programs we were hearing. Today's children, by contrast, have radio, TV, telephone, cellular phones, and Internet in their bedrooms, away from parental eyes and ears.

The only telephone in our house was of a candlestick design with no dial or buttons. When we picked up the receiver, a woman's voice asked, "Number, please." We then said the number we were calling, such as "PASSAIC 2-5164." She then connected us, which started the other phone ringing. She was alive, not computerized as are many voices on the telephone today. Because our telephone was primarily for Daddy's business, Mart and I were forbidden to use it. Mamma's sister Anna was a telephone operator but not in Clifton.

Early in the morning, the milkman delivered milk in returnable glass bottles. Some grocery stores brought orders to customers' homes, having received the list of items needed by telephone earlier. Mail carriers, usually only men, delivered mail twice a day! In my hometown, with a population of approximately thirty thousand, we could mail a birthday card in the morning and know that the celebrant would receive it in the afternoon of the same day. (By contrast, as an adult, I mailed a check to a plumber in my community, but the mail service took eleven days to reach him with my payment.)

Neighbors knew each other's names, jobs, children's names, churches attended, etc. They socialized with each other by visiting on front porches or in backyards in summer or indoors during winter and watched out for each other's safety.

In those days, most married women were full-time homemakers. Very few drove automobiles. Families usually had only one automobile and maybe a truck for the husband's work.

Children had small toys, such as tricycles, scooters, balls, roller skates, a few table games, and dolls and a carriage but did not have expensive items equivalent to today's computers, trampolines, swimming pools, private phones in the bedroom or cellular phones to carry with them, CD players accompanying them outdoors and plugged into an ear, etc. Mart always wanted an Erector Set and Lincoln Logs but received neither because of prices. He had Tinkertoys instead. The Great Depression was but a few years ahead, and Daddy's work in construction was seasonal at best until it stopped completely. The previous overview was based on our experience in our community, not necessarily a national picture.

Mamma used a non-electric Singer sewing machine with a foot treadle to make clothes or items for the house. Food was prepared from scratch with few, if any, convenience items available. She prepared dough for baking in a non-electric bread mixer. The dough was kneaded by turning a handle at the top of the round bucket until all ingredients were well mixed and formed into a ball. Then the dough rose in that bucket overnight. A woolen shawl, used for this purpose only, covered the bucket to protect the dough from cool drafts while it sat on a shelf protected by three walls. In the morning, Mamma removed the dough from the bucket and divided it into two equal portions. She placed each amount into a bread pan and allowed the dough to rise in its respective bread pan, covered again by the shawl. When the dough filled each pan, Mamma placed both pans inside the preheated oven to bake. The house filled with a wonderful aroma while the bread baked!

When one of the loaves appeared on the table, Mart and I called out, "Crust!" whereupon Daddy sliced off the the crust and gave each of us a half. Daddy loved the crust, too, but rarely had the joy of eating the fresh first slice.

As I am writing these lines on my talking computer, my electric Pillsbury bread baking machine that also talks is preparing a cinnamon/raisin bread. After the kneading and rising phases, the baking stage will produce that delectable aroma of baking bread, described to arouse old memories dormant after all these years! Only once a year at Easter, Mamma made a special bread in the usual way with two additional ingredients and a slight modification. Beforehand, she purchased at the pharmacy a pinch of saffron leaves, derived from the spring flower, the crocus. Her handbag was scented for weeks just because of transporting the leaves from the pharmacy to home.

With the leaves, she brewed a kind of tea with sufficient water to equal the amount she used each time in making two loaves of bread. She strained the tea afterward to exclude the leaves. She also added seedless raisins. In the process, the dough acquired the color of saffron. When fully baked, the bread was luscious in taste, fully aromatic because of the saffron. This annual treat was truly memorable!

The first kitchen table that I remember was a round, wooden one with a pedestal in the center underneath. Coffee was made in a percolator on a burner. The pot had to be monitored to prevent it from spewing water and grounds.

The kitchen had a single sink with a drain-board and basket for placing dishes once washed. Behind the kitchen was a pantry with shelves on either side and its own window and swinging door. Kitchen dishes were stored on shelves behind doors with windows. Below those shelves was space where bread dough rose under the shawl. Below that were drawers down to the floor. Our ice box stood between the kitchen door and the outer door in a kind of air lock. In very cold weather, we did not use ice because that space between the two doors was very frosty.

At one end of the kitchen three doors formed an "N". One went to the basement, one to the staircase to the bedrooms, and one to a closet.

The door to the basement gave me the greatest problem. When Daddy went to the basement, he always latched the door to keep it closed. Mamma, by contrast, never latched the door. When I came through that area from the dining room or back door, the basement door was likely to be ajar, moved by a draft of wind. I hit the edge of the door, usually with my face.

Countless times, Daddy reprimanded Mamma for not latching the basement door to prevent me from hurting myself by hitting it when I had expected that door to be closed. Unhappily, Mamma's behavior did not change. Did she not understand what Daddy was saying, or did she not care how many times I hurt my face?

The completely finished basement of the house had a coal-burning furnace in the center. Because of that fact, we had a coal bin and a wood bin. Between them was a preserve closet to store cans and jars of food, a bag of potatoes, and other fresh vegetables or fruit that did not spoil quickly when kept cool. Although the kitchen pantry was additional storage space, the preserve closet permitted the family to have more food on hand than the pantry alone could accommodate with its warmer temperature.

A truck parked in our driveway in order to unload coal. With a chute from the body of the truck down into an open window in the coal bin, the driver shoveled coal into the chute where it slid down into the house.

With his truck, Daddy brought home wood a cord at a time and dumped it into the backyard, from where we children carried arm-fuls to the other side of the house to drop the wood through an open window into the wood bin.

During one of these episodes, my mother had been instructed by Daddy to open the wood bin window. However, she propped open the window by a piece of wood between the sill and the pane. When I came along to drop my load in, one of my pieces hit the stick prop-ping the window open. The window slammed shut, shattering the panes. Daddy did not punish me but reprimanded Mamma for not using the hook from the ceiling to hold the window up and out of the way.

Outdoor life was quite different from life indoors. Daddy cleared snow from sidewalks and driveway with a shovel, not a power snow-blower. Mamma or Daddy mowed the lawn with a push mower, not a power machine. Mamma or Daddy watered the grass with a hose held in hand and aimed at various arid areas to reach all the lawn; au-tomatic sprinkler systems were not yet heard of or were too expensive for our neighborhood.

Our backyard contained a detached, brick garage that accommo-dated Daddy's dump truck and our family's secondhand Buick. The third stall stored mower, hose, shovels, rake, ladder and whatever else needed a resting place when not in use. Later, that space served as rentals for various individuals who had no other garage.

Housewives adhered to a schedule for accomplishing certain routine tasks each day. Monday was usually reserved for laundering clothes. This was a day of physical labor. In the basement, Mamma had two laundry tubs and a washing machine with a wringer. The cleanest items went into the washer first according to categories: bed linens, white wearing apparel, light-colored items, towels, dark-colored articles, Daddy's work clothes, throw rugs, cleaning rags, etc. The articles went through the wringer and into the first tub of rinse water, then into the second tub for further rinsing, and then into the laundry basket. Mamma carried the heavy load upstairs, through the kitchen, and out onto the small back porch when weather permitted. With clothespins, she hung items on the rope clothesline. Because the rope was on a pulley, she pushed the hung clothes away from her to the left while empty rope approached from the right. A housewife's pride centered on having items duly pinned in the correct group—socks by socks, shirts by shirts, aprons by aprons, etc. The day's work involved several trips from the basement to the porch and back to the basement. Dry clothes were removed from the line as soon as possible to make room for wet clothes.

When my mother was recovering from a heart attack in 1938, Daddy did the laundry. A neighbor housewife offered to hang the clothes for Daddy after seeing his first efforts. His clothes were not in categories. He refused Ann's help with, "The same wind is blowing on all the clothes. When I take them in, I will sort them and put them where they belong."

The last job related to laundry day was the emptying of the tubs and washing machine. A bucket had to be placed under the machine's drain to catch the water. Once the last bucketful drained out, clean water had to be inserted into the machine to rinse away soap and scum.

When I was older, that was my job, especially during summer vacations. I was happy to have a job, because Mamma prohibited me from doing many chores in the house. I was permitted to dry dishes and put them away, but I was prevented from using the gas stove.

When the weather was inclement, clothes were hung on lines in the basement. Even in winter when moisture was not falling, clothes were hung outdoors. They smelled fresh when brought indoors later. On very cold days, the clothes froze on the line and had to be hung in the basement to thaw.

Sometimes clotheslines broke, dropping the clothes to the ground; then the clothes needed to be laundered again and hung in the basement until Daddy installed a new rope line.

With prolonged immersion in water and soap and exposure to outdoor cold temperatures, Mamma's hands were often rough and chapped. During the Great Depression, Mamma could not afford to indulge in hand cream or lotion to counteract the condition of her skin. Unfortunately, we had no gas or electric dryer in the basement to simplify the work for Mamma. Needless to say, all the clothes that were outside had to be brought indoors in an orderly manner. When I was present, I folded towels and put them away, and delivered underwear to each bedroom, placing the garments on each bed. I carried the laundry basket to the basement to place it near the tubs.

Tuesday was used for ironing. In order to do ironing, Mamma had to make a few changes in the kitchen by pushing the table away from its usual location and toward the sink and placing chairs wherever they best fit temporarily. Between the two windows was a narrow door. When open, it revealed the ironing board, with one end permanently mounted in the wall. When the other end came up to make a kind of table (wide near the wall and narrow at the other end), it was supported by two metal bars also in the wall. The iron was electrical and its base triangular in shape.

Some articles, previously sprayed with starch water, were rolled up to retain moisture. A spray bottle of starch water was nearby in case a garment was too dry for desired results after ironing. When ironed, those articles acquired a crisp finish as for men's shirts, some dresses and blouses, and dresser scarves and tablecloths. After ironing wearing apparel, Mamma hung them on hangers or on the back of chairs until the time when she had all on hangers and placed in closets.

Some articles such as men's trousers required pressing. This involved placing a damp towel over the area being ironed to create moist heat to achieve the necessary creases in the appropriate places.

Mamma did all ironing while standing. In summer, the heat of the iron rose to reach her neck and face. Ironing all the articles that required ironing was a long, tiring job for Mamma and other women in the neighborhood.

Why was ironing such a big job? Most fabrics were forms of cotton, which dried with wrinkles, unlike many fabrics today that require no ironing or only a small amount. When Mamma completed this weekly chore, she then collapsed the ironing board, closed its door, set the iron somewhere to cool before returning it to its rightful storage site until the next Tuesday, returned the table and chairs to their proper location, and then began preparation of supper.

Wednesday was mending and/or sewing day. What is the difference? Mending included attaching buttons, repairing hems and seams, reattaching straps, etc. Sewing, on the other hand, meant making an entire article, such as a dress for me, an apron for Mamma, pillow slips, etc.

Thursday involved cleaning the three bedrooms and bathroom, washing windows when necessary, changing bed linens, and cleaning the staircase down to the main floor.

Friday was similar cleaning but on the first floor. It included vacuuming the rugs, dry mopping the bare floor, dusting, polishing furniture, mopping the kitchen floor, etc.

Saturday included planning menus, grocery shopping, baking such goodies as an apple pie or chocolate cake for the weekend, and so on.

Sunday dinner was always in the dining room. We ate all other meals of the week in the kitchen. Then the week repeated its routine in predictable monotony. As someone has aptly said, "Housework is so daily."

Our social life was quite predictable as well. On Friday evening we visited one set of grandparents and on Saturday evening the other. Sunday morning was for Sunday school and church. On Sunday afternoon, we sometimes had guests or visited friends or relatives. Switching from my family and my house, let us look at my neighborhood.

Houses were different from each other, individual and distinctive, unlike in today's projects and planned communities, where the houses have the sameness of cough drops or buttons down a shirt front. Some of the houses were for one family, with bedrooms upstairs or on the main floor. Some houses accommodated two families, upstairs and downstairs. Some constructions of houses were of wood or brick or stucco. Each house had its own choice of color. Some houses were on one lot, some on two. Most did not have fences.

When we moved into our new house, we had no neighbors on the kitchen side of the house up to the corner. Later two houses filled in that area. Our block had three houses on the other side of our property. Altogether, we had six houses in the block on our side of the street. Our block was five-sided, involving Highland Avenue where I lived and going to the left from our front yard to Ward Street, Gregory Avenue, to Burgess Place, to Third Street, and back to Highland Avenue. A tour around the block revealed one store, a metal business, and a church with its parsonage next door. The remainder were private homes.

Adults in our neighborhood (called Dutch Hill) were blue-collar workers, primarily of Dutch descent but with Irish, Polish, German, and Jewish families mixed in with us. All adults had less than an eighth-grade education. Many of the neighbors had noticeable accents, but all were citizens.

In the early years in this neighborhood, my sister, Ida, was too young to be a playmate for me. When she was two years old, I was four and a half. Mart had many companions, all of whom were boys. There were few girls my age with whom to play. I yearned to have my own friends. More often, I played alone. I explored the neighborhood fearlessly. One day when the house directly across from ours was under construction, I wandered over to the site, attracted by the sounds of activity and the presence of other children who were watching the workmen. Walking toward the noise without being able to see down to my feet, I fell into the hole that was to become the basement. Fortunately, because the concrete had not yet been poured and set, I was uninjured. Even though the experience was frightening, my desire to explore freely was undiminished. I am confident that this early investigation on my part helped to develop in me both orientation and spatial relationship skills.

Mart was always good about making sure that I was not left alone away from home. I especially remember a time when he seated me in an aisle chair on the girls' side of the Sunday school classroom and then went to sit with the boys. As more girls arrived and invited me to sit near them, I gladly moved closer. Shortly after the class started, my brother began to cry. Quietly slipping over to where he was seated, the teacher asked him why he was crying. "My sister is gone. I don't know where she is!" he cried. Apparently, he had been so preoccupied with the boys that he had not noticed when I had changed chairs. Later, when he discovered that I was no longer where he had seated me, his immediate reaction was panic. The teacher gently reassured him that I was safe and showed him where I was sitting.

I remember another time when Mart and I walked into the woods near our house. When Mart returned home without me, Mamma became frantic. She assumed that Mart had deliberately deserted me in the woods. Before Mart could explain that I was with Marie O'Brien, an older girl, Mamma exploded! Typically, Mamma reacted without listening for an explanation but assumed that she already knew the facts in the case. So Mart was "guilty" of an offense he had not committed, just because Mamma recklessly concluded that a mother always has the right answer. Unfortunately, I think she was more concerned about explaining the situation to Daddy than whether I was actually lost or in danger.

Another memorable event in this house was when Mamma and

Daddy decided that Mart and I should have our tonsils removed. During this time in medical history, physicians thought tonsils were unnecessary organs that should be surgically removed before becoming infected. It was common then to perform such surgery with a child lying on the kitchen table. As Daddy held my legs and Aunt Nellie my arms, I protested just because of being restrained. After the doctor began to administer the anesthesia, he asked me to count backward from ten to one. Wanting to prove that I was smart enough to do that, and after taking a deep breath, I started counting: "Ten, nine, eight ..." and I was out like a light. After the surgery, somebody carried me upstairs to my bed. After Mart's surgery, the doctor left; Aunt Nellie went home; Daddy returned to work. When I regained consciousness, I was in my own bed. My throat was very sore; I did not talk much. Mart was also awake, telling Mamma his throat hurt. Even though she cautioned him not to talk, he continued complaining. Later, Mamma gave us ice cream. Cool and smooth, it slid down our sore throats. How wonderful to have a legitimate reason for eating ice cream—it was not even a birthday or Fourth of July!

Tragically, Mamma continued referring to Ida as her "normal" daughter and to me as her "blind" daughter. She could have said "younger" and "older" instead. I felt a sense of shame, as though something about me was somehow bad because I could not see. Another reason I hated to hear the word *blind* was because I could see some things and did not consider myself blind. I thought the word blind meant inability to see anything. In truth, I was blind by a definition used by medical personnel and agencies to identify which individuals are eligible to receive specific services designed exclusively for the legally blind population.

By definition, legal blindness includes those individuals whose central visual acuity is 20/200 or worse in the better eye while wearing corrective lenses OR whose range or field of vision (above, below, and to either side of each eye) is greatly restricted. This limitation is often referred to as tunnel vision or gun-barrel vision or soda-straw vision.

This is also legal blindness even when the person can read print or identify colors. The restriction in range is a profound limitation.

Mamma, however, constantly reminded me by saying such things as, "You're blind! You can't do that!" or "You're different from other girls," or "Don't forget you're blind—you can't do the nice things other children can do," or "Don't try that. You are blind. Blind people can't do that!"

Employing the word blind is appropriate when necessary but inappropriate when doing so overshadows the total person.

Think of any other adjective, such as tall or fat or pimple-faced or shy. Whenever the mother refers to her child, she should not say, "my fat daughter," "my shy son," or "my tall daughter." How would mothers like to be referred to by their children as "my fat mother," "my not-so-bright mother," "my uneducated mother," or "my mother who is not a good cook?"

Most mothers would reprimand their children for referring to the parent in such disrespectful or demeaning words. Parents, if you would not like to be addressed that way, then do not do it to your child. Respect works in both directions. Negative words hurt and leave indelible scars whether addressed to children or adults.

My mother was fat, and if I had constantly reminded her that she was fat, she would have punished me for being disrespectful. Yet, she never recognized her negative words to me as put-downs and slurs.

Children do not need to be bombarded by the word *blind* in order to grasp the truth. Bit by bit, I began to discover that other children, even younger ones, could do what I could not do: enjoy catching a ball rolling on the floor or traveling in the air, thrill with excitement when looking through a window to discover the first snowflakes falling to the ground, insist upon using a specific color to paint a picture, proudly reach the stage of being able to write with a pencil, read words wherever found, happily recognize friends and relatives by appearance even before they speak, or naturally reciprocate someone's wave of the hand in greeting even from a great distance. Vision—or the lack of it—was the difference between them and me.

I was learning what I could and could not see. For instance, although I could see a car drive into the yard and see where it parked, I could not visually distinguish the model of the car or identity of the driver or passengers. By contrast, my brother might call out, "Uncle Dick and Aunt Nellie are here." Similarly, at night in the dark, although I could identify street lights or headlights on vehicles but not soon enough for safety, I could not see sidewalks or curbs because of night blindness due to damaged rods in the retina. I also could not identify colors because of damaged cones in the retina. To me, things were either light or dark. A man in trousers and shirt would appear to be light in the upper portion of his body and dark in the lower area. I could see the white lights on Christmas trees but not colored lights.

When people less familiar with me saw me moving about in my house or yard, they expressed the belief that I could see quite well. What they did not realize was that I had memorized the territory. Light coming through windows during the day or electric lights in the house at night also helped me move about more easily.

When I was in unfamiliar surroundings, the limitations of my vision became quite obvious. I remember shopping with Mamma and wandering away while she was busy at the counter. Suddenly, I was tumbling down a flight of stairs at the back of the store. Thankfully, I was not seriously injured. Mamma often said that she wished she had a nickel for every bump I had received. I am grateful for those bumps, though, because they mean I was active and curious, experiencing life. As someone so aptly put it, it is better to wear out (doing things) than to rust out (doing nothing). In all of this, I was discovering me: *Who am I? What can I do? What can I not do? How do people react to me? How am I different? How am I similar to other children?* These were valuable lessons.

In addition to the problems of mobility, blind children lack the advantage of learning by observing others. Children having normal vision learn countless behaviors by watching and imitating others, especially those a bit older or larger. The expression "Monkey see as monkey do" may have originated from that fact. If one child deliberately walks in a silly manner, another child is likely to mimic. Blind children, by contrast, cannot observe others to acquire new skills and information. Think of all the competencies a seeing child acquires primarily as a result of observing others: walking in a natural gait, shaking hands eagerly in response to another's extended hand, skillfully using a spoon in the correct grasp, competently holding a sandwich without losing food, learning to smile at appropriate times to reveal emotion, holding the head erect as seeing persons do, facing the person to whom he or she is speaking, climbing stairs correctly when legs are long enough to have only one foot on a step, etc. Armed with the knowledge that vision enhances learning, parents and teachers must be the blind child's "eyes."

Do not assume that because your blind child does not act like other children, he or she is mentally retarded, emotionally disturbed, or autistic. Teach your child, sometimes literally with your hands on him to demonstrate the desired response sought.

To grasp the importance of this, pretend in your mind that you are visiting an exotic country—Mongolia, Nepal, Sudan, Peru—but for the duration of your tour you wear a blindfold one hundred percent of the time. When you return home, friends inquire about your journey: Describe the houses. Describe the vehicles. Were mountains part of the scenery? Did you like the food when you could not see it? Was there a national costume that everyone wore, or did individuals dress in various ways? How did natives greet each other?

Because you are an adult, you might ask questions to gain information, ask permission to touch things, ask someone to provide description, etc. A young blind child is likely to be less resourceful.

When your blind child demonstrates gaps in his or her acquisition of acceptable skills, intervene to show the proper behavior rather than merely accept improper behavior as inevitable because of blindness.

Your child in later years will be very embarrassed and humiliated to learn that when he or she was eleven years old, you continued to permit him or her to ride in the child seat of the supermarket cart, just because your child had been doing so since age one. Wanting to continue to ride there when eleven is inappropriate, and you, as parent, must terminate the practice when it is no longer age-appropriate. The blind child cannot look around to see that only babies are in this kind of seat and that eleven-year-olds, even when they can still fit, are completely in the wrong place. Making the child happy by permitting inappropriate behaviors is woefully wrong. Instead, use your energy to prepare him or her for life's demands. Your responsibility is not to prolong childhood and dependence but to prepare your child for adult roles as a man or woman, not a child in an adult body. An employer will not hire your son or daughter merely to be charitable to a blind individual when your son's or daughter's behaviors are bizarre, weird, odd, and really strange. Teach your child in order to promote independence, social acceptance, self-esteem, and pride in fitting into the world of individuals with normal vision.

Unhappily, my parents had no guidance from a professional in the blindness field. If a legislator or agency executive is reading this book, note the importance of providing parents of children who happen to be blind with qualified preschool and child development counselors who are thoroughly knowledgeable about the rearing of such children. You will then be able to spare many families from emotional pain and inappropriate child management. These counselors do not make only one home visit to solve all the problems. Instead, a given counselor may visit once every two weeks or even once a week to discuss a specific aspect of child behavior or parental attitudes.

My situation might have been improved had my parents graduated from high school or college. The reality is that my parents' formal education was woefully inadequate for rearing even a "normal" child. We have training programs for many jobs, such as driving a car, working in a restaurant, and learning to be a secretary, but no training for every individual who will be a parent. Even rearing a normal child today is extremely problematic; rearing a child with a disability is overwhelming, frustrating, and lonely.

If part of Mamma's problem stemmed from feeling guilty for causing her child's blindness, I attribute no guilt to her. I maintain that her body was incapable of having two children only thirteen months apart. Four months after Mart was born, her pregnancy with me began. Mart was not receiving the full nutrition that he required as revealed when breast milk was withdrawn with a pump and examined when deposited into a glass. It resembled water rather than milk. I, too, was not receiving full nourishment as an embryo because she was nursing Mart. The eyes begin to form very early in pregnancy. Other women seem to be able to have children close in age, but I believe that Mamma was not one of them.

When she married, she weighed one hundred and ten pounds. By the time Mart was born, she weighed one hundred and eighty pounds with height of only five feet four inches. She was fat the rest of her life until six months before she died.

Gaining weight rapidly, as she did, is unhealthy. Then not losing weight after three pregnancies did not improve the situation.

Her ignorance was not limited to child rearing but also included health during pregnancy and physical health and sound nutrition at all periods of life. How ready is a ten-year-old (fifth-grader) to assume adult roles of mother, nurse, family nutritionist, and monitor of child development from stage to stage? Her source of "knowledge" was her own mother, with even less education. Mamma had received the equivalent of a fifth-grade education.

Although she could read, she mispronounced many words. She did not read to us children. She "read" magazines to herself only when they had pictures.

Mart began public school in September 1926 at School No. Fifteen, located a bit more than two blocks from home. Although I was eager to attend school, I had to wait for that experience to begin until I had turned five. Because my life at home was not the happiest, especially when alone with Mamma, I anticipated life in school to be very exciting with teachers who would accept me and be pleased to teach me. I was hungry to learn. Surely, teachers like pupils who want to learn!

TWO

◇◇◇◇◇◇◇◇◇◇◇

In September 1927, knowing nothing about special education, my parents enrolled me in the same elementary school that my brother attended. (I imagine my father was responsible for placing me in school, whereas Mamma would have argued, "What's the point of school for Grace? She's blind and can't learn!") Although I could learn from what I heard, I could not participate in the many visual activities, such as coloring worksheets and pictures, chalkboard work, and reading. I had some residual vision, but it was insufficient to use in those tasks.

My teacher made no attempt to test my abilities to determine what I could and could not learn by asking me to recite the days of the week or months of the year or my age or name, fruits, vegetables, count to ten, etc. Like so many other adults, she must have assumed I was mentally retarded because of being blind. They go together, don't they?

Because day after day I was excluded from all activities, I soon began to dread going to school. The teacher did not call on me for answers or participation in discussion even when I raised my hand but merely let me sit all day as an outcast.

I remember so clearly the day my teacher distributed our first book of the basal reading series to teach us to read. When I realized that she had not given one to me, I thought she had accidentally overlooked me. I said, "I don't have a book."

"No, and you're not getting one! You can't read!" she responded. How many children in the room at that moment could read, but they received books?

I was crushed. What difference would it have made even if I held my book upside down? At least I could be holding a book instead of being identified as class fool or idiot. If I had a book, my mother could read the story to me and describe the pictures to prepare me for the next day's lesson.

I never felt comfortable or welcome in this school. Somehow, I sensed I did not belong there. Although I could not articulate then what was happening, as I can now, I clearly felt rejection and humiliation. At home, when Mart was learning from what Mamma and Daddy explained to him, I understood the same information. I knew I could learn if someone would just work with me. Why did my teacher not put forth the effort to try to teach me? Why did she not even try?

My teacher not only lacked training to reach the visually-impaired child but also ingenuity, creativity, and curiosity. She and teachers like her permitted their assumptions to override the necessity for pedagogic evidence. For instance, when I could not count the lines on the chalkboard for arithmetic, the teacher never used tangible objects to evaluate my understanding of quantity. In order to demonstrate my comprehension of number, I could have counted pencils or crayons or keys or blocks to group, such as "Show me two. Now add four more. How many do you have altogether?" In her thinking, I am sure, the visual channel was the only entrance to the intellect.

History of public school teacher preparation in the 1920s and earlier indicates that the pedagogic program as designed then was immutable and rigid, claiming to meet the needs of all children. Unhappily, "all children" excluded any child who could not learn from that untouchable program. Such children (hearing impaired, vision impaired, developmentally delayed, learning disabled, etc.) were brutally labeled "unteachable misfits."

When these teachers were college or normal school students, the *abnormal* child was seldom, if ever, discussed; rather, a child must fit into the program as it then existed. Just as with me, it was easier to let me sit doing nothing and ignore me, rather than address my evaluation and educational needs. Evaluation and identification of needs would require modifying the sacred program. To exclude problem children was easier than trying to educate them with appropriate methods and materials. To call me unteachable was a simple solution to a huge problem. Then special education was swept under the rug, the program could claim stupendous success in American public education. An analogy would be for medical doctors to refuse to interact with sick individuals and then proclaim publicly that all Americans are healthy.

The program was more important than the individual child. The sacred program must not be tampered with or modified for the needs of a single child.

When the child could not conform, that child was excluded and banished with no education, since he or she could not perform as a *normal* child was expected to do.

Individual classroom teachers were not totally at fault. This is how most teacher trainers thought and transmitted their "wisdom."

In spite of the label affixed on me, I knew instinctively that I was capable of learning.

For a short time, assuming that smaller classes and Christian teachers might be to my advantage, my parents enrolled me in a local Christian school. Unfortunately, this school was no more successful than the first. I soon returned to the same public school with an even more intense hatred for it.

I tried to resist attending. I remember the morning, while we stood on the front porch, when Mamma said, "Here comes a policeman. Now you have to go to school!"

A man spoke, "What's wrong, little girl?"

I did not know whether he was really a policeman but responded,

"I hate school, and you can't make me go!" School had become intolerable.

The principal had the practice at promotion times twice a year of visiting every classroom to read a list of names. When students heard their names, they knew they were being promoted. Those children who had not heard their names also knew the meaning.

My teacher asked the principal, "What do we do with Grace?" Both adults were close enough for me to reach out to touch them.

The principal said, "Keep promoting her until she graduates when we will be rid of her!" Those words stung like a whip. I did not like him any more than he liked me. I was promoted to second grade but was still in prison.

Home and school are very precious areas for young children. They are tangible signs of love, acceptance, and ability. For me, neither home nor school represented love, acceptance, and ability. Mamma did not want me at home, as I perceived that environment, and principal and teachers did not realistically want me at school. *Where do I belong?* Although the principal and teachers did not know *how* to teach me, they had no right to treat me with disdain and as a non-person. Their professionalism was absent. I daresay the principal never consulted anyone in the school district to ask for information to help this "blind/ retarded" child in his building. No professional should resort to rudeness and insult in matters relating to children.

At this same time, when my sister was almost four years old, I was almost six and a half. She developed appendicitis and underwent surgery with ether as the anesthesia.

When my mother arrived at the hospital one morning to visit Ida, another mother was already there. She told Mamma that when she had arrived earlier, Ida was lying on the floor; she had picked up Ida and placed her in bed. No one knew how long Ida had been on the floor. In short, the result was that Ida developed pneumonia and died!

On the evening before the funeral, many adults were in the house to comfort my parents. I was standing alone in the kitchen when Daddy entered, leaned on the oven, and wept noisily. I was near enough to touch his leg and wanted to hug it, but his audible sobs stunned me into inactivity. I had heard children and women cry but never a man. Daddy's pain paralyzed me. I knew why he was weeping (because of Ida's death), but I had not known that men cried. I was learning a frightening lesson about human emotion.

The evening after the funeral, only Mamma and Daddy were downstairs in the living room while Mart and I were upstairs in our beds. My room was at the head of the stairs that descended into the living room with no wall separating stairwell from living room.

Mamma was crying; I understood that. Then she asked, "Why did God take Ida and leave Grace?" Daddy did not answer with words, though he may have shrugged his shoulders or put a hand on Mamma's hand. I have always cherished his silence.

Mamma's question burned an indelible scar into my heart and mind. Miserable, I cried into my pillow, realizing that *Mamma loved Ida more than she loved me. She wished I were dead and buried in the ground! She loved Mart and Ida, but she did not want me!* I would have understood the question, "Why did God take Ida?" if it had ended there. She did not say, "Why did God take Ida and leave Mart?" The message was abundantly clear. Mamma's question created a Grand Canyon between us.

Later, whenever she did something for me, such as sew a dress, buy me new shoes, or curl my hair with a curling iron, I thought, "You are not doing this because you love me. You are doing it just to impress other people with what a great mother you are. I heard that question. Other people would not be impressed if they knew that question!" *That question* became an insurmountable blockade between us for many years—perhaps always.

I was certain now that I did not belong at home where I was not wanted. I did not belong at school where I was also unwanted. *Where do I belong?* I was despairingly lonely.

Then something fortunate happened in my favor that changed my life forever.

Our family physician, Dr. Stoltz, was making a visit in the home of a woman, a stranger to us. The doctor noticed something unfamiliar on her dining room table and asked, "Is that some form of art?"

The woman explained, "No, that is Braille. Some blind people read this with their fingertips. I am a transcriber for the American Red Cross. I am copying from this print book to make a Braille book."

The doctor asked, "Do only blind adults read Braille?"

"No. Blind children in school learn to read and write Braille," she answered.

"I know a family with a blind child, but she is not learning to read this way."

"The child should be learning Braille now. Let me contact the individual at the head of the American Red Cross to find out important information," she volunteered.

She made that telephone call. The American Red Cross then telephoned the American Foundation for the Blind (AFB) in New York, who then telephoned the New Jersey State Commission for the Blind in Newark, who sent Miss Lydia Hermann, a field worker to my home.

The purpose of the visit was to determine why I was not receiving special education. My parents said that they did not know about special education.

"What is special education?" my father asked. Miss Hermann explained that special education is for blind children in a different way, that the teacher can teach blind children to read and write Braille and other subjects.

"What is Braille?" asked Mamma.

"It is a system of raised dots that blind persons can feel with their fingertips and learn to read books." She showed a sample of Braille and read it with her fingers. Miss Hermann, in fact, was blind, too. "Your child should be attending this school," she explained.

"Where is that school? It must be far away from here," my father asked.

"Actually, it is very close. It is in the next city, Paterson (adjacent to

Clifton). The teacher has a group of blind children in a public school. I urge you to visit it and then enroll Grace in it," Miss Hermann encouraged. She supplied my parents with the name of the teacher, address of the school, and its telephone number. She suggested that my parents phone for an appointment to visit.

"Did anyone from your local public school or the superintendent's office tell you about this class for blind children?"

"No, no one told us anything."

Miss Hermann said that she was going to visit the superintendent that afternoon.

My parents learned later that the worker, in fact, had visited the superintendent and asked why he had not shared the information about the class for blind children. He pretended ignorance about the class. Miss Hermann told him that she already knew that Robert Potter from Clifton was already attending the class and that Clifton was paying Paterson to educate him. Sputtering for an answer, the superintendent, Mr. Smith, said, "The girl's parents never asked to enroll her in the Paterson class."

Miss Hermann challenged him by saying that as superintendent he was obligated to share with parents information that he had that would benefit a child.

"Besides, how could the child's parents ask about something they did not know exists?" He was trying to save money by not having to pay Paterson to educate another child from Clifton—save money at the expense of a blind child, by depriving her of appropriate education. He was in a precarious situation, lying, claiming innocence and ignorance as Superintendent of Public Instruction. If the Commission had taken him to court, he surely would have been charged with dereliction of duty.

After learning about the superintendent, we can understand why my principal acted as he had toward me. He knew that the superintendent was supporting him in rejecting this blind child. Collusion was afoot!

My parents made an appointment for the three of us to visit this school.

Located in an Italian immigrant neighborhood, the three-story brick school building accommodated several special education classes besides two kindergartens and two rooms each for grades one through eight.

Miss Katharine Taylor greeted us warmly, while my parents sat and observed all the activities in the room. Miss Taylor took me on a tour of the room: from the piano near the door, past bookshelves with very large books, a double sink in the corner with chalkboards over and beside the sink, more bookshelves, a supply closet in the next corner. Then we approached five large windows with a radiator beneath. All the while, Miss Taylor tenderly held my hand. However, when she moved my hand forward and said, "Here is the radiator," I jerked my hand back and away from hers. She calmly and gently reassured me that she was not going to put my hand on the hot radiator to burn me but just let me feel the warm air without touching the radiator, so that I might know where the radiator was. I believed her, won over by her sincerity. We continued the tour hand-in-hand again, finding huge wooden maps on easels and a sandbox. The last wall contained the coat closet for children and a locked closet for Miss Taylor's personal possessions: coat, handbag, umbrella, etc.

Meanwhile, my parents were witnessing other children on various grade levels from kindergarten through eighth at work: using a noisy machine to write Braille, using a device for arithmetic, using an ordinary typewriter, studying one of the large three-dimensional maps, silently reading a Braille book. Of course, my parents did not then know what the children were doing except for writing on the typewriter and feeling a map. A child left the room independently to attend a class on his grade level with children who had normal vision. Another child returned to the room at the end of her class somewhere else in the building.

Miss Taylor then seated me at a desk and placed a Braille book before me. "I can teach you how to read this book, Grace," she promised. Inside my head, I heard bells, whistles, and musical chimes and saw flashing lights to announce that at last I had found a teacher who could teach me!

I examined the page, discovering bumps in many places. I said, "This book has bumps all over it."

Miss Taylor said, "We call those bumps dots, and even today I will teach you some letters," whereupon, she pushed the book aside and placed a card before me. It held a single dot that Miss Taylor called *a*. Then she showed me a different card with two dots in vertical arrangement, called *b*. The third card contained two dots in horizontal arrangement, called *c*.

After that, she showed me the cards in random order several times. At each presentation, I correctly identified the letter! My parents, teary-eyed on the sidelines, watched in awe and disbelief.

Miss Taylor explained to my parents that besides the seventeen rooms for normal children from the local neighborhood, the building accommodated rooms for children with disabilities. In addition to her class, the building had two classes for children with poor vision who could use large print and excellent illumination. Other classes included two rooms for mentally-retarded children, one room for deaf children and two rooms for hearing-impaired children, two rooms for children with orthopedic disabilities and a room for physical therapy, and two rooms for children recovering from tuberculosis or who had been exposed to it at home. Their school environment was cold and circulated fresh air to breathe. The children often sat in sweaters or coats.

In one room, hot lunches were prepared for special education children who did not go home for lunch, as did the normal neighborhood students. Besides the hot dish, students ate sack lunches brought from home. Milk and graham crackers were available morning and afternoon. The room was not large enough to accommodate all special education children. Therefore, some classes ate in their respective rooms, as did Miss Taylor's children.

An auditorium, gymnasium, manual arts room, and home economics room also existed. Besides the office suite and teachers' room, the nurse had her room. The basement was used for playing in inclement weather.

Outdoors were equal but separate playgrounds for boys and for girls. Thus ends the tour of this very unusual educational facility.

Visually-impaired and blind students participated in manual arts and home economics. Only blind and visually-impaired students were integrated daily into classes for normal children for specific courses, such as English, history, geography, health and science, and mental arithmetic.

In Miss Taylor's classroom, we learned special education skills: Braille reading and writing, arithmetic on a variety of devices, typewriting, map reading, organizational skills, working independently, working in small groups, telling time, etc. Throughout the month, the same Miss Lydia Hermann, blind, referred to earlier, came to our classroom to teach us basket weaving, basic hand sewing, knitting, and crocheting. Mr. Walter Fritz, also blind, came to the building once a week to give piano lessons to those children whose parents were willing or able to pay for lessons.

On our return ride home that April day, my parents expressed their favorable impression of Miss Taylor. They said that I might be enrolled in that school in September. Those were fighting words for me. No, I could not wait until September. I had found the right teacher after waiting so long. I had much catching up to do. I must start in Miss Taylor's class right away! I became a pest at home until my parents promised that I would start in Paterson's school on Monday!

What was my transportation to and from school? When my father was not working, he drove me in our Buick. When he was working, Mamma accompanied me on public transportation on a bus. Clifton School District paid my parents three dollars per week for transportation: twenty cents for Mamma's round trip in the morning and ten cents for my ride in the morning, the same amount in the afternoon, and sixty cents a day for five days a week.

Now consider School No. Fifteen in Clifton and School No. Two in Paterson. They coexisted a few miles apart. Their contrast in philosophy and practice were staggering! Clifton's actions screamed, "Get handicapped children out of our schools; those children do not belong here. They are unteachable misfits!" At the other extreme, Paterson's school welcomed children with a variety of disabilities. Not only did Paterson educate its own residents but eagerly accepted children from the greater surrounding environment. Furthermore, blind and visually-impaired pupils were educated together in an integrated setting with normally-seeing students from that school's local neighborhood.

While Clifton educators, on the primary level, were thinking and saying, "It can't be done," Paterson was already immersed in doing it!

Even as a five- or six-year-old child in Clifton's neighborhood school, I instinctively knew that I was in the wrong school, that other qualified teachers existed to teach me, even though I at that moment did not know who such a teacher was or where that teacher worked. Never did I believe that I was unteachable. Persons like Miss Katharine Taylor did not come from normal schools or from ordinary colleges with teacher preparation courses but from Columbia University! In spite of the wait that I had to endure before finding Miss Taylor and the emotional pain heaped upon me by principal and teachers, I eventually received far superior education in Paterson than even my brother received in Clifton.

Another pedagogic contrast then to today's practices with, say, Mexican children in our public schools where U. S. teachers teach in Spanish is that the children in School No. Two came from Italian-speaking parents who knew no English. An older sibling often served as translator between parent and principal or teacher. The school offered no classes taught in Italian. The Italian-speaking children were saturated in English in the confines of the school setting. When these children graduated from eighth grade, they had no more accent from another language than I did whose parents spoke only English at home.

I loved Miss Taylor deeply for many reasons. She accepted me wholeheartedly as Mamma never had. Miss Taylor could separate my blindness from me, the person. She saw me as a child with an eager mind for learning. I would have gone to live with her at a drop of the proverbial hat. She turned my life around from my hating school to loving school when both teacher and school were appropriate. She never yelled, never raised her voice in anger but, at the same time, was fully in control of her class. She radiated love and acceptance of her students. She saw our potential without feeling sorry "for these poor blind children, what a pity!" She set expectation levels, and we worked to achieve or surpass them. Her classroom was a healthy environment for physical, emotional, and intellectual growth. She was a gifted teacher. Often, she would say, "Grace, you can become whatever you want to be as an adult." I had never heard that at home. In my life, she was the first adult who offered me hope for the present and future. What an impact she has had on my life, then and afterward.

As an official student, I was learning more about this school. Because of the large enrollment of normal children, each grade had two sections: 4B for the first semester of fourth grade and 4A for the second, for example. These ran concurrently. Furthermore, 4A operated in fall and repeated in spring semester with the same teacher. Likewise, 4B, twice a year, was taught by another teacher twice a year. This system applied to all grade levels. With this arrangement, children could be admitted to their appropriate grade whenever they moved into this school's official neighborhood. Because students could begin a grade in either fall or spring, the school had two graduations from eighth grade each year, in January and June.

Miss Taylor assigned me to the first semester of second grade for the end of that academic year. In September, I was in the second half of second grade. I had no difficulty beginning there. Although in the

Clifton school I did the arithmetic mentally, I had to learn now how to write it. Other information that I had heard, I learned but could not write the words in the Clifton school. Now, with Miss Taylor's instruction, I was learning how to compute in written format and to read and write Braille words and sentences.

Two methods then were different from today's teaching. One relates to writing Braille. We started with slate and stylus instead of the Braille writer, the equivalent to a typewriter for print. With the stylus, we had to punch every dot we needed. On the machine, all the necessary keys can be pressed simultaneously to make a given symbol. The great benefit of Miss Taylor's sequence was that we thoroughly mastered slate and stylus writing, untrue for many of today's blind students who may be introduced to slate and stylus in twelfth grade. They never become proficient in writing with slate and stylus but must carry a Perkins Brailler (weighing ten pounds) from classroom to classroom in public schools or carry an expensive electronic device for writing. Besides mastering the skill, we appreciated advantages: Slate and stylus are portable in pocket, handbag, or briefcase. They are much less expensive than Braille writing machines or electronic devices. Slate and stylus are much less noisy than a machine.

We began using Braille writers in fourth grade. Writing this way is faster.

The second difference in methodology was in Braille reading. We began with Grade One Braille (grade here has nothing to do with grade levels in school). For three or four years, we used Grade One Braille; this is where all words are spelled out as in print. Then we changed to Grade One and a Half Braille for about as long. Grade One and a Half includes forty-four Braille contractions which may be likened to business shorthand signs, though different. For instance, in Grade One Braille the word round is spelled out as in print, round. In Grade One and a Half, the same word is written with the ou sign as shown within parentheses in print as r(ou)nd. Others of those contractions include the er sign, ar sign, ing sign, gh sign, etc.

Just before leaving Miss Taylor's class at the end of eighth grade to enter high school, we began Grade Two Braille with 190 contractions. The word *round* now appears as r(ound).

The disadvantage to changing codes is that students achieve speed and proficiency in Grade One and are then introduced to something different that reduces speed and proficiency. When skills become polished again in Grade One and a Half Braille, then comes Grade Two Braille that destroys skills once more. This is at the time when students have more to read as they enter high school. Here is another example of the changes encountered: *would, w(ou)ld, wd.* The parentheses indicate where a contraction occurs.

Why are contractions used at all? Contractions serve a definite purpose in enhancing mastery of Braille in both reading and writing. The areas under the reading fingertips (usually index fingers) are very small when the fingers are stationary. When Grade One Braille is used, the fingers must travel farther to reach the end of the word to identify it, as illustrated by the examples above. Think of longer words with no contractions, such as individual, hospitality, educational, misrepresentation, uncompromising, etc. A given contraction shortens or shrinks the distance; hence, the word is identified sooner, thus increasing speed. A few more examples may clarify this point: *abv = above, afn = afternoon, k = knowledge, imm = immediate, ll = little, r = rather.* With contractions, both reading and writing times are reduced. Contractions are necessary and extremely helpful.

In Miss Taylor's defense, I must say that the sequence was not her personal choice or method. The books used in schools for blind children were published according to this sequence at the American Printing House for the Blind in Louisville, Kentucky. Even if Miss Taylor had taught us Grade Two Braille initially, we students would have had no books at our grade level in school in Grade Two Braille.

Today's readers begin with Grade Two Braille and have primary-level books available in Grade Two Braille. Thus, students build speed and proficiency without disruptive setbacks, without unlearning and relearning, as when I was a child.

You may wonder whether first-grade children have to learn all 190 contractions before moving into second grade. The answer is no. Certain contractions are not in primary-level reading vocabulary. So the child does not learn that *nec* is for *necessary* until that word occurs in the reading experience. Learning the 190 contractions is spread over several years. Currently, every book and magazine in Braille is published in Grade Two Braille. For some multi-impaired Braille readers, some books are available in Grade One Braille only, but this is a tiny percentage of all Braille publications for children and adults.

When I began learning to read Braille, Daddy was tuned in to what was happening at school. Wanting to help me learn, he bought an alphabet made of wooden cut-out capital letters. At first, these were loose in their box in scrambled order. When I picked up individual letters, I was neither sure of its name nor how to hold it in its upright position, even though I could recite the alphabet forward and backward. After Daddy recognized the problem, he nailed the letters in upright position in alphabetical order onto a board. He even painted individual letters in a variety of solid colors to make the total teaching aid visually attractive. For instance, A was green, B red, C yellow, etc. Because I could recite the alphabet, I soon learned the shape of every letter. The lower-case letters came much later, because I had no tactual representation of those letters. Embossed capital letters were in my environment in the form of names of gas stoves, electric ranges, refrigerators, bathroom doors, cookie boxes, bars of soap, and other items.

I was learning! I felt like a sponge, soaking up everything I could.

Miss Taylor was a steadying and positive influence in my life. When a child was talking instead of working, Miss Taylor said, "Empty barrels make the most noise." When she had given a directive, such as, "Billy, sit up straight," but he later slouched, she said, "A word to the wise is sufficient." She could snap her fingers louder than anyone I ever knew. That sound signaled for us to work diligently and not dawdle. When a specific child was doing something amiss, she merely pronounced the child's name. He or she usually knew what behavior needed to cease. When she was working with one child, her eyes monitored the rest of us.

Our classroom, in some ways, was like a one-room country school, with all grades—kindergarten through eighth—represented but with only one teacher. At last, I was in school and learning and loving every minute of every day. Besides learning the basics in communication and computation, I attended my grade with seeing children for a variety of subjects.In those days, we did not have social studies but history and geography. In mental arithmetic, no one was permitted to use pencil and paper. Our brain was the only tool.

On Friday afternoons during the last hour, Miss Taylor read aloud to all of us, such books as Dickens's *A Christmas Carol* and *Dr. Doolittle*. As she read, she asked someone to define a word or someone else to explain why a character did or said something.

On Friday afternoons, we were required to leave the room tidy and neat. One of those times, I chose to work on the top of the piano, arranging books in piles by size. Then I returned to my desk. Later, Miss Taylor, who had not left the room, said, "I wonder who is responsible for the top of the piano." I said nothing. The word *responsible* sounded ominous to me. At home, when someone was responsible for making a mess or for breaking something, the guilty one was in real trouble. So I thought that I must have done a messy job on the piano and was in deep trouble. I remained silent. Miss Taylor then said, "I'd like to thank the person who tidied the piano; it looks very neat and attractive. I wonder who did it." Then I eagerly raised my hand to claim the credit. She duly thanked me. I learned that *responsible* has a good side, as well.

While I was still in second grade, our class went to the nurse's room for weight and height checks by Miss Hunt. We took off our shoes during weight measurement. I could do that. When Miss Hunt was finished with me, I put my shoes on and asked Miss Taylor please to tie them. Another student, named Sarah, offered to tie my shoes and did an excellent job. I was embarrassed in not being able to tie my own shoes.

That evening at home, I asked Daddy (not Mamma) to teach me how to make a bow, because I needed to learn how to tie my own shoes. I told him what had happened at school that day. "And Sarah is in first grade and is only six years old. She has less vision than I do."

Daddy used heavy twine and the back of a chair. He taught; I learned. In short order, I was tying my own shoes. My parents had assumed that a blind child could not tie shoes and, therefore, never attempted to teach me to do that.

Miss Taylor taught me specific tasks so that I might do them as my regular jobs. They included using the paper cutter to trim off Braille writing in order to salvage the remainder of the pages. Even today, I trim paper with scissors in order to save usable paper for future use. To do that, I fold the paper at the end of the writing and then insert scissors in the crease so made. Braille paper is expensive. She taught me stewardship.

She taught me how to open and close the big windows by using a pole to pull down or push up the upper sash. Related to that was adjusting the window shades that were mounted at the center of the vertical distance. One set of cords raised or lowered the upper shade while another set of cords regulated the lower panel.

A third job, when Miss Taylor suggested it was for me to go to the next classroom to borrow from Miss Fisher the key to turn on or off our overhead lights. When I inserted the key into the appropriate hole and pushed, I achieved the desired result. Then I returned the key.

My favorite job was to prepare Miss Taylor's coffee for lunch. With a small saucepan in hand, I walked to the lunchroom to heat water until I heard it bubbling. I then carried the pan of hot water back to Miss Taylor's desk where I had previously filled a spoon with a perforated lid with instant coffee. The coffee was the first of its kind, and it left a residue in the cup if deposited before pouring the water, because it did not dissolve as later products do. With the lid on the spoon closed, however, water could enter the coffee to flavor the water, but the grounds could not escape the spoon. Then, with the spoon already inserted into the cup, I poured the hot water into the cup. She trusted me not to spill water on her desk where papers and folders lay. (Mamma would not permit me to do this job for her. Even when I told Mamma what I did every day, she did not relax her rules about my not helping with food preparation involving hot items. She reminded me of the saying, "Don't confuse me with the facts. My mind is already made up.")

When I was a bit older, another job was for me to help kindergartener Dorothy with her snowsuit—to take it off and hang it up and later to put it on her.

When I was nine, my maternal grandfather gave me his player piano, because every time I visited him, I tried playing the keyboard. He sensed that I had talent to play it.

At home, I had a Victrola in my bedroom. I liked one song in particular. I hummed the first note down the stairs to the piano and hunted for that note until I found it. Then I ran upstairs and played a phrase, ran to the piano and found the keys for that phrase. I continued this process until I had learned to play the whole song with both hands. The song was "Whispering Hope." Much later, I learned that I was playing it in two sharps!

After that, I began receiving lessons from Mr. Walter Fritz who came to my school once a week. I continued lessons with him for the next eight or nine years, going to his home after I left Miss Taylor's class.

When I was ten or eleven, I was working at my desk, and Miss Taylor was teaching another child, when a man walked in and merely said, "Good morning," to Miss Taylor without saying her name. Then he focused his attention on me. He asked me questions about temperate zone and frigid zone, etc. He asked me to define several terms related to that topic. He asked whether I could demonstrate what I was talking about. I had a circular piece of paper in my drawer and retrieved it. I folded it in half and again and again as needed. Then I flattened out the paper and pointed to the equator and the Tropical Zone on either side of the equator. Then the South Sub-tropical and North Sub-tropical Zones came, moving away on each side from the Tropical Zone. Then the North Temperate and South Temperate Zones came, even farther away from the equator. Lastly, came the North Frigid and South Frigid Zones, farthest from the equator.

After asking a few more questions, such as, "In which zone do you live?" he departed as suddenly as he had arrived.

Afterward, Miss Taylor said that she was very proud of me for the way I had interacted with the gentleman and how I had given so much correct information. She said, "I did not know, Grace, that he was coming; I did not know he would choose you to quiz. That gentleman is Mr. Thompson, the Superintendent of Schools for Paterson. You make me a very proud teacher." I was happy that I had not disappointed or embarrassed my favorite teacher.

I must explain here how Miss Taylor and the other teachers worked together. Whichever teacher had one of Miss Taylor's students, she communicated frequently as did Miss Taylor with her. When a test was scheduled, the teacher sent a print copy of the test for Miss Taylor to Braille. Then that student answered either in Braille or on the typewriter. When the answers were in Braille, Miss Taylor wrote with pen on that same sheet, writing exactly what the child had answered, even when incorrect. Relative to the zones of the earth lesson, the teacher let Miss Taylor know that she had introduced this topic, discussed it in class, and made a diagram on the board for the seeing children. She communicated, "I don't know how much Grace gained from that lesson."

In response, Miss Taylor said, "I will work with Grace to teach her that kind of information," whereupon she cut out a circular piece of paper to represent the earth. Then she began folding the circle to show me the equator and further folds to show me additional zones, their names, neighbors, etc. Then when Mr. Thompson made a surprise visit, I used a flat circle not yet folded to show him that I understood. Actually, that unfolded circle was meant for me to take to class to give a demonstration to the class with my other teacher. Miss Taylor cut out a new circle to take to class after Mr. Thompson's visit. Whereas the zones lesson with Miss Taylor came after the seeing children's lesson by one day, many other times Miss Taylor was able to teach me before my other teacher introduced that topic. I think, too, that teachers assigned to School No. Two were screened to determine how well they fit into this unique school.

Although we children were dismissed at three o'clock, I am sure that Miss Taylor never left the building for home until after five o'clock because of all the preparation she had for each student for the next day.

In my last year with Miss Taylor, she shared secrets with me. I certainly would not betray her by telling other children. For example, just before Easter vacation began, our principal, Mr. Rich, was having one of his frequent assemblies in the auditorium. Miss Taylor whispered to me, "You stay here when I take the class to the auditorium. I will come back very soon." I had no idea what was afoot but trusted her implicitly.

When she returned, she asked, "Would you like to help the Easter Bunny?" Of course, I would! Then from her closet she produced the right number of empty baskets and an assortment of Easter candy.

After washing my hands, my job was to put an equal amount in each basket. When finished, I placed a basket on each desk.

Then she and I went to the auditorium to hear the latter portion of the program. My classmates never realized that I had been missing part of the time.

When the children returned to our classroom, they discovered that the Easter Bunny had visited our room! I said not a word about the conspiracy.

All special education children need a Miss Taylor in their lives as a catalyst for good. Any special education teacher may be the first positive influence in a child's life. Celebrate that impact! An educator is a change agent. Capitalize on your privilege to show a child possibilities available to him or her, rather than only despair, negativism, and futility generated at home by one or both parents.

Sometimes we children gathered at Miss Taylor's desk after lunch. One day I said, "I wish I had curly hair like yours, Miss Taylor. Mamma says that straight hair is ugly. I wish I had been born with curly hair."

She said, "Grace, straight hair is not ugly. It depends on how it is cut and styled; straight hair can be very attractive when the hair is a pretty color and shiny, just like yours. Curly hair wants to go in the same way all the time. I cannot make it go in a different way for a different look."

After I had learned in health class that we should go to the dentist at least twice a year to have our teeth checked for caries or other problems, I told Mamma that I needed to go to the dentist. She asked whether I had a toothache. No, but I want to have my teeth checked for caries or other problems.

Her response was, "When you have a toothache, I'll take you but not before." She had a rule in the morning that we must brush our teeth BEFORE breakfast! I protested with, "I did not eat anything while I was in bed." When I tried to brush my teeth *after* breakfast, she complained that I was wasting toothpaste, because I had already brushed my teeth before breakfast. Then I went to school with a dirty mouth all day. No wonder I had caries and lost some permanent teeth before I became an adult. It was a consequence of not being checked periodically by a dentist.

She added, "We can't afford to go to the dentist." Yet soon after that conversation, she took me to a beauty shop for a permanent. The condition of my teeth did not show as far as the public was concerned, but the public saw my hair! Mamma was consumed with the drive to please the public. Mamma said countless times, "What will people think?" I wanted to scream, "Why don't you care about what *I* think?"

By contrast with Mamma, I met a delightful couple who visited our class. On their first visit, Mr. and Mrs. Dixon sang a duet for us; both Sarah and I exclaimed together, "Frank and Flo!" who sang regularly on the radio. They often spoke of Nora who was at home. They arranged transportation so that all of us might visit at their home after school. They did not live in Paterson but in Glen Rock. When we arrived, one of them said, "Here comes Nora." I was expecting their daughter. Instead, Nora was their very friendly but well-behaved dog!

Miss Taylor told me that the Dixons wanted to adopt me. I strongly believe that they had visited my parents. When Mamma and I were alone, Mamma brought up the topic of adoption and how great it would be to live with a different father and mother who were rich. How did she know they were rich?

By contrast, Daddy never mentioned adoption.

I am convinced that Mamma would have preferred the Dixons to adopt me; then Mamma would be rid of me. I think that she was nudging me to clamor at home to be adopted. She may have thought that when I created a big enough demand, Daddy would consent to adoption. Although it sounded attractive in order to have a different mother, I did not want to lose Daddy. So adoption never occurred. I truly believe that I would have had a more positive home life with the Dixons and perhaps more opportunities to develop interests and make social contacts than those available to me from a financially poor and uneducated, uncultured home environment. To contemplate my potential life with the Dixons is both very pleasant and inspirational. In retrospect, I wish it had happened.

Not everything was academic at school. Miss Taylor's students were included and involved in drama and assembly programs. In one play which was to be a program in the evening for the public, I was the leading lady, an old woman, sitting in a rocker knitting while reviewing memories. I easily memorized my lines. As I spoke, I was mentally reading down the page, turning pages as needed.

In the afternoon rehearsal before the public performance, Miss Taylor, at the back of the auditorium, said, "I can't hear you, Grace." I explained that I was talking as loudly as I could. When my voice began to fail altogether, she advised me to stop talking and not talk at home, with the hope that my voice would return.

Because I had no understudy, Miss Taylor must have been experiencing panic. Happily, when I returned in the evening, my voice was back in full volume.

At the end of our parts, Sarah and I had to exit from backstage by using the fire escape from the auditorium, cross the concrete playground, and enter a door left unlocked for us. Once inside, we returned to Miss Taylor's room to change into our going-home clothes.

At another time, we were in a production of *Uncle Tom's Cabin* in various lesser roles. In one scene that did not involve blind students, a slave was to faint but be caught and supported by others. In the public performance, something happened that had not occurred in rehearsals. Those who were to support the fainting slave missed, and he fell to the floor, uninjured.

To digress from school to focus the camera on my father instead of my mother, I will relate an anecdote from home. One day I overheard Daddy talking on the front steps with the man who lived across the street. They were talking about this man's new baby son, born with cleft palate/cleft lip. Unwilling to accept his child, the father wanted his son to die. The baby was having difficulty feeding, either by breast or bottle, because of his inability to form a vacuum for sucking.

I heard the father say, "I just want him to die. What's the point of his living this way?"

Daddy quickly asked, "Can doctors do anything for him?"

"They say they can operate and close the holes, but I don't want to put my baby through surgery. I just want them to let him die!"

With much emotion, my father responded, "Be grateful that doctors can help your child. Let them operate. I wish a doctor could say to me, 'I can help your daughter's eyes with surgery.' I'd jump at the chance! But no doctor can help my child."

The neighbor soon consented to surgery for his son.

I was so glad I had overheard this conversation. It helped to cement in my heart that my father loved me in spite of my blindness. Nor did Daddy say, "I wish Grace had died and not lived as a blind person."

I feel that if Mamma had been involved in that exchange with the neighbor, she would have said, "Yes, it is better to let your baby die. I wish Grace had died; then she wouldn't be here now."

Returning to school, associating together as a group helped us to learn from each other. If Miss Taylor had tied my shoes that day in the nurse's room, I would have continued thinking that tying bows was impossible for blind children. We learned that age, grade level, and amount of residual vision did not necessarily predict what each of us was able to do. This mutual learning environment is something missed by children in an itinerant teacher program (to be discussed later in the book) in which a blind child usually has no blind peers from whom to learn, in a school for seeing children as I did in Paterson.

I was thrilled when two or three years later Miss Taylor assigned me—not Sarah—to help Dorothy with her snowsuit prior to going to the playground or going home at dismissal time. Daily, I was teaching this little girl how to manage the snowsuit herself by my consistency from day to day—applying task analysis.

Miss Taylor had a gift for preserving a child's self-esteem when something went awry. One example was when I was in a spelling bee in her room. The word assigned to me was *heel*, which she pronounced and used in a sentence. I knew the difference between *heel* and *heal*.

In my haste, I spelled *hell*. Immediately, I recognized my error and flushed with my hand to my face. Saying nothing to me to embarrass me further, she gave the same word to the opposite team.

Another example of her gift to support children rather than tear them down was on a day when she sent me to one of the classes for orthopedically-impaired children to borrow a wheelchair for one of our boys who had sprained his ankle the day before at home. Gladly, I completed that errand.

Then Miss Taylor said, after thanking me, that she needed someone to push David to the boys' bathroom. When I offered to do it, she merely said, "You have helped already by getting the wheelchair. This time, we will let someone else help him. I think Richard would be happy to help David."

She never went into a lecture about girls' not going into a boys' bathroom. She handled the situation without having to embarrass me. She retained her self-composure and allowed me to feel good about what I had done, even though my comment was innocently inappropriate.

In addition, Miss Taylor was a master of establishing schedules, akin to a juggler keeping all the balls in the air. For her children who were being integrated into classes for normal children, she needed to communicate with each teacher to learn when specific subjects were scheduled: ten-thirty for English, one o'clock for history for Grace, etc. and similar schedules for others of her students. She worked out such schedules for each of her students. She had to prepare Braille schedules for her students. Then she had to consider when Richard or Susan, for instance, would be in the special education room in order for Miss Taylor to schedule what she would teach Richard or Susan during that time. In addition, she had to know what the other children would be assigned to do by themselves when she was working with Richard or Susan. All day long, she was multitasking, accountable for each child's respective learning experience. Nothing was left to chance.

When I was much older and talked with her about her experiences, she shared that she volunteered often at faculty meetings to do this or that in order to build positive relationships with the total faculty, so that when one of her students was assigned to one of the generalist teachers, that teacher would not feel imposed upon, as sometimes happens in other schools. The general educator sees the special educator with only ten or thirteen children while having thirty or more normal children. Being a special education teacher at first glance looks easy. The generalist then may conclude, "Why should I have one of her students in my room when she has it so easy to begin with?"

By being an eager beaver in the total life of the school, Miss Taylor was communicating that she appreciated what the teachers were doing for her program and that she was not lazy or seeking the easy way out.

Some of Miss Taylor's students were multi-impaired. Some of them were not integrated. Miss Taylor regulated the amount of integration that a given child could handle. She provided much more integration for those capable of succeeding. Her goal was to promote her children's independence, not to prolong their dependence on her.

Sadly, some special educators seem to think that they must "protect" their charges as much as possible and drown them in dependence on their special education teachers. In truth, an excellent special education teacher promotes the child's independence, advancement, resourcefulness, ability to be stretched, and preparation for demands ahead. An excellent teacher loves her children but also shoves them.

Our classroom was the same size as others in the building, but the children's desks were larger to accommodate bulky equipment and typically large Braille books. Our desks were not bolted to the floor as in classes for normal children, to enable Miss Taylor ease in rearranging desks according to the number of children enrolled. One child might graduate, and his desk was removed until, say, two new children arrived, when another arrangement of desks became necessary.

In classes for normal children, desks, bolted down, were arranged in five columns with seven desks in each. Usually, all desks were occupied.

Another new experience came my way through my family's optometrist. During my last year with Miss Taylor, Dr. Silverstein introduced my parents and me to Feinbloom Lenses. Those were adjustable telescopes in two barrels. They were not appropriate for walking, because jostling disturbed their focus. When I stood still and looked through them, I saw things I had never seen before. Dr. Silverstein allowed us to take a unit home for several weeks as a trial period.

From my front porch, I could count the steps at the front of the house across the street! When I was in our backyard and a neighbor raised his arm in greeting, I imitated the motion that I had seen him use.

Dr. Silverstein came to Miss Taylor's class to work with me. He never exerted pressure to buy and never tried to interest Miss Taylor in order to promote the lenses among her other students.

He and I went to the windows on the side of the building. He asked me what I saw. I told him that I saw a man walking away from us on the main sidewalk. Urged on by Dr. Silverstein, I explained that the man's shirtsleeves were folded above his elbows, that he looked fat. This was the first time that I had seen anyone in three dimensions or in depth perception. Before that, what I could see was only two-dimensional.

I enjoyed seeing new things with these lenses. However, the barrels were heavy and had to be supported by my hand to keep them in place and in focus.

When my family went for a drive, I tried to use the lenses to see new things. However, the movement of the car, hitting bumps, or swerving threw the lenses out of focus. The lenses did not help me to read print.

Toward the end of the trial period, Mamma asked whether I wanted to keep the lenses, though they were expensive—$150! She said that if Daddy bought them, I had to use them. From my past experience with Mamma, I knew very well how she could nag. I could not look through the lenses all day; I had other things to do: read, play the piano, play with my friends, listen to the radio, etc. Yet I could already hear my mother asking, "Why aren't you using those glasses? We paid a lot of money for them."

So I told her, "They don't help that much. Let's not get them." Now the pressure was off.

Long before then, my father had bought me a portable typewriter and a Braille Writer, long before the Perkins Brailler was manufactured. Today the Perkins is the Cadillac of Braillers. The one Daddy bought me operated like a Mack truck, and the paper went crooked on the bottom line, though that machine was the best at that time.

Though those purchases were a financial sacrifice for my father, he saw them as his parental duty.

Today many families feel that Social Services or service clubs should buy whatever their blind children need; yet they buy expensive items for their seeing children. I admire my father's determination to provide for his child, though money was scarce. Because of money spent on me because of blindness, my brother received few extras that he would have liked to have.

In January 1936, I graduated from eighth grade with my class of normal students. This meant that I would be leaving Miss Taylor's instruction and entering Clifton High School as the only blind student in a large school.

During those years, three experiences with Mamma stand out in my memory. In June in Sunday school each year, students were rewarded with books for perfect attendance. Although I received a book, I could not read it. Only one summer, Mamma offered to read my book to me. We sat on the front porch in the afternoon. After several of these enjoyable sessions, Mamma said, "Last night I finished the story and will tell you how it ends." I was furious and bolted away from her. First, I did not believe that she had actually finished reading the book. Her telling me how the story ended would not be based on the book but be her simplistic creation of an ending. I was so angry with her for deserting me in the middle of a story. Never again did she read a story to me!

A second episode during these years was when Ruthie and I were playing in the backyard. We wanted to jump rope. Because we were only two persons, I tied one end of the rope to the outdoor faucet. Then one of us turned the rope while the other jumped. Because I could not see the rope itself, I watched Ruthie's arm turn the rope, thus knowing when to jump in.

Suddenly, Mamma burst out through the back door, accusing me of ringing the buzzer. (We had a buzzer at the back door and a bell at the front door.) I told Mamma that I had not rung the buzzer but was down here on the sidewalk playing with Ruthie. Mamma said I was lying and went indoors. This occurred several times more. Each time Mamma accused me of lying. Finally, after another outburst from her, she sent Ruthie home and said I was a bad girl.

In the evening, she told Daddy how bad I had been. Daddy came outside where I was alone and asked me what had happened in the afternoon. I told him about jumping rope and that I had never rung the buzzer.

He examined the outdoor faucet and then went to the basement. The buzzer sounded again, and Mamma came out again, yelling, "I told you so! She did it again!"

In time Daddy returned to me from the basement and explained that he had found the problem. When the faucet was jiggled when the rope turned, a pipe rubbed against the wire that controlled the buzzer.

He explained the situation to Mamma. She never apologized for punishing me or calling me a liar.

The third of these three occurred shortly before Christmas. When I came home from school, Mamma wanted to know what I was carrying. I explained that it was my Christmas gift from Miss Taylor. She asked what was inside. I said that I did not know but would find out on Christmas Day when I opened it, just as Miss Taylor had directed us to do.

Mamma ordered me to open it now. I protested that Miss Taylor had told us to save it for Christmas Day. No, Mamma insisted. Furthermore, I should thank Miss Taylor. I assured Mamma that I had thanked Miss Taylor.

Then she ordered me to telephone Miss Taylor to thank her. I protested again. Mamma became angry and ordered me to obey her and to call Miss Taylor to thank her and stop being selfish.

In tears, I phoned Miss Taylor for the scarf. She said, "Grace, you were to wait until Christmas."

I explained what had happened between Mamma and me. She apparently heard my pain and said soothingly, "I understand, honey. You were getting two sets of instructions, one from me and one from your mother. I understand, dear. Have a Merry Christmas, sweetheart." I believe that she truly did understand my predicament and how Mamma refuses to listen to me.

Why did Mamma make such a big issue of this matter? What was her psychological or psychiatric problem? Mamma was an enigma. Why did she distrust me when I explained so many things? She preferred to believe I was evil!

So many of these unhappy incidents I never related to Daddy, because I knew that Mamma would be punitive when she and I were alone. Consequently, Daddy never knew about much of Mamma's abusive treatment of me.

THREE

THE TIME HAD COME for me to transfer to Clifton High School in January 1936. My brother and I traveled together on public buses to and from school.

My years with Miss Taylor had revealed that I was above average in intellect, though some would still prefer to believe otherwise.

Having learned the skills of reading and writing Braille, typewriting, using specialized equipment for mathematics (before the introduction of the Cranmer Abacus or talking calculator) and independent study skills, I was ready to compete with seeing peers in Clifton. Now I would have the opportunity to prove myself in Clifton High School on Piaget (pronounced by locals as Pie-ay-jet) Avenue.

Even if I had attended one of the secondary schools in Paterson, which fact was unlikely because of the expense to the Clifton School District, I would have had no more contact with Miss Taylor there than in Clifton. The two placements would have been quite similar though Paterson had more experience than Clifton in having one or more blind students in its high school.

To provide me with a reader, the New Jersey State Commission for the Blind contracted with Miss Julia Hoffmeister, my homeroom teacher, for one hour daily. I was in her German courses for three years. She arranged our schedules so that we had the same free hour in order for her to read to me then.

Several of my teachers questioned my abilities. (Either they also believed that a blind person cannot be very bright or word from School No. Fifteen had reached some of the teachers to the effect that, "We had her in first and second grades; she's mentally retarded.")

My instructor of English told me that she did not think I was doing my own homework. To expose me, she decided to give me an oral final examination in freshman year (ninth grade). After maintaining my same high standard on the oral test, she was finally convinced that my homework was truly my own.

A year later in a class called Problems of American Democracy, when the class had a test, the teacher said I should take the test home, do it there, and then submit my paper to him the next day. I followed his directions completely. When he later returned papers to the class, including mine, so that we would know our grades, he asked us to pass the papers forward for him to collect in order to enter grades in his record book (not a sound practice to give papers to students without first entering grades into his record book). A week or so later, he said he had lost my paper and asked me what my grade on it was. I told him ninety-six, the actual grade. His response was, "You didn't get ninety-six. I'll give you eighty." I received eighty on my report card for that marking period! He never seemed well organized, so I can accept the fact that he had misplaced or lost my paper. He had a doctorate! Again, someone did not believe that I could excel.

By contrast, Mr. Charles Hartzell assigned an excellent student to sit beside me in biology laboratory to describe what she was seeing in the microscope and in the manual; Mr. Hartzell also discussed the assignment with me to supply necessary information. Apparently, he believed in my ability to learn science.

Someone made a wise decision to have mathematics teachers teach me on an individual basis. I had four years of such courses: two years of algebra, one year of plane geometry, one semester of solid geometry, and one semester of trigonometry. So much of mathematics is taught via chalkboards with teachers' pointing and commenting: "This is equivalent to that" or "This formula is derived from that calculation" or "When you divide this into that, this is the result," etc. A student who is blind cannot learn from that kind of presentation. Mr. Adams or Mr. Applegate taught me each course.

At first, I was asked to submit only answers; however, when my answers were usually correct, the teacher assumed that someone at home was solving the problems and giving me the answers to type. My brother was having difficulty with his own math homework. Neither of my parents could do algebra with their very limited education. The answers were *my* work.

About this time, when I still did not have a Braille textbook, an older student, Martin Brown, offered to help me understand algebra. He came once or twice, if I recall correctly, until I terminated that arrangement for a valid reason. With so many teachers already suspicious about the authenticity of my homework, they would surely reject my work as my own should they learn that Martin Brown was trying to be helpful while I did not have a Braille textbook. My teacher then changed his requirement from writing only answers to typing out the entire solution to all problems. Although it was time-consuming to work out the solution in Braille or on other specialized equipment, I then had to copy from that to typewrite it.

My typewriter contributed further to the difficulty by lacking a plus sign and a half-line spacer. For superscripts or subscripts, I had to estimate a half-line distance up or down and hold it with one hand, while the other typed the necessary key.

When I completed one problem, I had to guide my mother through it to show her where to insert plus signs with pen. Cumbersome though the process was, I did it. Then my teacher was persuaded that I was doing my own work, but he did not return to accepting only answers.

The absent half-line spacer also affected German when I needed to add umlauts.

My parents had selected and purchased the typewriter, not knowing the requirements for mathematics and foreign languages.

A greater problem was the fact that I did not have a Braille algebra textbook. Naïve, I went to the principal's office to report to Mr. Walter Nutt that I did not have a Braille algebra textbook although it was available for purchase from the American Printing House for the Blind (APH) in Louisville, Kentucky. He assured me that he had ordered it. At home, I wrote a letter to APH urging that my book be sent quickly because the semester had already been in session several weeks. In response, APH wrote that the school system had not placed an order!

I returned to the principal's office to show him the letter from APH. He sputtered in embarrassment. I never did learn whether he had not placed the order or whether he had sent the order to the superintendent's office for approval and processing, where it was refused. (This was still the same superintendent referred to in Chapter Two.) Nonetheless, I received the textbook in a relatively short period of time. This is what Miss Taylor meant by making us children independent. Rather than merely accepting algebra without a textbook, I should assert myself when that specific textbook was already available for purchase but someone had not ordered it. The principal or superintendent did not expect seeing students to take algebra without a textbook but expected me to do so, because my textbook was more expensive.

One day when I was waiting in the principal's outer office for Mr. Adams to arrive for my algebra lesson, the secretary told someone in my presence how many dollars I had already cost the school system. She quoted some very high number, much higher than the price of my algebra textbook. She must have included the tuition paid to Paterson for my special education instruction.

I had a few Braille textbooks in high school; some were in process by volunteer Braillists who tried to keep ahead of my needs. This works better when the teacher begins on page one and continues without skipping chapters, as sometimes happens when a teacher may use chapters one through five and then jumps ahead to chapter eight. The Braillist then would be unable to supply me with appropriate pages in a timely fashion. Books prepared by volunteer braillists cost my school district zero dollars.

Unfortunately for Braille readers, not every textbook in print is available in Braille. For those that were not, I had to rely on Miss Hoffmeister's reading to me. With only one hour daily for such reading, I was deprived of a second reading of the same chapter. Seeing students have the luxury of rereading more difficult material. One might ask, "Why did Miss Hoffmeister not tape record material?" The fact is that reel-to-reel or cassette recorders were not yet available.

Besides Braille and live reader, today's students have available to them cassette recordings, digital recordings, computer accessibility, technology to convert material on the Internet to Braille or audio recording, The Library of Congress holdings for visually-impaired or blind patrons, Recording for the Blind and Dyslexic, and whatever resources individual states have available. The contrast between the 1930s when I was a student and 2007 when today's students are on high school campuses is the difference between black and white! Frankly, I become irked and impatient with blind students today when any one of them complains about "how hard being a blind student is today!"

Another problem facing me was my ineligibility then to use The Library of Congress Division for the Blind national network of libraries throughout the country, containing Braille books and recorded books on 78-rpm discs called talking books, available since the early 1930s. The Division for the Blind is now called National Library Services (NLS). Earlier I wrote that Miss Hoffmeister could not record her reading because such equipment was unavailable. Now I refer to the libraries for the blind and their recordings. This is not a contradiction. The recorded books at that time were produced by commercial equipment not available to individuals.

I was ineligible because the law stated that the service was exclusively for blind adults, not blind children. In 1952, that law was rescinded, permitting minors to use the library's resources; by 1952, I was thirty years old! The recorded discs were manufactured by commercial equipment not available to individuals. We had to wait until reel-to-reel and cassette recorders were invented and released for recording purposes by individuals.

By contrast, children attending boarding schools for the blind had large libraries of Braille and talking books on campus to meet students' requirements for both textbook and recreational reading. Braille classes like Miss Taylor's, however, had almost no space for recreational reading to be housed in one classroom. I was not an adult. Now on the secondary school level, I had no access to a source from which to borrow books except from the Commission's limited library. If my school could not buy a Braille textbook because of its unavailability, I had to rely on a live reader.

During elementary and secondary school years, I had four magazines available to me: *Our Special* (a woman's magazine), *Ziegler Magazine* (an adult magazine), *Searchlight Magazine* (designed for children and youth), and *John Milton Magazine* (a Protestant magazine).

I imagine the law barring children from using the Library of Congress network of special libraries affected many other high school students who, as Braille or large-print readers, were graduates of special education classes in public schools throughout the country. Because students in residential schools for blind children then comprised the larger group of students compared to us who were attending public high schools, the minority group was sorely neglected for many years until someone in authority pressed to rescind that law and to broaden use of the special libraries to any blind or visually-impaired individuals, regardless of age. Students who attended boarding schools for blind children usually remained at those schools until graduating from twelfth grade, whereas we who attended public high schools ended special education at eighth grade. When we transitioned into local public secondary schools, each of us was usually the only blind student in the student body of our respective schools.

In your community, can you imagine a public library's barring children from using its materials? If this were to happen, what would be the consensus of the residents?

Whereas most of the states had their own residential schools for blind children (their only option for educating those children), New Jersey chose not to erect such a campus for its residents for a valid and farsighted view. A residential school campus is a very expensive undertaking usually with only one option open to children and their parents. Expenditures include: administrators and teaching staff, clerical staff, educational books, equipment and supplies, construction of one or more buildings for academic classes and activities, custodial staff—all necessary for any school whether for disabled or normal children. In addition, they must fund dormitories, houseparent personnel to supervise children when not in class, around-the-clock health service, three meals a day seven days a week, food service personnel, maintenance of buildings and grounds—all for a relatively small student body.

Without such a campus, New Jersey (through establishment of the Commission for the Blind in 1910) could choose the most appropriate program for each child. If children needed residential schools, New Jersey enrolled them in the ones that were nearest to their homes and that provided the most appropriate services for each student. The following nearby states had schools: Massachusetts, New York with two schools, Pennsylvania with two, and Maryland. Massachusetts' Perkins School for the Blind had a large enrollment because it educated children from Maine, New Hampshire, Vermont, Rhode Island, Connecticut, and some from New Jersey in addition to those from Massachusetts. When a child lived within commuting distance of a school offering special education for Braille or large-print readers, the

Commission chose that option if it met the child's needs. The choices were primarily made by parents with counseling from the Commission. Perhaps if my parents had had an ongoing relationship during my preschool years with a qualified counselor who had known my mother's opinions and practices, I might have been enrolled in a residential school. When children were enrolled in residential schools then, New Jersey paid the receiving states for educating New Jersey's residents.

The leaders of the Commission believed early in the value of integration for specific children who could benefit from it. Sadly, today many school districts "integrate" children who are incapable of benefiting from association and competition with normal children, while requiring one-on-one caregivers in the classroom while being integrated and who even with caregivers are disruptive in classes for normal students. Many of these special education children, though of school age, are not toilet trained but still wear diapers, cannot talk, cannot do the academic work, are hyperactive and noisy, cannot comprehend class discussions, etc. This is not the most appropriate placement for these special education children.

Many years later when someone from Colorado proudly told me that Denver schools began integrating blind students in 1948, I had to hide the humor, as I saw it, while remembering that New Jersey had been doing so since 1910. This supports my previous statement that a boarding school limits options to only one for many children for many years.

The Colorado residential school was founded in 1874. Even early in the twentieth century, transportation and communication were very primitive compared with today's possibilities. Transportation then was primarily by horse and wagon. Because of winter weather many parents could not travel to Colorado Springs in December to take children home for the holidays; even at Easter break long trips were uncertain because of the weather. Consequently, many children did not have physical contact with their families between early September and late June.

Similarly, many families lacked telephones; some children lacked even that communication with home. When parents wrote letters to their blind children at school, they took into consideration the fact that an employee of the school would be reading aloud the letters to specific children. Because of that fact, certain news about the family was omitted from letters.

When children went home for July and August vacation, sometimes they were more like guests than members of the family. Seeing siblings had already formed friendships with neighborhood children and preferred them to the brother or sister who was regarded as much more like a stranger than kin.

Today, many more blind students are attending local public, private, or parochial schools than when I was a public school student. Also, many of the blind children enrolled now in residential schools are multi-impaired and unable to be integrated because of multiple problems better handled at a residential facility. Because of improved pediatric medical care, many blind babies are surviving but in addition to visual disorders are sustaining problems such as mental deficiency, emotional disturbance, autism, schizophrenia, cerebral palsy, and/or hearing impairment.

Today's curricula at some residential schools no longer resemble programs of fifty or seventy years ago when course content was equivalent to any strong academic elementary and secondary schools for normally-seeing students. Besides rigorous academic courses, students participated in quality music education, used power equipment for industrial arts, operated power sewing machines, learned knitting and crocheting skills, prepared complete meals using electric or gas stoves, learned housekeeping skills in home economics classes, participated in sports practicable for students with poor or absent vision, etc. Many of the graduates from the boarding schools later graduated from colleges and universities to enter professional fields.

With that necessary historical digression, let us return to Clifton and my high school years. Although Mamma did a small amount of reading to me, she was not a fluent reader. Because of her oncoming heart attack in 1938, she easily became breathless and had to stop reading. She also frequently mispronounced words. I remember the time when we students were assigned to memorize the Gettysburg Address. She read it while I Brailled it. Instead of saying *dedicated*, she said *dictated*. That was what I wrote and memorized. In class when each of us was called upon to stand to deliver the speech, other students said it before I was called on to do it. Mentally, I quickly made the switch, replacing *dictated* with *dedicated*.

My social life was limited. Although I made friends among my peers, I lacked mobility skills to socialize outside of school. No civilian blind adolescents or adults were being taught orientation and mobility with the now traditional long cane; mobility, in general, was not addressed for civilian blind.

During World War II (after I graduated from high school), blinded military personnel had specific needs met in learning Braille, typewriting, personal-care skills, job preparation, food preparation, etc. Richard Hoover (with three careers in the blindness field: physical education teacher, rehabilitation counselor during the war, and afterward, ophthalmologist) recognized the basic need for mobility. To meet that need, he developed a course with sequence and scope related to teach independent travel skills to the adults (not adolescents) in his group. He abandoned the short cane that some agencies issued to blind clients without instruction in its proper use. Hoover designed the long cane, measured from the individual's sternum down to the ground with consideration of the length of stride. For approximately twenty years after the war, no blind civilians received similar training.

In the 1960s, two universities initiated graduate programs to prepare seeing professional orientation and mobility (O&M) instructors to work with blind civilians, using the long cane. As a civilian, I received no training in mobility with a cane until the 1970s!

Wanting the ability to travel independently, I then recalled an earlier experience. On a summer evening when I was twelve, my parents and I were sitting on the front porch. I heard someone walking past the house but thought little of it. Afterward, my parents told me that a blind man had just walked by with a dog guiding him and asked whether I would like to have such a dog.

The idea to me then was abhorrent—it was like walking the streets with a big sign reading, "I AM BLIND!" No, I did not want one of those dogs!

Now in high school, I recognized the value of using a dog guide. I had matured enough to realize that I *am* blind and that I need to use a dog just as I already was employing Braille books and a Braille writer.

While still a freshman student, somehow I learned where The Seeing Eye, Inc. was located (in Whippany, New Jersey, at that time) and wrote to request information. When I discovered that the dog cost $150 and that the school preferred that service clubs not buy the dog for the blind person, I wanted to earn the money myself rather than expect my father to spend his money.

I ordered leather supplies from a source in Connecticut to make belts, wallets, change purses, keycases, etc. Friends of the family heard about my project and offered to take samples to show at their worksites. Some of the high school teachers (none of whom was my teacher) became interested and promoted the undertaking among their friends and associates. In time, I realized a profit of $150 and thought that I would stop making leather articles, but teachers and others encouraged me to continue in order to save money for college; I was already enrolled in a college-preparatory program.

I was too young then to receive a dog. The Seeing Eye letter had suggested that I wait until after I had graduated from high school before securing my dog.

A brief word here will supply background on the dog guide movement.

Dog guide use began in Germany soon after World War I for blinded military personnel. Later, someone read to Morris Frank in Nashville, Tennessee, an article from *The Saturday Evening Post,* telling of a program in Switzerland. Enthralled by the facts, he wrote a letter to inquire whether he might go there to learn how to use a dog guide. The school accepted him. After he completed training, he returned to the United States on a ship that docked in New York Harbor.

He traveled the busy streets successfully, thanks to skillful maneuvering by Buddy, a German shepherd.

Morris Frank was so enthusiastic about a dog guide's potential for improving independence in the lives of individuals who are blind that he visited the American Foundation for the Blind (AFB), located in the same city, to introduce his dog as a vital tool for many men and women.

Instead of appreciation for the impact that dog guides possess, Morris Frank met with ridicule from the one person with whom he spoke. With his dog he returned to his home in Nashville.

At that time, he could walk the streets with Buddy but was barred from entering with his dog stores, hotels, restaurants, businesses, buses or streetcars, trains, airplanes, etc.

Society was not ready to admit a dog guide where a blind man needed to go. Hero and pioneer for individuals who are blind and yearn for travel ability, Morris Frank was undaunted. Though disappointed with the lack of acceptance displayed by citizens in his own country, he was firm in his belief that dog guides are invaluable for providing independence to blind men and women. He saw the problem as not the dog's but society's. It needed to be educated to appreciate the service rendered by Buddy and multiply that by other dog/person teams who would demonstrate dignity and courage to travel when impaired or absent vision would prevent safe travel without dog or cane.

To that end, Morris Frank gathered around him a group of forward-looking individuals to establish a school to train dog guides and to instruct students in proper handling and responsible care of their dogs. The school, the Seeing Eye, Inc., began in Nashville in 1929. In time, the area's heat and humidity proved to be inappropriate for working with dogs and students. Then the school moved to Whippany, New Jersey, in the Morristown area; then it moved in the 1960s to the opposite side of Washington Valley where it has been ever since.

In 2004 the school celebrated its seventy-fifth anniversary as the first school of its type in the United States.

This is not the end of the positive influence exerted by Morris Frank. For twenty-five years, he worked for the school to educate society about dog guides. He traveled many thousands of miles in those twenty-five years to speak to various groups, encouraging them to admit dog guides and masters as employees or representatives of other businesses, customers for services or products, travelers as daily commuters or long-distance tourists, etc.

Morris Frank was a speaker at countless conventions of various organizations, such as railroad transportation, hospital administrators, restaurant managers, hotel administrators, bus transportation owners, airline transportation, owners of small businesses, large department stores, college and university presidents, insurance companies, police and firefighter chiefs, city mayors and managers, newspaper editors, radio station managers, etc.

The goal was to reach employers who in turn would share with employees what they had learned from Morris Frank. The wall of resistance and ignorance had to come down, replaced by open doors as much for blind individuals as for other seeing minorities. Morris Frank's aim was to speak persuasively while supplying factual information to remove opposition superseded by respect and acceptance of dog/person teams. (The next chapter provides information pertaining to my day-to-day instruction at The Seeing Eye.)

Public education is an ongoing necessity, because those who were children are now adults and in positions to permit or bar dog guide/ master teams from entering, whatever the type of site. With that in mind, many dog guide/person teams either offer their services or are invited to speak to classes of children or adolescents so they can learn not to fear dog guides but also not to interfere when the team is working. Thus, these students become adults who already are aware of dog guides and know their lack of threat to people in whatever venue. The same or other teams speak to or give demonstrations to service clubs.

At this stage of my life, two thoughts were at the front of my mind: securing my dog guide and attending college. At home when I commented to Mamma, "When I go to college ...," she began yelling at me, "Knock that crazy idea out of your head! You are not going to college. No one in our family has ever gone to college. Who do you think you are? Besides, you are blind. Blind people don't go to college!" I knew she was wrong; I knew blind persons who had graduated from college.

Daddy heard this tirade and entered the kitchen. "Stop telling her she can't go to college. She makes great grades on her report cards. I don't know all the answers or where the money comes from. Mike [another truck driver] has three children in college, but he's just as poor as I am. I will ask him some questions."

He came home later with some information, "Mike's twin daughters and son receive something called scholarships. The money to pay bills comes from somewhere. Mike doesn't have to pay anything for his three children in college." Although this information was optimistic for me, it was not specific enough for me to be sure that scholarships could apply to me. In time, I would receive answers.

Meanwhile, the high school principal requested that I teach Braille to Victor, a student a year behind me. Victor's vision disorder was retinitis pigmentosa that was beginning to affect his ability to read print and would probably deteriorate even more. We met one period a day.

Several times during the next summer, he came to my home to visit. We sat on the front porch in separate chairs and chatted. He did nothing offensive or suggestive such as hold my hand or sit close. That was not the kind of relationship we had.

Mamma, unfortunately, would not believe me and was anything but subtle. Coming to the front door, she exclaimed in an unnatural voice, "I don't know where the evening has gone. It's already ten o'clock!"

Quietly, Victor said to me, "I get the hint," whereupon he departed.

Afterward, Mamma went into a tirade about not marrying him because I would have blind babies. Yet she knew nothing about genetics. She assumed that everyone who was blind, regardless of the cause, automatically would have blind children. In spite of the fact that I assured her we were just friends, Mamma had to "nip it in the bud." Oh, how I wanted independence from her!

One evening in 1938 at supper, Mamma complained that she felt sick. She left the table to lie down. She mentioned having pain on the inside of her left arm. Daddy quickly phoned our family physician, Dr. Peter J. De Bell, who, surmising a heart attack, told Daddy to keep her quiet until he arrived. Dr. De Bell later diagnosed the condition as angina pectoris, a cardiac problem. This was when Mamma was forty-three years old. Besides prescribing medications, the doctor insisted upon bed rest for several months. Daddy hired a housekeeper until Mamma was able to resume her responsibilities.

Eventually, Mamma improved, although she was never completely the same again healthwise. Although losing weight and exercising were options in order to regain strength and vitality, Mamma made no effort to do either. In fact, she resisted any changes, especially in her food choices. To her, eliminating any food was punishment; she did not understand the value of certain foods and the hazard of others. Consequently, she did not lose weight.

Many times I had tried to help Mamma see that doing something different would only benefit her, but she was unable or unwilling to make an effort to change her lifestyle. Furthermore, taking suggestions or advice from her "blind/retarded" daughter was the last thing she would consider. With so much internal drive within me to succeed, I failed to understand Mamma's complacency except as ignorance. Yet, in spite of the difficulties I had experienced with her over the years, I wanted to see her health improve.

This same year, I was permitted to join church, four years after I first wanted to do so. Age twelve is common in most churches for children to become members after months of instruction. Mamma said for four years, "You don't understand something as important as church membership."

This year, my brother, now seventeen, was interested in joining the class to learn about church history, Christian beliefs, meaning of church membership, sacraments, etc. Because he took that step, I was permitted to do so also. I think that one or both parents felt that the older child should do it first. If I had done it first, Mamma especially would have been embarrassed by the fact that her firstborn was not interested.

I recall several Good Fridays during my high school years when I suggested to Mamma that she and I go to church in the afternoon for the Good Friday service. She would not, explaining (lying) that only adults go to that kind of meeting. She was not interested in attending but gave me a false reason for staying away from it.

Because of Mamma's oppressive influence, one thought permeated all of my thinking: being able to come and go as I pleased was enticing. I became convinced that a dog guide would be the means to break my mother's deadly hold over me.

I felt that Mamma violated my right to privacy, relative to receiving mail. Whenever mail arrived for me, Mamma always opened and read it before I came home from school—another of her bad habits. I felt victimized. Why could she not wait until I had arrived to let me open my own mail? She knew she would be the one to read it to me; she would not have been deprived of any information if she had waited. Her behaviors revealed how little she valued her children's rights or feelings.

At times when I received several cards for a special occasion, Mamma handed me each card after she had read it to me or removed a check as a gift. Each time, I slipped a hand inside the card to determine whether it contained Braille. After seeing me do this, she accused me of being selfish and greedy. "Isn't it enough that people send you a card? Do you expect everyone to send you money also?" Mamma had no understanding of blindness.

At last, a big day for me arrived! After I arranged for an interview at The Seeing Eye, my parents drove me to Whippany on a Sunday afternoon (so Daddy would not need to miss work). Miss Elizabeth Hutchinson, Director of Student Services, conducted the meeting. Because we had previously completed the paperwork, she already had my medical and ophthalmological reports and letters of recommendation as well as other necessary forms.

She led me outdoors where she performed several tests as part of the Juno Walk. How fast could I walk comfortably? How were my reflexes and reactions relative to stopping suddenly, swerving or turning sharply? How good was my orientation in relation to the building we had exited? What kinds of things could I see on the campus?

When we returned to her office, she assured us that I would be an excellent candidate for a dog guide.

The next matter to consider was that of scheduling me into a training class. Because I was set to graduate from high school in January of 1940, Miss Hutchinson assigned me to the April class after that.

Although this was not in the immediate future, it was thus settled that I would obtain a dog guide! After this, whenever I felt frustrated and angry with Mamma for stifling me, I told myself that it was only a matter of time before I would experience freedom. This was only one of the aspirations growing stronger within me.

The other, of course, was that of attending college. Even though no one from either side of our family had attended college, I knew I had the ability and yearned to see this dream fulfilled.

Determined as I was to attend college, I wrote to the Dean of Admissions at the new teachers college in Paterson. I received an application and other documents. One of the questions asked about disabilities; we answered it honestly. Later I received a letter from the dean, saying that a blind person cannot be a teacher.

I assumed that he was concerned about finding me a teaching position. To calm his concerns, I wrote to him again, explaining that I did not expect him to find me employment but that I wanted the opportunity to earn my bachelor's degree as a teacher.

He wrote again, repeating that a blind person cannot be a teacher. That door slammed shut!

When my pastor, L. J. Borst, heard about my rejection by the local college, he told us that he was a member of the board of admissions of Central College in Pella, Iowa. He was confident that he could have me admitted there.

He explained the procedure that the board followed. Each application was considered by itself. In addition to the paperwork submitted, any board members might speak in behalf of the applicant. Then the board voted to accept or reject that applicant.

Armed with necessary documentation, off to Pella he went with high expectations. At the appropriate moment, he presented my name, application, and background information , and my membership in his congregation. No one else on the board was acquainted with me. Then it was time to vote. After the ballots were counted, Borst was the only one to vote for me! The consensus of the others was, "What's the point of educating a blind person?"

Neither of the two colleges had referred to my academic record as being weak or unsatisfactory, because it was neither weak nor unacceptable. The two colleges did not demean me when they refused to accept me as a student. Instead, they demeaned themselves because of their own ignorance about the abilities of many blind individuals and their prejudice against minority groups. I daresay that what happened to me at the hands of these two colleges was happening to other individuals, such as an African American, a Jew, someone from the "wrong" Protestant denomination, or someone with an artificial limb. This was in late 1939. If they held such a very low opinion of blind individuals, how poorly did these Christian clergymen relate to blind individuals in their respective congregations?

Borst returned home very disappointed to have to inform us that Central College had refused to admit me. Another door slammed shut!

I discussed the matter of two rejections with Miss Hoffmeister, who told me that I would be required to take the College Entrance Examination. Convinced that this was what I wanted to do, I contacted the New Jersey State Commission for the Blind to determine how I might take that examination.

Miss Josephine L. Taylor, Director of Educational Services (not related to Katharine Taylor) explained that the procedure required that I come to the Newark office of the Commission and, in a room by myself, read each Braille question and then typewrite my answer. The process took a full morning and afternoon.

Because Daddy was scheduled to work on the designated day for the examination and his work was seasonal at best, someone else would have to drive me to Newark. Who would that be? Mamma's uncle, George Meyers, was retired and available.

After we arrived at the Commission office, Uncle George was prepared with reading materials to sit somewhere to spend the day reading, while I was assigned to another room to work alone all day.

At noon, someone alerted me to eat the sack lunch that I had brought from home. Then I plunged into the remainder of the test.

After I completed the test, someone from the staff using the official print answer form entered my typewritten answers and then mailed the form to the central office for all tests taken by seeing students for official scoring.

When the Commission received the results, I was notified that I had performed exceedingly well—well enough, indeed, for the Commission to sponsor me financially (from rehabilitation funds) for college for four years! In time, I learned the rest of my good fortune: besides the Commission's assistance for tuition and reader service, I also would receive a county scholarship and a college scholarship. In short, all my expenses, except for clothing and incidentals, would be met for four years!

After the two rejections, Miss Hoffmeister recommended New Jersey College for Women (NJC), Rutgers University, in New Brunswick.

I wrote for information and an application form, which we completed and mailed. Then I waited, expecting another letter of rejection.

Instead, the news was that I had been accepted! I still had to have an interview, but the admission was official, nonetheless!

Not only had I been accepted but I also had the wherewithal to attend college! I still had to graduate and obtain my dog guide. God was working out my future by removing what had seemed to be obstacles or stumbling blocks. *Thank you, Father.*

When Miss Hoffmeister told my mother that I would receive scholarships, Mamma said, "We will not accept charity. If we can't afford to send Grace to college, she won't go to college!"

Miss Hoffmeister explained that scholarships are not charity. She added that scholarships are given to only the strongest academic students and that receiving scholarships was an honor, not a disgrace or embarrassment.

Mamma had difficulty grasping the significance of this fact. Who would spend money to send a stranger to college? She could not fathom that.

As graduation approached, the principal and Miss Hoffmeister wanted me to attend a few classes during spring semester to remain in student mode to prepare me that much more for college in September. In April, of course, I would be excused to attend The Seeing Eye while I trained for four weeks with my first dog guide.

My head was spinning and my heart singing: *I am going to college and I am getting a dog guide!* Things were coming together so beautifully, and I had not even graduated yet. Now graduation seemed to be a steppingstone or bridge to bigger events ahead.

Before commencement evening, I had a dream that I ranked fifth in my class. That was meaningless, because I did not know my status in my class or who might be ahead of me. It was a silly dream.

As the class would be entering the auditorium in single file, I did not want to have someone beside me as a guide; that would spoil the whole processional. I told the teacher in charge of rehearsal that I had a different plan.

I had brought with me a spool of heavy thread. The girl ahead of me held the spool while the girl behind me wound the end around her finger. Midway along the thread, I made a loop and inserted my finger. The teacher was pleased when the technique worked splendidly in rehearsal, and she approved it for the official processional.

After returning home after graduation ceremonies, my brother was examining more closely the student rankings. Excited, he said, "Sis, you are *fifth* in your class. Your name is seventh in the list, but there are two ties that place you officially fifth in your class!" Fifth in a large high school class! I, "the blind/retarded kid!" As a blind student in Clifton High School between 1936 and 1940, I was in a minority of blind students who were *not* educated in a residential school but in a day program in a typical high school for normally-seeing students.

In January, my parents and I drove to New Brunswick. I was recovering from the flu. Our Buick had no heater, so Daddy borrowed his brother's automobile because of its heater and the need to prevent me from becoming chilled.

New Jersey College for Women changed its name later to Douglass College. The dean required an interview with every new student. During the interview, the question of blindness never entered the conversation. Because this institution had had many students with impaired vision since its founding in 1918, my blindness was not a concern. My dog guide that I expected to have in September was to be the first on that campus.

Unlike the early part of this book, which relates my disappointed expectation that going to School No. Fifteen would be a happy experience because of my eagerness to learn, this chapter shows the fulfillment of my realistic expectations in both securing a dog guide and entering college. God was opening doors to indicate where He wanted me to go.

FOUR

◊◊◊◊◊◊◊◊◊◊◊◊

On a Saturday afternoon early in April 1940, my parents and I drove
to The Seeing Eye in Whippany, New Jersey. The campus is now located on the opposite side of Washington Valley.

My instructor met us at the front door and led us from the lobby,
up the circular staircase, then to the right to the end of the corridor
into my room, which I shared with a woman from Alabama. The instructor suggested that I unpack and promised to return to give me a
tour of the building (that I would be using).

When he reappeared, he led me to a common recreation room for
my class's use on the same floor. Here, men and women could gather
to converse, play the piano or radio, play table games, read, have instructional sessions, etc. He showed me the location of the public telephone on the wall outside the recreation room. We then descended
the stairs. Because it was a winding staircase, it was valued as a teaching tool. At the bottom, he showed me where to deposit my outgoing
mail in a basket but cautioned me to be careful as I approached the
shelf because of its sharp corner at face or head level. (All hazards in
the greater environment cannot be removed because of a blind person
who resides or travels in the community.)

We turned right and proceeded along a corridor to the dining
room where he led me to our table and to my specific chair. The other

class used another table. (When he "led" me, it was not by the sighted-guide method of today. Instead, without touching me, he used phrases, such as "turn right" or "stay on the rug" or "turn toward me" or signaled by tapping something noisily, such as the back of my chair.)

We retraced our steps to the lobby and the front door and went outdoors and down the steps to the sidewalk. Outside, he did the Juno walk with me—the instructor assumed the role of the dog by leading me with the U-shaped harness handle. What he was doing was similar to what Miss Hutchinson had done outdoors with me, described in the previous chapter. The goal was to gather performance information about my gait and reflexes (helpful information when he needed to select from his string of ten or twelve dogs [German boxers, German shepherds, and retrievers], both male and female, the one best suited to my characteristics.) How well did I follow, stop suddenly, and swerve or turn unexpectedly, as one might have to do when traveling with a real dog guide? How much pulling on my left arm could I tolerate?

(In the early years, most of the dogs had been purchased by the school or were donated by specific kennels. Today, the school has its own breeding station at another site with German shepherds, Labrador retrievers, and golden retrievers being the primary breeds.)

The instructor had already trained his dogs for three months before I arrived. (Now training of the dogs prior to the arrival of human students takes four months.) He was thoroughly acquainted with the working style of each of his dogs. His job was to pair us for the best total combination of characteristics. In certain traits, such as speed of walking, dog and person should be the same. In other points, such as excitability, they should be opposites.

His string of dogs would serve eight students in his class. (Now the maximum class size is four.) Having more dogs than persons ready for assignment allows for satisfactory matches for each dog/

person team. The unused dogs one month are available for the classes scheduled for different instructors the next month.

When my class ended in late April, my instructor started training a new string of dogs for three months beginning in May before having his next class of students in August. He taught three or four classes in a calendar year, depending on when his vacation was scheduled.

I must clarify that the school then had more instructors than mine and his partner for that month. Every month except September has classes with two classes and two instructors each month except September. Today, twenty-four students come each month with six classes and six instructors each month. Each instructor trains his string of dogs for four months and then has a class. Instructors start training dogs in different months of the year. In a given instructor's schedule, he/she has students in the fifth month. Each class for persons begins on Saturday. I hope that that elaboration gives a clear picture of the schedules each instructor follows. Nowadays, if I am assigned to a January class, it means that my instructor trained his/her dogs in September, October, November, and December to have them ready for his human students in January.

Now let me return to my room on my first day at Headquarters. Returning to my room, I waited for the call to come to the dining room for the evening meal. Although instructors and supervisors were stationed along the route to the dining room, we were not taken by the hand and led. When a student seemed confused or walked in the wrong direction, an instructor offered verbal assistance with very explicit directions. Many lay persons do not know how to give helpful information. Telling someone, for instance, "over there" is not specific for a blind individual. One expects to see a hand point in a specific direction with the word "There."

Once everyone was seated in his or her assigned chair at the table, the instructor introduced everyone in his class and read aloud the menu.

Well-trained waitresses served us at the table. The food was unfailingly delicious and generous in portion size.

By sitting in an assigned chair for three meals before we met our dogs, we were better able to lead the dogs on leash with less confusion for the dogs. Later when each dog wore its harness to the dining room, it would know exactly which chair to use as a destination.

Relative to social climate, staff and students were addressed as Mr., Mrs., or Miss. Yet the atmosphere was never stilted or stiff. It seemed perfectly appropriate. We students called each other by given names. In more recent years, classes are more informal with staff and students on a first-name basis, if students approve.

After supper on that first day, the instructor directed us to gather in the recreation room for an orientation meeting. This included the school's history (as given in the previous chapter), house rules, daily routines, procedures for being introduced to our dogs the next afternoon, and distribution of leash and harness for each dog.

On Sunday morning two main activities were afoot: Instructors conducted their Juno walks not completed the day before and met with supervisors and the Director of Training to discuss dog assignments to specific students. After the noon meal, instructors directed us to wait in our respective rooms until summoned to the recreation room to meet his or her new dog and then return to the student's room.

When my name was called, I eagerly approached the designated rendezvous with my first dog guide! After I sat, my instructor suggested that I say, "Rachel, come!" She rushed to me with curiosity. Rachel was a German boxer (with very short, smooth hair, just a stub of a tail, erect ears, and an affectionate tongue quick to explore me. She was a bundle of energy. I snapped my leash onto her collar as instructed. I was then directed to stand, hold the leash in my left hand with my arm against my side, and lead Rachel to my room, where we would spend the afternoon becoming acquainted.

I sat on the floor in order to be on the dog's level. Rachel seemed completely happy being with me and showed no signs of wanting to return to her trainer. I talked to her so that she might become familiar and comfortable with a new voice. I stroked her smooth body, scratched behind her ears, rubbed her strong legs, let her lick me and enjoyed observing her stubby tail wiggle-waggle furiously in excitement and pleasure.

This well-behaved canine was my ticket to freedom and independence. "Oh, Rachel! I have needed you for so long. We will have many adventures together! You will go places with me completely unknown to you, but we will go together. You are half of the team; I am the other half. Furthermore, my instructor and the supervisors have prepared you for me, though they didn't know that while training you. We were made a team this morning when the decision was made to put Rachel and Grace together. You are at one end of the leash; I am at the other end. We need each other to be a team and to have a lifetime and bookful of experiences that I cannot do without your teamwork. Because you lead, I follow. You need me for your meals and water, exercise, a place to live, and for love and reassurance; I need you for so much more than that—to do the kinds of thing I know I can do but Mamma thinks otherwise. You and I are going to college in September. I want to be a teacher, even though two colleges think that a blind person cannot be a teacher. I want to teach children. Who knows what will follow after that? Are you willing to put your faith in me? I'm ready to put my trust in you, Rachel. Watch it, world; here we come!"

With the knock on the door, I called out, "Come in." My instructor was ready to take Rachel outdoors to *park* to relieve herself. I would be taking her in the future, but for today and tomorrow morning, we students had the luxury of valet *parking*!

After Rachel returned, supper was called, the instructors monitored our behavior as we proceeded to the dining room and led the dog on leash only, with the command, "Rachel, heel." When I found my chair at the table, I tapped it and said, "Good girl!" This would help her to identify my chair when later, in harness, she led me into the dining room. I put her at *rest* facing out from under the table. She lay very still for the duration of the meal. At the end of supper, we returned to our room to continue becoming acquainted with our dogs.

After being taken to park at eight o'clock that evening, our dogs stayed with us overnight for the first time. At five-thirty Monday morning, my instructor came to take Rachel to park while I dressed for the day. When Rachel returned, I made my bed, tidied the room, and waited for the breakfast call.

While we were in the dining room, my instructor told us which four teams would be in the first half of the class to go to town in the station wagon (now minivan) and to be ready to leave at 7:55 at the front door.

Four students and four dogs went to town for their maiden walks. Because this was the first walk for each student with a new dog in harness, our instructor took one dog/person team at a time this morning.

As we walked around the block, we made only right turns at corners. We do this somewhat differently from the way that seeing persons turn corners. We walk to the curb, feel it with a foot, praise the dog, and make the appropriate turn. The dog has been trained to go to the curb first before turning. Curbs become landmarks. If we blind persons attempt to turn corners the way seeing persons do, we have to estimate how close to the corner we are. If we estimate incorrectly and give the command, "right," we might end up in someone's yard or in a gasoline station or in a parking lot, etc. Furthermore, estimating the distance from the corner is not workable in territory not previously traversed. Therefore, going to the curb before giving the command, "right," is much more precise. When the dog stops short of the curb and the person does not easily reach forward with the foot to find the curb, the master encourages with, "Rachel, hopp-hopp" which means move forward a short distance so that I can find the curb. When the dog moves forward and master finds the curb, praise is given.

When we give a command to the dog, we use the dog's name first, such as, "Rachel, right."

At the curb, three options are viable for an experienced dog guide user: forward to cross the street, left, or right.

In making a right turn, the person turns his or her body one-quarter turn away from the dog and then commands, "right." Then the dog turns to the right and lines up beside the master. This is easier than left turns.

When the student turns one-quarter turn to the left toward the dog and commands, "left," the dog (which is usually on the person's left side) turns away from the master to lead.

Throughout our training, we students learned to use certain inflections in our voices to convey happiness, enjoyment, and encouragement. Also, we used hand gestures to indicate left, right, or forward to combine with the verbal.

Our instructor followed and observed everything that the team did or neglected to do. He gave reminders as well as praise or even reprimands. This feedback is essential to stop inappropriate management of the dog. At this early stage of training, the dog is more highly qualified than students are.

This new experience was exhilarating for a blind adolescent— walking in strange territory but not holding a human guide's arm while walking at a faster rate than one goes when unassisted. *Look at me! I am walking fast and straight along the sidewalk! I am doing it!* "Thank you, Rachel! This is great! Rachel, you are a *good girl*! You stopped correctly at the curb. *Good girl*! You deserve a pat on the shoulder."

Then we were back at the station wagon. Lots of praise for Rachel! We went all around the block on our first walk!

We waited until the next team exited the vehicle before we entered, saying, "Bon voyage! Have a great walk!"

After our instructor walked each team on this same route, we headed back to Headquarters, so that the other four students could go to town for their maiden walks. Not every student was a beginner like me. Some students were training with their second or third dog. Nevertheless, this was their maiden walk with this new dog.

Back on campus, as we approached the front door, for safety, one student rattled the door handle, opened the door outward, went through, and allowed the door to latch with a click before the next student stepped toward the door. This procedure prevented one student from walking into the edge of the open door held by another. Also, by not reaching for the door handle before hearing the door latch, one's fingers and hand were not pinched and injured.

We entered the lobby with ear-to-ear smiles, I am sure, because of our successful trips in town. Success begets self-confidence.

Although I had not known before going to The Seeing Eye how the dog worked, I was already beginning to comprehend the process. I needed to communicate with the dog by using words in her listening vocabulary: *come, sit, down, rest, fetch, out, good girl, left, right, forward, hopp-hopp, steady,* etc. When I know how to reach my destination, I convert that information to the three basic commands—forward, left, right—a block at a time. Rachel would not understand the command, "Rachel, grocery store" or "Rachel, bank." Instead, I must know the lefts, rights, and forwards involved in order to arrive at the grocery store or bank. Furthermore, these commands work in any location, even foreign countries. Even if Rachel understood "grocery store" and "bank" in Morristown, she would not know how to find those destinations in my hometown. Consequently, the same commands that work in Morristown work successfully anywhere else. As motorists, you want traffic signs and traffic lights to mean the same thing from state to state; just so, we users of dog guides want commands that work anywhere.

Of course, the master of the dog must give commands. When the dog and I leave the house, the dog does not know whether I will be turning left out of the yard or right. When we reach the first corner and toe the curb, the dog does not know whether I am going to say, "Forward," "Left," or "Right." She does not know beforehand whether I am going to visit my friend, Sue, or go to a bakery or to a shoe store or to a beauty salon or out for an exercise constitutional. The dog is not my brain. She is a canine tool that I use for independent travel.

When you get into the driver's seat of your automobile, the vehicle does not "know" where you intend to go. You "command" the car by using the ignition, steering wheel, gears, turns, speed, etc.

Each dog is trained in Morristown but then will move to a new community and may move several more times in its life. For instance, Rachel was trained in Morristown, would move to Clifton and then to New Brunswick to the college campus and who knew where after that! Wherever a team lives, when the person and dog leave home on an errand, the dog does not know beforehand the destination. Teams are encouraged to vary routes at home (not during training in Morristown) to keep the dog curious and alert rather than limit the dog's experience to only one route to each destination.

After the last four students returned in the morning, we fed our dogs and took them to park, an asphalt-covered area on campus.

During lunch, our instructor assigned each of us to the first or second trip of the afternoon. The assignments changed each trip. For instance, in the morning I might be with Stan, Bill, and Carl. In the afternoon I might be with Carl, Steve, and Doug. I might add here that women were in the minority in the early classes. In my first class, women students numbered only three, while men were thirteen. Throughout the four weeks, we were in various combinations. Changing the membership of teams working together is good for the dogs rather than working with the same team exclusively every time we worked in town.

The duration of our stay at the school for training was a week longer for students securing their first dog than for those with prior experience. Students training with their first dog stay in training through Thursday of the fourth week and return home that day.

In the afternoon of that first Monday, our instructor took two teams together to work the same route used in the morning. When we worked with two teams together (as we will for the duration of our training), one team started first and waited at the curb at the end of that block for the other team to arrive soon after and align itself beside the first team at the curb. The second team followed soon after but did not crowd the lead team. This walk was not a race. The second team stayed behind all the way to the curb where it came abreast of the first team.

Then our instructor might direct what had been the second team now to lead in the next block. Dogs must learn they cannot always be first. They must follow in a self-controlled and orderly fashion.

After the second trips of the afternoon, students fed their dogs, took them to park, did the obedience exercise, and then groomed their guides. Of course, all activities were supervised, because our mishandling of the dogs might damage the dogs' training or confuse them with unfamiliar management.

At the evening meal our instructor told us of a scheduled evening meeting in the lounge at 6:45. At that meeting, students may again practice the obedience exercise. The instructor may discuss the two sets of walks that had occurred that day and any topic he deemed appropriate that early in training.

Eight o'clock was time for the last park opportunity. Once indoors again, we were given the rest of the evening as personal time, though many students prepared for bed and retired. It had been a long and busy day!

I will not take you through every day of the four weeks in detail as I did the first Monday. Now that you have seen a typical day, I can just say that the other days were very similar. The two major differences from day to day or week to week were the variety of routes taken and topics addressed in instructional sessions in the recreation room.

A route was usually walked three or four times. Then came the solo trip. What *solo* meant was that two teams walked the same route again but with no assistance from the instructor or from supervisors stationed along the route. In fact, students did not know where any one of the training staff might be stationed to monitor students' management of dogs.

The purpose of solo trips is for students to demonstrate how well they can manage the dog under all conditions when the instructor is unavailable.

Even when teams turned too soon at the wrong corner but then recognized the error by encountering something unfamiliar, such as a downhill slope or a noisy business and corrected the mistake by retracing their steps back to the route, this was considered a successful trip.

In addition, each route became longer and more complex or more complicated. The first route, for example, was in a quiet, residential neighborhood, going around the block, making only right turns. Gradually, subsequent routes introduced left turns, crossing streets without traffic lights, crossing with traffic lights, more pedestrian traffic, wider sidewalks, business areas, broken pavement, going up or down hills, walking beside the road with no sidewalk, walking in a city park with distractions by wild life, crossing streets with heavy traffic, etc.

The last week was an assortment of requests by students of experiences desired before going home. These might include a bus ride, a train ride to the next station and return, walking through a train terminal, going to New York City to use subways, finding a designated coffee shop, shopping in a department store, using a revolving door or elevator or escalator, exploring a mall, etc.

We had trips to town on Saturday mornings, but Saturday and Sunday afternoons from two to four o'clock were reserved for visiting hours for relatives and/or friends. Those hours were strictly enforced.

When my parents left me after their first visit while I was in training, they went to their car, fully expecting to see all students come out the front door en route to the park behind the building. My instructor waited and waited for my parents to leave the campus. When it was apparent to him that they were not planning to leave, he walked outside to their car to explain that students would not be coming out until all visitors had left the campus.

One of my parents said, "We won't speak to Grace. She won't know we are watching."

The instructor explained further that visitors are not permitted to watch students while working with their dogs. He suggested that after I come home with my dog, they may watch me to their hearts' desire, but not here at the school. "Now please leave."

Sunday mornings had no trips to town except when diabetic students required exercise.

On the Thursday designated for returning home, a few students might have transportation provided by relatives or friends who came to the school. Instructors and others of the Training Division transported students to bus stations, railroad stations, and Newark Airport and waited with them until they boarded. Members of the staff checked to be sure that the dog was comfortable and adequately provided for during this trip. For dogs traveling on airplanes, this was their first experience on a plane. Most of such dogs settled down as if planes were no different from buses or trains.

On the next day, instructors completed their written reports about student performance; they also sanitized the dogs' park, making it ready for the next class, arriving on Saturday. The two instructors moved their personal belongings out of their respective rooms and took them home. During the first week of class, the two instructors stayed overnight at the school for a solid week, having only phone contact with their families. Beginning with the second week, two instructors alternated nights in going home and being back at the campus by five a.m.

The housekeeping staff gave the building an extra thorough cleaning, though it was cleaned every day. Student rooms were made ready for new arrivals the next day. On Saturday, the cycle repeated itself for the next class.

A word about the building might be interesting. Originally, headquarters was a large private home that was converted into a school as much as possible. Offices were on either side of the lobby. The kitchen and dining room were at the back. The second floor was primarily bedrooms and recreation rooms for students. The third floor contained living quarters for instructors who had classes for almost a month.

The basement provided students with laundry equipment for washing, drying, and ironing.

A room in the basement was available for grooming dogs when weather outdoors was inclement.

A nurse was on duty for each shift, especially important for diabetic students. Other students might need a nurse for sore feet or ankles, for blisters, for colds, etc.

In time, as the student enrollment increased, wings enlarged the building's ability to accommodate additional students.

On the campus were other buildings that students did not visit: garages, kennels for dogs at various levels of training, a quarantine clinic for dogs when ill, a building for equipment and supplies for maintenance of buildings and grounds, and canine health care center for routine maintenance, etc.

I was blessed to have met and interacted with the founders of The Seeing Eye, Inc., a privilege denied more recent students and staff members because of retirement and death of those distinguished pioneers. I have already referred to Elizabeth Hutchinson, Director of Student Services. One of her tasks was reading mail to us.

Mr. Willi Ebeling was a charming gentleman with a German accent. He managed the financial affairs of the school.

When I first met Mr. Ebeling, I offered him my check for $150 to pay for my dog. I explained how I had earned the money. He said that I did not need to pay for my dog then, that I might use that money for college expenses. I explained that I had a total scholarship and that I wanted to pay for my dog then. He said that I might wait until I was a teacher and earning a salary before paying for my dog. I insisted on paying immediately.

Because Morris Frank worked for the school for twenty-five years, I had the privilege of association with him during my class sessions when he was on campus and not traveling.

William G. Debetaz, a delightful gentleman with a French-Swiss accent, came from Switzerland to be Director of Training, a position he held for approximately forty years until he retired. In that time he contributed invaluable service to training dogs and instructors as well as educating students, a necessary first step to launch the school.

Incredibly astute about dogs' interpretation of situations, he taught me to get inside my dog's head and look through its eyes at a given scenario that was problematic. This insight on his part, shared with me, resolved problems soon after they arose.

Jack Humphrey was a supervisor of training. He reminded me of an Army sergeant in his interaction with students, but he was usually justified in his approach when students had done something wrong.

Recounting an incident will convey his manner of interacting with students. As supervisor, he knew the next day's itinerary for students. To create a realistic situation that students sooner or later encountered, he parked his vehicle across the sidewalk we students were using that day and turned off the engine. Soon a student came along to find a barrier. The student, a man, put out his hand to discover it was some kind of vehicle, whereupon he audibly complained about why someone would park across the sidewalk when blind students were using that sidewalk as part of the day's route. He continued to complain without demonstrating resourcefulness.

Irked by the student's behavior, Mr. Humphrey, from inside the vehicle, boomed out with his sergeant-like voice, "Instead of grumbling about the vehicle, use your dog and walk around it!"

On a few occasions, I had the great privilege of meeting Dorothy Harrison Eustis, who had visited the school in Switzerland to observe how the dogs were being trained and how they functioned when fully trained. Afterward, she wrote an article published in *The Saturday Evening Post*. It was that article that someone read to Morris Frank in Nashville, Tennessee. That article ignited a fire in Morris Frank's heart and mind. He then wrote a letter to the school in Switzerland to request permission to go there to be trained with a dog. The rest, as they say, is history.

Of all the agencies with which I have had personal and professional association, The Seeing Eye, Inc., is number one on my list for several positive reasons. The Seeing Eye genuinely respects the men and women it supplies with dog guides. Sadly, some employees of other agencies work for blind individuals but neither truly respect their clients nor consider them equal to themselves. Some agencies provide drab and unattractive surroundings for clients, because "clients can't see their environment anyway." The Seeing Eye, Inc., by contrast, insists upon visually-attractive surroundings for its students, with pictures and mirrors on walls, fresh flowers on tables in the dining room, attractive décor in each room, etc. As the first school of its type in the United States, it certainly set high standards for subsequent schools to emulate.

Its professional staff members are highly qualified, dedicated, and committed to their students and dogs.

I will relate an experience that I had in a very large city when I visited a state agency for the blind. I was curious about whether I might work for this agency as a rehabilitation teacher, then called "home teacher."

The director of the agency met with me. Blind himself, after discussing my credentials, he said that I was highly qualified to work for his agency. However, if I worked for him, he said that I must forfeit my dog (reason No. One for not wanting to work for him)! Then he summoned his secretary to bring him an application form to give to me.

When she appeared, she attempted to take my handbag out of my lap, saying, "I'll put the application in here for you, honey, so that you don't lose it,"(reason No. Two)! Those two factors were reason enough to justify why I did not apply for the position.

My response to the secretary was, "If I am qualified to work here, I am also qualified to take care of the application and put it into my handbag myself, honey."

The director had not trained his secretary to adopt a different attitude toward employees or prospective employees. I had to conclude that her behavior and attitude were exactly what he wanted in a secretary.

Although in later years I have lived closer to other schools providing dog guides, I, as a satisfied consumer, have returned each time to The Seeing Eye for my next dog.

The staff's enthusiasm is contagious. Furthermore, staff members, especially of the Training Division, remain for many years with very little turnover. Attrition is usually for retirement, not for changing jobs outside the blindness field.

I also firmly believe in students' paying something toward the expenses for their dogs. The price for the first dog is $150, and $50 for each later dog; those prices were set very early in the school's history but have not been raised since then.

The actual cost of preparing one dog guide now is $50,000 or higher! The cost per dog is determined by adding all expenditures incurred by the school in a fiscal year and then dividing that sum by the number of dogs trained in that year.

This was the only school of its kind in our country in 1940, when I went the first time. What a unique experience to be a student then as a female adolescent when female students were definitely a minority group! The school did not discriminate against female students.

Instead, men were more likely to be employed then and have need of dog guides. Females were more fearful of traveling alone.

Let us return to matters of training. One aspect of using dog guides has not yet been addressed: How do blind people use traffic lights that they cannot see? The assumption by the public is that dog guides differentiate between green and red traffic lights and know when to go and when to wait. No, the dogs do not read lights. Instead, blind pedestrians must listen carefully to the flow of traffic in order to interpret the red or green light. This is true whether the person who is blind uses a dog guide or cane.

For instance, imagine that my dog and I are standing at the curb with Madison Avenue in front of us and with Broadway on our left side. When traffic is moving on Broadway, I have a green light. When traffic stops on Broadway but starts on Madison, I have a red light. So I must pay strict attention to what vehicles are doing—not only going in straight lines but when making turns at intersections. Dogs can determine by vision sooner than blind persons can know by listening that vehicles are turning a corner toward us.

Even if I tell my dog, "Rachel, forward" when I have a green light, she will not leave the curb when she sees a vehicle moving toward us. This behavior is called intelligent disobedience. As I sense the vehicle is approaching, I praise the dog and wait until the vehicle passes and the noise has dissipated before I repeat the command.

Once we are in the street headed for the opposite up-curb, the dog is in control, slowing down when necessary, swerving, stopping abruptly with nowhere for me to go except up on my toes in order not to advance, if required. Once on the sidewalk again, I give praise and the next command of "left," "right," or "forward" for a block when I have no destination in that block except to reach the next corner and its curb as a landmark.

If my destination is within the block (such as a shoe store or pharmacy), as I approach it, I alert the dog with the words, "Right, right, right" or "left, left, left" with the words drawn out. The words are meant to be suggestive rather than an abrupt turn. When the dog has been to this destination earlier, she will zero in on it this time.

If it is the first time for the dog, we might go to the wrong door if several storefronts are side by side. I will inquire within. When we enter the correct one, I praise the dog so that the next time, she is likely to come directly to the one that I desire.

If other pedestrians are available, I might stop one to ask for information or assistance in finding that address the first time.

Knowing how to ask the correct question is crucial. If I stop in front of a store, not knowing what it is, and ask another pedestrian, "Is this a shoe store?" indicating the building, he might say, "Yes, it is." Then later, after I am inside, I learn that it is Fit Right Shoes, but I wanted Smith's Shoes. A better question would have been, "Do you have time to show me where Smith's shoe store is in this block?" The pedestrian might walk me to the entrance, or he might offer, "It's that direction." At that juncture, I need to determine with a gesture which direction I think he had indicated: "Do you mean that I should go that way?" When he says, "Yes," I thank him and continue my walk. Even though this means I must walk in the correct direction and ask another pedestrian, I am making progress toward my destination. (Think of situations while you are driving. The first question that you ask someone may not supply all the help you need. Then you ask someone else later for additional information.)

When possible, we ask friends before we leave home for the specific street address or ask for information, such as, "Is it closer to Brook Street or to Empire?" Or we might even phone the store for more information. Once we have located a specific address, we use existing landmarks, such as an exhaust fan, a noticeable crack in the sidewalk, a driveway, etc., to use next time when approaching that same address.

Another kind of problem is caused by some drivers who can add misinformation without knowing it. Perhaps a driver recognizes my dog as a dog guide and is curious about how these dogs work and assume that the dogs read traffic lights. So the driver decides to wait to see what the dog does when the light changes to green. However, because I am taking my cue from this vehicle and not from the light, we do not move forward when the light changes because the vehicle had not moved. Furthermore, the dog waits for my command, "Forward." (When more vehicles than one are available, I gain additional information from the others that may help me.)

The driver then concludes that my dog is not well trained and may tell many people about seeing this dog that was apparently ill-equipped to be a dog guide, because it did not go forward when the light turned green. Drivers can help us most by doing what good drivers should do at all times. Then we pedestrians who are blind (whether with dog guide or cane) receive clear signals.

Unhappily, some drivers have not been pedestrians in years and are unaware of the problems they can create for pedestrians, even those with normal vision.

Specifically, drivers who whiz around a corner behind pedestrians do not allow for missteps when the curb is extra high or broken. Another situation is when plows have pushed snow against curbs; pedestrians then need to climb the bank of snow and ice in order to reach the sidewalk. If the walker slips and falls, he or she will be under the wheels of the vehicle. Caution on the part of drivers is in order.

What does a blind person do at a corner without a traffic light? Blind pedestrians must listen to all vehicles from all directions—left and right, ahead and behind—before leaving the curb. We must ever be vigilant. *Will this vehicle turn in my direction?* When a noisy vehicle, such as a truck or bus, approaches, it obliterates all other vehicular sounds. So we must wait until the environment is reasonably quiet again before determining when to cross. Someone's noisy lawn mower or a worker's air hammer creates too much noise for a decision about when to cross. The safe thing to do might be to turn the corner without crossing a street and go to a quiet corner to cross and continue en route after the detour.

When you observe a pedestrian with dog guide or cane waiting at the curb an extra long time, this behavior does not necessarily mean that he or she is confused or disoriented; instead, it probably means that the person is waiting until some noise not obvious to you dissipates. Waiting is precisely what this person needs to do. Seeing persons can cross streets in loud noise; blind persons cannot; safety is primary.

On usually busy streets, blind persons are wise not to cross without a traffic light. Walking to an intersection with a traffic light in order to cross with it is an intelligent maneuver. Also, when a blind person is a passenger on a bus coming home and needing to get off at Ward Street and cross Main Street (quite busy), he would do well to leave the bus earlier or later at a traffic light intersection to cross the busy street there and walk the extra distance under more favorable conditions.

A specific law permitting drivers to turn right on red lights is to the disadvantage of blind pedestrians. The vehicle turning right then gives no information about the traffic light: is it red or green? Drivers may turn right when the light is green or when the light is red.

In the past, a traffic light gave equal time in each direction: north-south and east-west streets, with the same amount of time to wait or move. Nowadays, many traffic lights give less waiting time to drivers on busy streets and more to less-traveled side streets. Consequently, crossing the busy street on foot or on wheels provides few seconds to accomplish the task. Although that is an advantage to drivers on the busy street, it is a definite disadvantage to all pedestrians crossing the busy street. This means that pedestrians have much less time to cross busier streets.

Another technological problem for pedestrians is when busy streets may not be stopped by a red light when no vehicles are on the side street. Only when a vehicle triggers a cable under the side street does a red light signal for the busy street to stop traffic. In other words, a pedestrian may have a very long wait before traffic stops on the busy street to permit him to cross.

Another problem for blind pedestrians is that automobiles are less noisy than heretofore. Electric cars are just about inaudible! They are practically noiseless, when hearing vehicles approach is crucial.

Not all blind adults use dog guides for a variety of reasons:

More legally blind individuals use canes because more of them have useful residual vision and may not qualify for dog guides. Fewer legally blind persons are totally blind.

To use dog guides successfully, persons must be physically able to be active to follow energetic dogs, have employment, have reasons to leave the house to travel alone. Having very little useful vision promotes greater reliance on the dog's guidance rather than trying to depend on one's limited vision. Maybe a person sees better on a bright, sunny day while someone else sees better on a day with less glare and intense brightness; this reliance on the dog enhances the dog's usefulness and self-confidence. Someone who is eighty-seven years old and gradually losing vision is less likely to qualify for a first dog, though each applicant is considered on an individual basis, rather than following strictly formulated rules on paper.

Diabetics are good candidates when all other factors have been met. Having a dog guide permits the diabetic to walk outdoors for exercise to control sugar levels. Using the dog for exercise to maintain health is an excellent reason for a diabetic to have a dog guide in addition to the other reasons.

The youngest student might be sixteen or seventeen years of age though valid exceptions may exist. The teenager must be mature enough to maintain the dog's training and be consistent from day to day.

When an individual continues using dog guides throughout his or her life, age is less of a factor relative to securing the next dog, though the school requires a medical evaluation of the student each time a new dog is sought. In ten years or so since the previous medical report, changes may be occurring and should be considered as factors that may influence a decision to grant another dog guide. Health changes in the student can occur since the training with the previous dog.

At this writing, I am eighty-five years old and have been using dogs for sixty-seven years! My present dog is my ninth!

Why do some blind individuals prefer the cane for mobility? One answer is personal choice. Some persons may have distorted impressions about having a dog guide and opt for the cane. For instance, without obtaining official information, some cane users may believe that dog guide and master must never be separated. With that misinformation, cane users feel that the cane is preferable. In fact, dog and master may be separated for such reasons as attending a concert or drama or dance with a spouse or friend as guide, going to a dinner party with a companion when the dog will be under the table all evening, going shopping for clothing with a friend and having to use small fitting rooms, using a swimming pool with a spouse or friend, etc. However, one cannot leave the dog unattended all day unless in the care of a responsible adult who will provide appropriately for the dog's needs.

Afraid of dogs or reluctant to trust the dog with their safety when crossing streets or stopping at the top of a flight of stairs, these persons prefer to use a cane or only a human guide.

Feeling negatively about having to take the dog outdoors in all kinds of weather to go to its "park" to relieve itself or disliking canine accidents or canine medical expenditures, these users of canes see no advantages in using dog guides. (Expenses caused by dog guides are included in human medical expenses according to the Internal Revenue Service.)

Users of canes come home and may stand the cane in a corner until the next trip out. For some, it may mean coming in from work on Friday evening and not leaving home again until Monday morning.

Some individuals enjoy sleeping late on days off; this is not advisable with a dog guide that requires more or less a regular schedule each day.

Some visually-impaired individuals see well enough in daylight to travel safely but do poorly in the dark. Using a dog under those conditions is inadvisable; the dog is likely to be handled incorrectly during the day and then expected to work properly at night. This tears down the dog's understanding of when to work and when not to work.

Individuals with sufficient vision for travel may not view themselves as blind and not needing dog guides; they are correct on the latter point. Also, usable vision is a hindrance to efficient use of dog guides. When the person can see the curb or flight of stairs before the dog stops to signal them, the person can confuse the dog by stepping up or down before the dog signals. In time, the dog's training deteriorates from non-use or from confusing behavior of the master.

The public is requested to ignore a dog guide when it is wearing the harness and working. This means not whistling at the dog, not patting it, not feeding it, not deliberately standing in its path just to see what the dog will do, not grabbing the person's left arm to steer the team, not grabbing the harness handle to steer the dog, etc. When you think that the person seems to need help, do not assume you know what kind of help is in order. Instead, ask, "May I help you?" The person can either explain what kind of assistance is necessary or decline your offer.

To illustrate that point, I draw from personal experience. One day I was standing at a corner in Philadelphia. A man came by, grasped my arm and said, "I have time to help you," while trying to propel me to the curb. I insisted that I did not need his help. Ignoring what I had said, he again stated that he had time to cross the street with me. Freeing my arm from his vise-like grip, I informed him that I was waiting for a bus and had no need to cross the street.

When you attempt to give directions, talk directly to the person and not to the dog. For instance, when I enter the room with my dog and you want to show me where an empty chair is, talk to Grace rather than say, "Rachel, bring her over here. Over here, girl. Rachel is a good dog!"

When you think I am too strict with my dog, don't argue with me about how I should give her more freedom to wander about and visit with other people or have a little snack. I have been taught how to manage my dog in various situations. It is imperative that I maintain her excellent training to prevent others from interfering, adding to the risk of the dog's being negligent, thus causing me injury. It may be my bone that is broken, not yours, when she fails to signal a down staircase because you have distracted her.

I think of a woman who, when I had completed shopping in a store, criticized me when I gave my dog the command, "outside" when still far away from the exit.

The woman said derisively, "You aren't even close to the door. Why do you tell her 'outside' now?"

I explained that the dog needed to know where to go in the store. If I merely said, "Forward," the dog might think that we were going somewhere else in the store. "Outside" is a clear command that we are leaving the building. The dog is happiest when permitted to do what she has been professionally trained to do.

Relative to finances, what is the source of The Seeing Eye's income? Is there federal funding? Absolutely none. This is a private philanthropy. It raises money through public education and financial campaigns. Money is sent in voluntarily by donors who want to support the work of this school. Other sources are from wills, bequests, and types of charitable gift annuities. The board of trustees includes leaders who conservatively manage finances and investments, who regard seriously their stewardship of the school's wherewithal to operate and continue the school's mission.

Although additional schools for training dog guides now exist, they cannot be called The Seeing Eye, Inc. That name is exclusively reserved for the school in New Jersey. Each school must create its own name and have it registered. *Dog guide* is the generic term for all dogs that guide blind individuals. Just as a parking lot contains vehicles, not all of them are Plymouths. Similarly, Harvard would not want to be referred to as Yale or Yale referred to as Columbia. Just so, only certain dog guides can be called Seeing Eye dogs. Seeing Eye harnesses bear the name of the school. (Another distinction to be made among dogs is that dog guides are different from helper dogs or therapy dogs, companion dogs, or hearing dogs for the deaf.)

Many individuals are unaware of these various schools or their respective names but regard them as branches of the original school or know of only one school and assume that all dog guides come from it. Without consulting me, a colleague where I had worked made a financial contribution in my name to the school in Florida. Apparently, he thought that my dogs had come from it. Of course, no one at the Florida school was acquainted with my name.

Graduates from The Seeing Eye have a support system at their disposal. If we have a problem, we can write or telephone and expect prompt responses in the form of discussion of possible solutions, a visit by a qualified instructor, or correction of the problem at the school itself when the graduate has the time and is willing to return to the campus for possibly a week of intensive corrective work.

Our dogs do not have a designated birthday for retirement. Instead, they work as long as they are capable of rendering responsible and safe service. In terminal illness, such as certain cases of cancer, euthanasia is reluctantly employed. In other situations, such as arthritis with which the dog has great difficulty climbing stairs or boarding a bus, the dog should be retired to a less demanding lifestyle either in the same home or with someone eager to provide a home for a deserving dog guide. It now becomes a true pet, surrounded by affection and relaxation and medical care.

When I returned home after my four weeks of training, I introduced Rachel to our part of Clifton. We walked to and from high school to complete the spring semester. When Rachel stopped at the bottom of stairs before going up or stopped at the top of stairs before going down, Miss Hoffmeister and others interpreted the behavior as unwillingness to work. I explained that she was doing exactly what she had been trained to do and that she was signaling me about up-stairs and down-stairs. If she did not signal by stopping first, I would take a nasty fall.

In classes, Rachel behaved well as I had expected she would by lying in one place without a sound.

In church, Rachel disturbed no one. She came between two pews and lay down for the duration of the service without a sound.

For the first few weeks, Mamma was very apprehensive of my dog. I had to explain that Rachel was a German boxer and not a bull-dog, a different breed, and that Rachel would not hurt Mamma. In time, Mamma grew to love the dog.

The two novels that I have previously written, *MARISSA: Obstacle Illusions* and *MARISSA AND DAN: Grace Notes*, contain several accounts of my dogs that will not be repeated here, though other anecdotes will be included in this volume.

On a weekend my family drove to the seashore and walked the boardwalk. We stayed together until I said, "I'm going to walk alone ahead of you three." Rachel and I stepped out and maneuvered around other pedestrians. My father and brother were trotting after us. The family witnessed how well the dog could guide.

On a Saturday evening, I said I was going for a walk but would rejoin them at my grandparents' home. Immediately, Mamma wanted to know exactly which route I would use. This annoyed me, because my brother could leave the house without having to designate the route he would take.

When Rachel and I were about halfway through our route, I heard a very familiar sound approaching from behind. It was Daddy's Buick that had its own unmistakable sound. I waved at the car and called out, "Hi, Dad!"

When I arrived at my grandparents' home, Mamma said, "We can't get away with anything. You always catch us."

My parents had planned to observe us working that evening. That was why Mamma wanted specific information about the route I had chosen.

Life was changing because of Rachel's presence in the family. I was gaining independence, though gradually yet. Independence tasted very sweet and enticing! My independence was long overdue.

Rachel loved to sun herself on our small back porch. Even though she could have pushed open the door with her nose, she did not. Instead, she whimpered by the door. I let her out, and she lay in the early morning sunshine. When she had had enough, she whimpered to come in but did not scratch at the screen door.

I worked out an experiment with my brother to prevent an unwanted behavior. I suggested to Mart that as he walked down the steps of the back porch he slap his side and say, "Rachel, come." She bounded after him, whereupon I scolded Rachel for leaving the porch.

Days later, I had my brother repeat his behavior. Rachel did not accept the invitation to go with him. I praised her profusely. I had accomplished the desired end. Being tied does not show what the dog might do if not tied. I wanted her to know that going with someone, even from the family, was unacceptable unless I had given her my permission to go.

I now hasten to caution owners of dog guides not to follow my poor example. I was fortunate that nothing had ever attracted Rachel from the porch when not tied. I should have tied her to protect her from any danger that came into our unfenced yard.

I was excitedly anticipating college with my four-legged roommate. The two of us had a world to conquer. *College, here we come!*

Some minor changes in procedure and practice have evolved throughout the years since 1940 when I was first a student at The Seeing Eye, but the basic training protocol is the same.

FIVE

<small>◇◇◇◇◇◇◇◇◇◇</small>

In September 1940, the day finally arrived when we loaded as many of my things as would fit into our Buick and headed for New Jersey College for Women (NJC) in New Brunswick. About a decade later, the name was changed to Douglass College, named for its first dean. Even today it is still an all-women's college as part of Rutgers University. More graduates now would recognize it as Douglass than NJC.

I had been assigned to House L on Gibbons Campus. This three-story house accommodated only thirteen women. My room was at the front of the house on the first floor beside the living room. The other two bedrooms on first floor were singles as was mine. We had a communal bathroom on our floor. On second floor, eight women lived in four rooms, with a communal bathroom on that floor. The third floor had two rooms, usually a double bedroom and a double study for the house director and another senior of her choosing, with their bathroom.

The dean of women had earlier decided that blind students should have single rooms, so that working with readers would not disturb roommates.

In order to go to meals or to the main campus for classes from Gibbons, we students had to cross a highway, walk along a path across a field, and cross over a ravine via a suspension bridge. The only building before the bridge was the Music Building off to the right. Everything else was located on the far side of the ravine.

Later that fall, we had our first snow. I left my house en route to breakfast in Cooper Hall that morning, using the straight sidewalk to the highway. On the other side, I knew that snow covered the path to the suspension bridge. I wondered whether my dog could handle this snow problem. I had trained with her in the previous April but had no snow during our training, although she may have had experience with snow during her three months of training earlier. With some apprehension, I knew I had to try her in snow. Mustering my courage, I pretended having confidence in her. I commanded, "Rachel, forward," hoping that I sounded full of trust. She started with eagerness, but I was not sure where she might take me when she could not see the path.

Happily, Rachel was truly self-confident. I followed where she went but wondered about our destination. Then my boots sounded on the bridge! She did it! "You are an all-weather dog guide! Good girl!" After that experience, I never again doubted her ability to cope with snow!

For the first few days on campus, someone from House L walked with Rachel and me to breakfast. We sat at assigned tables with another freshman student as our waitress. This job provided the waitresses with their own meals as compensation.

The building, Cooper Hall, had a dining room for freshman, another for sophomore, another for junior, and a fourth for senior students, plus others for various additional purposes besides portions of the building for food preparation. Before waitresses served us, they ate in a separate dining room. We ate three meals a day and seven days a week in Cooper Hall. We had paid for our meals at the beginning of each semester. After December 7th, 1941, food was rationed nationally. Everyone used ration stamps. Cooper Hall used the equivalent of ration stamps for students. Our families at home had to declare their college student members and, therefore, received fewer food stamps. For instance, my brother was in military service, and I in college. Consequently, my parents received food stamps equivalent for only two, my mother and father.

Enrollment was approximately one thousand students, including only a few commuters who had to live with relatives and not in apartments with students. Even seniors who were not commuters had to live on campus.

I feel that NJC provided greater surrogate parental roles for its students than many colleges and universities do today for their students. By contrast to today's campuses, our parents had more confidence in the college's responsibility for its students. Many colleges and universities today may require that freshman live on campus, but students may live off campus after freshman year with no supervision by institutions. In my further comments about campus life, you will learn even more about the college's sense of responsibility as surrogate parent.

After breakfast that first day of classes, another student walked with us to my first class, and a third student accompanied us to the next class, etc. In a very few days, Rachel and I walked the campus independently, at least the parts that I used that first semester. Some courses were scheduled Monday, Wednesday, and Friday, while others were offered on Tuesday and Thursday. Each semester, my mental map expanded.

Other parts to learn besides classroom buildings included the campus post office, library, chapel, and campus bookstore.

Relative to the post office, I could not utilize the padlock on my box without vision. When I began appearing at the window to request my mail, the postmaster was irritated. One day he said in exasperation, "Unlock your box and get your own mail." Calmly, I explained that I was blind and could not use the padlock. He apologized. After that, he was most gracious to check whether I had mail, fetched it, and brought it to me at the window.

Relative to required chapel attendance twice weekly, the Tuesday service was led by a Catholic priest, Jewish rabbi, or Protestant pastor. These were not selected from congregations in New Brunswick but from other universities or prominent churches in the Northeast. Each week on Tuesday, the dean invited specific students to lunch with her and the chapel speaker of the day. Because written records indicated students' religious preferences or denomination, we lunched with a chaplain of the same denomination.

Friday chapel was more like an assembly program in high school. By that I intend no negative connotation, but it was not a worship service.

To provide the dean with chapel attendance records, each class had its assigned entrance into the sanctuary. Students had to sign colored chapel-attendance slips (one color for each class) and return them when leaving the building. In four years, I missed only one chapel service and that one for medical reasons.

Off campus, I learned the location of a few stores, but I did not have money to spend in them. I learned the location of a Reformed church in town. This pastor, Dr. Milton T. Stauffer, was also the editor of a Braille magazine, *John Milton Magazine (published by the John Milton Society in New York)*, a periodical covering topics on Protestantism. With my needs met on and off campus, I was ready to be an independent college student for four years.

For several Sunday afternoons at the beginning of my freshman year, Daddy drove Mamma to campus. The three of us sat in my room where Mamma put me through the third degree each week. She had not changed, even though I was then eighteen. Then Daddy announced that he was not driving to campus every Sunday. "Grace has more important things to do than sit here and answer questions." I could have hugged him for his wisdom, though Mamma, who did not drive a car, did not like his decision.

I blossomed in this academic life at college. I especially enjoyed living among other young women who considered me an equal. Here was no one saying, "You can't do that; you're blind" or "You're not like other women," etc. A heavy load was lifted from my shoulders when away from Mamma's negativism. I could now spread my wings and fly!

As a music major, I spent countless hours in the Music Building either for classes or for practicing on the pipe organs.

Mr. Earl Rudy was my organ instructor. He drove from Princeton to give lessons to several students on campus in New Brunswick. Although he had normal vision, he had studied in Paris with Dupré, a famous blind organist.

Dormitory life was supervised by the senior house director, Doris Cash, who was very pleasant, available to answer questions about campus life, and was responsible to the dean of women for the conduct of women in her house.

When we left the house in the evening, we had to sign out, indicating destination, time we left, expected time of return, and actual time of return. This applied even when we went to the library, Music Building, Science Hall, etc. Only with special permission from the dean of women might we leave campus in the evening Monday through Thursday evenings to attend a concert or lecture, for instance. On those four evenings, administration required students to be in their respective residences by ten o'clock.

On Friday and Sunday evenings, curfew was eleven o'clock, on Saturday, twelve-thirty. On seven evenings a week, signing out was mandatory.

During that first year while visiting my parents on a Friday evening during spring break, the three of us were walking home after visiting my grandparents. Subconsciously, I was pushing my father to walk more quickly. He asked why I was hurrying him. I explained, "I've got to be home by eleven o'clock!" He reminded me that I was not on campus. That shows how deeply ingrained were the rules in our psyches.

I never heard even one student complain about the signing-out requirement. I do not claim to know what the rules at Douglass are to-day. In an emergency from home, the students could be found quickly in order to relay a message.

Quite often in the evenings, someone in the house would take orders for food and then phone to have pizza or hamburgers or something else delivered. I never indulged for three reasons: I did not have money for such things; I had had three substantial meals already that day previously paid for at the beginning of the semester; I did not need additional calories.

Students in the house between seven and ten o'clock in the evenings were expected to be quiet to promote good study conditions.

We had very few automobiles on campus during the week except perhaps those used by commuters. Very few students in those days had automobiles, unlike today's campuses. On weekends, male students from across town at Rutgers drove onto our campus looking for dates.

I might explain that our campus was made up of four sections. Gibbons Campus and Douglass Campus were similar in design. Jameson Campus had larger dormitories that accommodated perhaps forty or fifty students. The fourth section was where the library, chapel, post office, classroom buildings, and science laboratories were located.

Freshman students had to become familiar with campus rules. One way to accomplish that goal was to identify freshman students to all other students and to faculty and staff by requiring freshmen to wear a green beanie and a sandwich sign bearing each student's name and requiring students to carry at all times for the first six weeks a small book containing campus regulations. Any upper-class woman or staff might stop a freshman to ask a question whose answer was in the book. If the student did not know the answer, she might be detained while she sought the answer in her book. My brother had made my sandwich sign and printed on it:

GRACE DONKERSLOOT
AND RACHEL

Earlier, when we had first applied for admission, photos were required. When we were accepted as students, Mr. Meder studied the photos to familiarize himself with incoming students. He looked at the picture and then at the back for the name and hometown. By the time freshman students arrived on campus, he could put names and faces together. He surprised just about all students when he met one of them walking somewhere on campus, and he greeted her with, "Good morning, Helene Watson. I understand that you are from Rutherford," or "Hello, Sallie Gustafson. You are one of our out-of-state students." He warmed our hearts; we knew we were not just numbers in a file somewhere.

Soon after I had arrived on campus, I learned who my readers were to be. These were freshman students taking the same courses as I and would be paid at the end of the semester for rendering that service. The money came from the New Jersey Commission for the Blind. That money had been part of my total scholarship funds.

About courses, Freshman College Algebra was difficult, not because of the content itself but because of Mr. Nelson's teaching presentation, typical of seeing mathematics instructors, as described in Chapter Three: namely, pointing to writing on the chalkboard and saying *this* or *that* and *here* or *there* and *these* or *those*. When my reader used her class notes and read from the textbook, I understood. At the end of the course, I passed while Pat, my reader, failed; yet whatever I had learned in that course, I had learned from Pat, not from Mr. Nelson. I could understand mathematics when presented in a style that I could comprehend or when I had a Braille textbook. (When I returned to my high school for a visit at the end of freshman year, Mr. Applegate asked what my major was. When I told him music, he said, "You can be a math major." I considered that a high compliment.)

By contrast, botany laboratory demonstrated how a faculty member could adjust his teaching style to meet the special needs of a student. Dr. John A. Small made teaching aids for me each week to acquaint me with the same information assigned to the rest of the class.

He used pie tins, rubber tubing, pipe cleaners, wire, string, wood, etc., to depict a specific type of cell or plant organ, etc. Each week, I eagerly went to his laboratory to discover more of his ingenuity and creativity. He was a gifted teacher. Three other days of the week, I attended botany lectures given by Jessie Fiske.

Before I graduated, I visited Dr. Small to thank him for his impressive teaching techniques. I added that I could imagine how much extra time and effort were involved in preparation for a given lesson just for me. He said that he was well repaid when he saw the light of comprehension on my face. He knew he had succeeded in reaching me.

Another course that I enjoyed was Freshman Composition with Mr. Raymond Milo Bennett. In high school, we had an abundance of grammar but less of composition. I improved greatly throughout the year in this course.

On my first day in that class, I had arrived before Mr. Bennett. I was ready to take notes with slate and stylus when he entered and walked to the front of the room. He checked his enrollment sheet against our sandwich signs. Mr. Bennett asked whether my name was Grace or Rachel.

I said, "Grace."

He then asked, "Why do you have RACHEL on your sign?"

I pointed to the floor where Rachel was lying at my feet and said, "Rachel is my dog, sir." He walked to my row and from the aisle saw my dog for the first time. (Rachel was the first dog guide at NJC.) He then returned to the front of the room and continued checking his enrollment before he began the class.

(Because of my signs, Rachel and I received friendly greetings from students, staff, and faculty. One typical greeting was, "Hello, Rachel!" with much gusto. "How are you?" Then almost as an afterthought, "Oh, hello, Grace.")

At the end of that session as I was leaving, Mr. Bennett rushed after me to apologize profusely. I explained that I knew he had not seen the dog and that he had not offended me in any way.

Near the end of first semester, Mr. Bennett announced that all students had to attend the last session, that it was compulsory for everyone. He did not explain why. He had previously informed us that we would have no final examination with him because of our many compositions completed during the semester.

On that last day, we were greeted by a treacherous sleet storm. Although I had left my residence early because of the weather, walking was exceedingly slow. I arrived in class after it had begun, contrary to my habit of being early if at all possible. Because we knew we would not be having a final examination with Mr. Bennett the next week, we were curious about what he had planned to do this last day and what was urgent about our being present.

Instead, he wanted to review types of questions that we might encounter in our other course examinations: compare/contrast, chronological development, outline of major and minor events, enumeration of cause or consequence, advantages/disadvantages, open-book questions, etc. He wanted to be sure that we knew the differences in order for us to answer questions on target. (Often, when students don't have clear answers and lack crucial information, they tend to write around the answer but not exactly address the question. They hope that a long answer will yield some points, even when the long answer is wrong.) I do not know whether every instructor of English Composition offered a similar last session or whether Mr. Bennett was the only one to discuss typical examination questions.

When that session ended, he met me at the door to say, "You shouldn't have come today; you might fall and have a nasty injury on the ice."

My response was, "You said that attending this session today was mandatory for *everyone*. I am part of *everyone*."

He said that he liked my attitude. After the second semester, I chose another English course with Mr. Bennett. I had learned very much from him.

In that second year, we were assigned a term paper. I wrote mine about Beethoven. In describing his face, I used the word muzzle. Mr. Bennett questioned why I used a word related to dogs. I explained that the word refers to Beethoven's jaw. He reached for his dictionary to find the definition. When he discovered that I was correct, he said, "You have taught me a new word. Thank you."

Even yet, when I write something of importance, I ask myself, "How would Mr. Bennett want it?"

Another professor of English was Dr. Oral Coad who taught Shakespearean Drama and Elizabethan Drama excluding Shakespeare. I had both courses with him. He spoke with a rather dull monotone; however, he injected humor. Only those students who were truly attentive appreciated the jokes. Other students whose minds had wandered heard some students chuckle but wondered what was so comical.

One comment that Dr. Coad made on the first day in his course bothered me as being negative. He said that only English majors could hope to earn A's. He seemed unreasonable if he truly believed that English majors were the only students capable of earning an A. Maybe he was challenging us who were not English majors to work hard enough to earn an A.

Although I had a year of World History, I do not recall the instructor's name or style of teaching. I have a vague recollection that it was a young woman, perhaps a graduate student. In American History, Dr. George Schmidt was my instructor. He had a delightful teaching strategy not identified immediately by students. He started a class by making a broad statement, such as, "Slavery was not bad. It had many virtues," or "If our tariffs are high enough, other countries won't bother to buy from us." or "The men who pushed for separation from England should have been hanged for causing so much unrest," or "As a Republican, I believe that …"

After making his pronouncement, he just stood there, looked

around the room at his students, and waited. In truth, he challenged us to defend the other side of the argument rather than quietly accept his statement. Once we students discovered Dr. Schmidt's agenda, the class became exceedingly interesting and volatile. However, when we debated with him, we had to have facts to support our position. The textbook or other historical sources were legitimate documentation.

After World War II began, many faculty members at Rutgers were either drafted or volunteered, leaving courses without instructors. When NJC was still offering courses that male students needed, they attended our classes.

We had some of them in Dr. Schmidt's course. When a group of us studied together for a final examination, the men tried to take over the leadership.

When I suggested three possible questions that Dr. Schmidt might ask, the men pooh-poohed those ideas. I did not like the men's put-downs of women students.

On the final examination, two of my questions were there in just about verbatim form. My third question was there with a different slant. I wondered what the male students thought then.

In many coeducational classes on college campuses, males dominate class discussion. Instructors, also male, tend to pay more attention to males, praise them for clear thinking and keen insight, but give little credence to female students.

Let me give an example from my personal experience with a male instructor. Just before leaving my dormitory at New York University in 1945, I heard on the radio that President Roosevelt had died.

When I reached our classroom, only the instructor was present. I shared with him what I had just heard. His reaction was, "No, he didn't. You heard wrong!" I was furious.

Soon after, a male student entered and made the same introductory remark. The instructor responded with interest, "Really? Tell me more!"

I was sitting there, but he never apologized to me.

From my personal experience at an all-women's college, I suggest to women that if they are serious about gaining a sound education (and not just a husband), attend an all-women's college instead of a coeducational institution. More women from the former become prominent leaders in their respective disciplines.

After having three years of German in high school, I opted for two years of German at NJC. Dr. Hauptmann was my first instructor. Then, he disappeared overnight! He was not available to complete the semester. The administration and faculty surmised that he had returned to Germany either because he was a spy or he knew his life was in danger if he stayed in the United States, enemy territory, under war conditions.

Later my instructor was Fräulein Schlimbach, who was also originally from Germany but apparently a U. S. citizen, because she seemed very secure where she was though we were at war with Germany.

During my sophomore year, I lived on Douglass Campus in a house next to the German House where students were required to speak German inside the house. Fräulein Schlimbach lived with those students to monitor their German usage.

Her suite was across from my side window. In the evenings in September, my windows were likely to be open with my desk lamp on. At eleven o'clock, Fräulein called in German from her window, "Grace, it is late; turn off your light and go to bed."

I did as instructed. On the next several evenings, the same thing happened. I was annoyed that someone should tell me when to go to bed.

I acknowledged her next greeting, responded in German wishing her goodnight, as usual, and extinguished my light, *but* continued to study! She was happy; so was I!

Before I graduated, I reminded Fräulein Schlimbach about it. She laughed uproariously when she had learned that I had turned off the lamp but continued to work in the dark.

Some readers might ask, "Why does a blind person have a desk lamp in the first place?" As blind individuals, we have been instruct-ed by personnel in the blindness profession not to sit in the dark regu-larly. When someone comes to our home or room and we open the door to invite the guest in, the guest is uncomfortable walking into a dark room. So the light is there for the comfort of our guests. Further-more, when a reader works with me at night, she certainly requires illumination in order to read to me.

During my college years, we had black-out practice frequently. The next day in class, I was the only one to submit assignments on time! Others reported that they could not do the assignment because of the black-out.

In our psychology course, Dr. Sidney Cook was the instructor. We were to discuss humor during one class session to analyze what was involved in humor. The session before, he asked us to prepare humor-ous samples on paper and place them on the table when we arrived next time.

I typed my sample. I think all students arrived early that day in order to place samples on his table before he arrived.

He came to mine as the third or fourth sample. It read:

I once had a classmate named Guesser;
His knowledge grew lesser and lesser.
It at last grew so small
That he knew nothing at all,
And now he's a college professor!

He slammed the paper down on the table and declared, "We are finished with our discussion of humor!"

Frequently, he referred to a disturbed person who put a gun to his forehead.

During that semester, he drove his car down a steep hill and put a pistol to his forehead!

It seemed ironic that a psychologist could not determine when he needed help for his own illness. If he knew that he was in need of help, I suppose he would not be ill. Self-denial is extremely strong. As someone has aptly said, "Suicide is a permanent solution to a temporary problem."

Psychologists with severe disturbances always seem more tragic as patients. They have studied psychology in depth but then cannot recognize their own illness. (In my personal life later, that fact was driven home by a member of my family.)

For my physical education requirements, I had two years of swimming and two years of eurhythmics. One day, the swimming instructor directed all of us to submerge in the water after taking a deep breath. Then I heard, "Grace, you can come up now," but I stayed under; after all, I still had breath to stay down. When I popped up, the instructor was impressed with my lung capacity. I was the last student to surface.

When I was eighty, a pulmonary specialist ordered a specific set of tests to evaluate my lung health. He was truly amazed by the results; even then my lung capacity was fabulous! I have never been a smoker, though I have inhaled much secondhand smoke.

Today, however, my breathing is often labored because of a cardiac condition.

In health course, the instructor produced a human skeleton. Eagerly, I examined it. I was fascinated and studied it meticulously. Some of the students would not touch it because of knowing it was from a human being.

Some said I was warped in my curiosity. I explained that they had photographs in their textbook and that this skeleton was my picture.

Two years of eurhythmics completed requirements for physical education and also met those for music majors. In eurhythmics, we moved about in a large room developing independence in arms and legs to accommodate two or three sets of rhythms—perhaps four-quarter time in the legs, eighth notes in the left arm, and half notes in the right arm, for example.

In this course, I met Virginia Shrope (later Mrs. George Kelcec) who volunteered to be my partner. We became very dear friends in the years that followed until even now. She currently resides near The Seeing Eye and visits me when I return to headquarters for a new dog. You will read more about Virginia later.

The instructor of eurhythmics came from Switzerland, if I remember correctly. When she wanted us to increase our speed, she called out, "Hopp-hopp," the same term that we use with our dog guides for the same reason.

The remainder of my courses related to music. I graduated with more credits than necessary by taking overloads along the way.

In spite of my experiences with extra courses, I have encountered blind students who enroll in nine or ten credits a semester and still complain about how difficult life is for a blind college student. What will they do when they eventually graduate but are then expected by their employer to produce a day's amount of work for a day's pay? College is a proving ground to demonstrate how one performs under pressure.

Being on an equal status with every other student was a delightful experience. No longer did I have my mother's critical and demeaning eye watching my every move so that she could tear me apart. She had never learned to be my friend, even when I was an adult. She refused to permit herself to become acquainted with her daughter. I was damaged goods; she would not let me forget that fact. Although I did not regard myself as damaged goods, her words and behaviors revealed her opinion of me.

I wanted others to see me as a person first—not see my blindness first.

I neither made a point of missing a deadline nor asking for an extension of time in order to complete an assignment. Asking for special exceptions was not my style.

The following anecdote illustrates that fact. In the spring of freshman year, we freshman students drew slips of papers for the next year's room assignments. The student whose slip read number 1 chose first where she wanted to live. My number was much higher. When my turn arrived, no room on Gibbons Campus was available, although a given number of rooms there were reserved for incoming freshman students the next September. Gibbons Campus was closest to the Music Building. My new room was on Douglass Campus, farthest from the Music Building. I accepted this development.

Later when the dean of women learned about this, she summoned me to her office to ask why I had not come to her before the drawing began, so that she could have reserved a room on Gibbons for me.

I said that other students had not received their first choice either but accepted the outcome.

The dean said that I was the first blind student who had not requested her intervention relative to room assignment.

I explained that with my dog I could live anywhere on campus and not find the address burdensome.

Some blind students capitalize on their blindness in order to escape deadlines or normal obligations.

I knew one such student who claimed that she had to miss a deadline because of not knowing how to change the ribbon on her typewriter. She also told her instructor that writing a research paper and using the library were impossible for her to do as a blind student. She was excused! I don't know whether that omission was reflected in her final grade.

Despite those negative impressions by blind students, a humorous encounter happened to me shortly before commencement. A student in my class said, "I wish I could have gone through college without ever taking examinations—like you."

Not understanding the point she was making, I asked her to elaborate.

She said, "Every time we have tests and finals, you are absent!"

Now I understood! Whenever my class had a scheduled test, my reader and I met in a nearby empty room to complete the test. We had few objective-type tests at NJC. Instead, I brought my portable typewriter and answered each question that the reader read aloud to me. At the end of the period, my reader delivered my paper to the instructor, still in the classroom. Of course, I was not visible as being present on test days.

However, if the student, concerned about my not taking tests, had been observant, she would have noticed that the instructor had returned a paper to me also.

My working with a reader in the same room as the class would have been unnecessarily disruptive with the clatter of typewriter and with reader whispering to me reading a question.

As mentioned in Chapter Three about scarcity of Braille textbooks on the high school level, the situation was even worse on the college level then. Conditions had not changed between my high school and college years. I was able to borrow a few talking books on discs, if the Commission's library had what I needed. In one of my English courses, I was able to secure from the same source Shakespeare plays on disc or in Braille; the latter I used in class. Not much else was appropriate for college courses. My primary books were in print, read to me only once. Present day students who are blind have many more resources available to them. I dared not ask a reader to come to my room to reread a chapter; she had her own studying to do.

I remember having a reader who, after reading aloud to me, said, "Now I must go home to study what I just read to you." Apparently, reading aloud did not help her to absorb the content of the material. When I describe what I did not have as a college student, I am reporting what were typical conditions for all blind college students in the 1940's in this country.(Consult Appendix to learn of equipment available today.) I marvel that any blind student in my generation was able to graduate from college and even with honors!

I used a portable manual typewriter. I devised a method for knowing when to quit typing on a page in order to have uniform bottom margins.

Behind my typing paper, I used a sheet of braille paper that extended a bit beyond the right edge of the typing paper. The braille paper had a line of Braille dots near its bottom. When I felt the line of dots begin to emerge, I knew how many lines I had left before ending that page.

I also learned to use carbon paper in case the ribbon failed or the machine was accidentally set on stencil. One can imagine the consternation experienced by a blind student upon submitting to the instructor a test or term paper only to be told later, "The last half of your paper is not legible!" A carbon copy can save the day.

I could not proofread page by page and use WITE-OUT™ fluid to make necessary corrections. When I knew instantly that the last keystroke was wrong, I used a square of CORRECTO-TAPE™, but that was the only correction I could make.

With a typewriter, footnotes were not at the bottom of pages but at the end of the paper. With a computer using synthesized speech today, I can place footnotes at the bottom of pages. Now, with a computer that speaks, deleting, inserting, proofreading, correcting, setting margins, setting up columns, using different fonts, colors, and making extra copies are all possible for blind operators.

Not every blind computer user takes a formal course in its use. Depending on the textbook used, some are complete, others of questionable assistance. I say jokingly that because I am self-taught, I have a stupid teacher!

I must add here that totally-blind computer users cannot use the mouse on the monitor. Instead, he or she must learn keyboard commands by pressing two or three keys simultaneously to effect the desired action. For instance, when I wish to go to a specific page in a document, I press Control and g together. Then the voice directs, "Enter page number." When I do so, it repeats the number, when I then press ENTER and press the ESCAPE key separately and wait until the wanted page is announced. Each command has its own sequence of key combinations.

Technicians who are acquainted with only the mouse procedures are of little or no help to blind users of computers. Instead, I need a textbook or a knowledgeable computer user to explain to me how to do a specific task without using mouse and monitor.

College was enjoyable and rewarding, in spite of all those hurdles. After the first six weeks on campus, each residence had its individual hazing—nothing violent such as what we read about on some campuses today. I was disappointed with how mild their treatment of me was. Someone removed my dresser drawers and replaced them in a different level in my dresser—the top one on the bottom, the second in the third position, etc. Nothing inside each drawer was disturbed. By contrast, some students found their shoes in the basement or their coats on the third floor.

Another phase of hazing involved spooky ceremonies in the Lodge on Gibbons campus. We were blindfolded and heard ghoulish moans and screams or had a finger inserted into "brains" or "intestines" that proved to be fruit cocktail or canned spaghetti, or someone passed a variety of odors under our noses while we were still blindfolded.

Greek societies or sororities, however, were not allowed at NJC; the founders of the college in 1918 considered them divisive and un-democratic. I agree.

Classes were stimulating, challenging, and of high academic standards. Some graduate courses that I later have had elsewhere were easier. When an instructor wrote on the chalkboard without including a vocal equivalent, a nearby student whispered to me the information. For instance, he might be discussing a person in literature or history or science and write the name on the board without spelling it aloud. My neighbor spelled it to me.

All of freshman year and the beginning of sophomore year were happy and quite carefree. When we returned in September, we noticed that several of our former classmates from the previous year were absent. Each class loses students each year for various reasons; students transferred, lost interest in college, had too low a grade point average to be permitted to return, married, etc. At that time, married students lived on campus without spouses.

After December 7, 1941, the climate on campus was emotionally charged, sober, serious, even somber. Students in any of the four classes were receiving word of wounded or killed relatives and friends. Students looked every day for letters from someone important in their lives.

Students helped in the war effort by cooperating with the American Red Cross by rolling bandages and donating blood. Because of the shortage of male students and employees on the campuses in New Brunswick, the Experimental Agricultural Station (now Cook College) called on NJC to help harvest corn; we did it on a Saturday.

Other evidences of the war were slogans, such as "Is This Trip Necessary?" to discourage civilians from traveling, thus limiting consumption of gasoline or occupying seats on trains already crowded with military personnel.

A popular song then was "Rosie, The Riveter," coined by Frances Perkins, Secretary of Labor. Because butter was shipped to the military, civilians were the first to use margarine. When I was at home during summers, my job was to knead the sack of white margarine to break the capsule inside to release coloring to turn the margarine yellow.

Nylon hosiery that had been introduced just prior to the war suddenly disappeared from store shelves because nylon thread was needed by the military for parachutes and other gear.

Because of the shortage of male employees, factories and industry in general, whenever feasible, hired women and persons with disabilities and began three eight-hour shifts to manufacture necessary war supplies.

Twice I worked in industry. I worked in an industrial laundry. The business even provided transportation for persons with disabilities. My station was beside the steam room. The supervisor brought me armloads of very hot cloths about the size of bath towels for me to flatten out, pile ten on each other, fold a specific way and stack a certain way. These were used to clean machinery.

Because my station was very hot all day, I asked my supervisor what the temperature was at my table. She told me one hundred twenty degrees! When I came out after work, the day always seemed cool regardless of the actual summer temperature! Because of the temperature at my work site, I had Rachel stay home with Mamma.

Another time, I worked in an electronics factory. My job was assembling starters for fluorescent lights. I commuted by public bus with Rachel who lay at my feet under my table at work.

Having lived through World War II, I am disappointed that with the war in Iraq since 2003, that the civilian population has not been required to experience any rationing of food, clothing, gasoline, tires, or any other commodities to help the war effort, except perhaps with the high price of gasoline. Families with relatives involved directly in the war effort seem to be the only Americans feeling the painful impact of the war. Why are the rest of us not compelled to sacrifice in lesser ways? The war is not THEIR war but OUR war, even though I have been opposed to it since President George W. Bush ordered an invasion into Iraq!

Returning to the topic of campus life, I can report that NJC closed to us students for summers. Instead, one of the scheduled activities I heard of was that the college conducted courses for bankers who stayed in our rooms. (Before we departed campus in June for the summer, we either took some of our possessions home or identified them with labels to be stored in the basement. Consequently, the banking contingent used our beds (but not our bedding), the college's table and chair, and closets.

I do not know who taught the courses—faculty from NJC and/or Rutgers or faculty from the banking world. Perhaps the arrangements were strictly a means by which NJC might earn additional revenue by merely providing space for classes, food service, and sleeping accommodation. In any event, the courses brought additional funds into the college each summer.

At home, air-raid drills and black-outs were as frequent as on campus. Black window shades were required to pull down over the shades already present to prevent any inside light from showing on the outside of the building. During these practice sessions at home, we sat in the kitchen, using only the gas light over the oven for illumination because it was less bright than electric bulbs and less likely to escape and be seen from the exterior of the house. Volunteer civilians and police patrolled neighborhoods to check on adherence to rules governing air-raid drills. Sirens sounded to signal the beginning and ending of drills.

Mail carriers of the U. S. Postal Service made a point of ringing doorbells when depositing in mailboxes letters from military personnel. Many civilians were writing letters to and receiving some from various areas of the world.

Women enlisted not only as nurses but in other capacities; women became pilots. However, women volunteers did not have the same rights and benefits as male peers. Inside our country, many civilian women worked in places like Washington, DC, doing clerical work and whatever else they could do to replace former employees then in the military.

My brother, Martin, entered the Army in December 1942 during my Christmas break from college. The four of us drove to Newark where Mart was to board a specific train.

Mamma and I, I thought, were standing on the platform against a building. Yet when I spoke to her, she was gone. With all the noise, I could not determine where she was. The next thing I knew, she was tugging on my sleeve and saying, "C'mon, let's go home!" I protested that I wanted to say goodbye to Mart and hug him.

Then she told me, "He's already on the train and gone!"

All that I can conclude is that she had me stand against the building and then left me while she joined my father and brother. I was furious that she did not consider me a member of the family but a no-body who did not belong in the family circle when bidding farewell to my brother! Again, she had made her feelings for me quite clear. She has created so much anger and anguish in me! She preferred Ida to me; she preferred Mart to me. That ugly question expressed by her when I was six resurfaced.

If I were a child today and if any of the incidents I write about now involving Mamma's mistreatment of me were revealed, she would probably be declared a dysfunctional and abusive mother. I wish the Dixons had adopted me.

Back on campus again and resuming classes after our first snow-fall, I quickly shed my wraps and set out my slate and stylus for tak-ing notes. About halfway through class, the student sitting beside me looked down and saw Rachel with one of my gloves in her mouth, not chewing it, just holding it. She whispered to me, "Feel your dog's face." It must have accidentally fallen from my coat pocket to the floor. Rachel had picked up the glove and waited for me to take it from her.

Rachel was excellent at executing the command FETCH.

While I was in training at headquarters, I took my outgoing mail to the mail basket. When I picked up the harness handle to continue on my way to the front door, Rachel brushed something against my leg. When I checked, I found an envelope in her mouth. Either I or someone earlier apparently had dropped it; Rachel, alert and enjoy-ing FETCH, picked it up from the floor, even without a command from me! She had learned the FETCH lessons very well.

As part of recreation, the college owned property some distance from the campus. On it was The Shack, an affectionate term for the fa-cility because of the primitive conditions there. One weekend in Janu-ary, Rachel and I were in a group going to The Shack.

At bedtime, I had Rachel stay inside The Shack by the fireplace along with some students while others and I slept outdoors in sleep-ing bags in a temperature hovering at zero degrees. We had to do our own cooking under crude circumstances. We were chaperoned by our class sponsor, Dr. John A. Small.

Another memorable event each year was a drama, one year performed by faculty about students and the next year by students about faculty. I hope that this tradition has continued into the present.

One year when students performed, they portrayed a faculty meeting and the necessity for Victory Gardens with questions about which vegetables should be included. One faculty member persisted in pushing for the lowly string bean while another faculty member advocated carrots.

One year when the faculty presented its play, it was about a weekend at The Shack. When it was time to prepare a meal, someone asked, "Where is the ground beef for hamburgers?"

Dr. Small answered that it was on the roof of the car to keep it cold and that inside the ice box would be too warm without ice for meat and that Grace's dog could not reach the meat on top of the car!

He brought the house down with his humor. We were so fortunate in having Dr. Small as our class sponsor.

In another play by faculty, the scene was a dormitory. Then Dr. Small appeared on stage announcing he had a telegram for a specific student, naming her. Then to the audience he said, "There's nothing important in the telegram, but I had to have a part in this melodrama!"

Another jewel in the necklace of memories was the social events occurring on the last night before Christmas break. The air was festive for several reasons.

On this evening, dinner included a Tapping Ceremony. The college had invited department heads to dinner, after which they proceeded through the four dining rooms and tapped the shoulders of certain students for recognition of their high academic distinction. I was thrilled when Mr. Duncan MacKenzie, Chair of the Music Department, tapped my shoulder for fellow students to witness!

After Dr. John Newton had died, Mr. MacKenzie, Newton's successor, invited me into his office. Because he was new at NJC, he was seeking feedback from students about courses and faculty and how the department might be improved and expanded. Afterward, he and I had a congenial relationship for the remainder of my time on campus. Even after I had graduated, we corresponded. His letters told me of changes on campus.

After dinner, many students rushed to their residences to dress for the Christmas dance. Not all students attended it, however, for a variety of reasons, I am sure. As a student body of a state university, we were not women from wealthy families; many of us were scholarship recipients with limited funds for dance expenses. More affluent families probably had their daughters enrolled at Smith or Wellesley College. Some of my fellow students did not own an evening gown and could not afford to purchase one. Boyfriends who might have attended the dance were away as military personnel. Some sweethearts had already been injured or killed. Some women did not have a special beau and were not looking very hard for one. Some were eager to attend graduate school somewhere and felt that boyfriends at that time might derail their plans for professional careers in medicine, law, science, and other fields where the master's degree and/or doctorate were required. In any group as large as our student body, one would likely find individuals who had little interest in attending a dance, even when men were available to invite. Perhaps, a few of our students even left campus for home after their last class.

We created our own evening of pleasure by having a house party or combining women from a few houses for it. Each person contributed snacks. We did not exchange gifts but shared experiences and told about Christmas and Hanukkah traditions at home. We did not dress up fancy but accepted each other as she was.

At midnight, we joined a larger group for caroling on campus, ending in front of the dean's home. The dean made an appearance and thanked us for including her in our midnight rounds.

Many of us did not go to bed that night. Instead, we welcomed home the princesses from the ball with eagerness to hear about each Prince Charming.

We eventually packed for going home, where we would spend our break until we returned on January 2nd second to complete the semester.

Some of my friends were engaged to be married soon after graduation. Others had already dropped out of college to marry before the men entered military service. High on my priority list was earning my bachelor's degree and becoming a teacher. Men were low on that list.

Two trips into New York remain memorable after all these years though they occurred during my years at NJC.

One was to attend a performance of *La Boheme* at the Metropolitan Opera House. The tenor's voice was liquid, lyrical brilliance. Rudolf Valentino would be welcome to sing under my window at any time!

The other visit was to attend Helen Hayes's performance in *Uncle Tom's Cabin*. I know that this was a one-of-a-kind performance for that lady.

In the play, she and her brother were in the living room chatting when he developed a coughing spell, obviously not part of the script. Helen Hayes, with great stage presence, called by name to one of the slave women off-stage, who appeared wordlessly. Helen said, "My brother needs a glass of water, please."

The slave returned with water but had much less poise, not even enough to say, "Here's your drink, suh."

I am positive that if we had attended the play the next day, the brother would not have had a coughing spell.

Back in class, I often wondered where I would be teaching after commencement. During my senior year, I contacted every residential school for blind children in the country to inquire about vacancies in the music department for the next September. The news was not encouraging. Many schools had no vacancies and anticipated none in the near future. Once music faculty had paying positions, they usually stayed until retirement. A few other schools reported that they filled vacancies with only their own graduates.

A private school in Mississippi for black blind children (the state did not provide a school for its black blind residents) offered me a position, not to teach music but academic subjects for "missionary pay."

Because of the paucity of job information, I telephoned the executive director of the New Jersey State Commission for the Blind for an appointment to meet with him. I took a bus to Newark and met with Mr. George Meyer to ask about teaching positions that he might have heard about.

Instead of answering my question, he asked what I had done to look for employment. I explained that I had contacted all the residential schools about music positions but had only one possibility and that one in Mississippi to teach academic classes but not music.

Mr. Meyer's reaction was, "Well then, you have a job. Why did you come here to bother me?"

I was shocked by his retort. As a blind person himself, did he believe that blind employment seekers should always take the first opening, without the right to explore other options? Seeing persons have that right to choose. Why should blind individuals be denied that same right? That job in Mississippi will reappear in the next chapter.

After I was at home during Christmas break, one evening Daddy and I tagged along while Mamma shopped for gifts. When we passed a store, I said the word CANDY. Surprised, Daddy wanted to know why I had said that. I explained that the electric sign showed the word in the window but that I could not see the candy itself inside.

Astonished, he asked, "You can see that?"

After telling him that I could because the letters were lighted and large, I shared with him how frustrated I had felt whenever we went to Dr. Glasgow for visual tests.

Our ophthalmologist gave me the typical Snellen central visual acuity test which I always failed because of being too far from the chart. Since I could not succeed at the standard distance from the chart, Dr. Glasgow ended the test. On one occasion, while he spoke with my parents, I moved closer to the chart and discovered I could identify letters on certain lines. In my excitement, I blurted out, "I can read the letters now!"

The doctor glibly dismissed my revelation by saying, "That's nice, but the test is finished." He never took time to determine whether I was totally blind or able to read the chart at a closer range.

I always left these examinations feeling as though I had failed. I kept thinking, *Why won't he listen to me?*

I recounted for Daddy a time when Miss Taylor's class joined another class for a special occasion at an ice cream parlor. As we approached the entrance, I said, "Push." Miss Taylor asked why I had said, "Push." (Probably she already knew why because she was extremely observant of her students.) After I explained that the plate on the door read *push* (but in a vertical arrangement) and pointed to it, she encouraged me to use my vision as much as I could.

When we departed, I saw on the inside of the door the sign that read *pull*, also in vertical arrangement. How different she was from Dr. Glasgow who, after concluding that I could not read the chart at his designated distance, assumed I could see nothing.

Today's ophthalmologists and optometrists are taught to measure even poor vision by allowing patients to walk close enough to the chart to read whichever lines are readable.

Then the central visual acuity measurement is recorded as 4/100, meaning that the patient read the 100-foot line at four-foot distance OR 3/200, meaning that the patient read the 200-foot line at three-foot distance, or whatever the actual measurement is for each patient. The measurement contains two elements: which line was read and from what distance.

To gain an understanding of the severity of the visual problem, remember that the 100-foot line is read by persons with normal vision capable of reading it at 100 feet away from the chart, but the patient with 4/100 vision must be four feet from the chart in order to read the letters. The second example means that persons with normal vision can read that size letter from 200 feet away, but the person with 3/200 central visual acuity has to be three feet away in order to read the same size letters.

If the same size letters were black on a white background on the candy store sign, I might not have been able to read that sign, however. Because the experience happened in the evening in winter and the sign was illuminated (getting much light into the eyes), I could read the sign. Nevertheless, I still could not read print books or newspapers because the letters were much smaller and not intensified by electric lighting.

I could read the largest letters in newspaper headlines, one letter at a time with the paper against my nose. I said that I could probably read better but that my nose got in the way!

When I was a child, Uncle John bought me a jigsaw puzzle that, when assembled, looked like a black and white checkerboard. That was the only puzzle that I could assemble visually, thanks to the strong contrast between black and white.

Over time, my vision gradually faded until before 1960 I was totally blind.

Commencement ceremony was in Voorhees Chapel. Afterward, a photographer was present to take a group picture of our Dean Margaret Corwin, President Clothier of Rutgers University, Sister Elizabeth Kinney (recipient of an honorary degree), and Mary Kravetz and me with our two dog guides. (Mary's dog was her second during our four years.)

The dean told me that she had wanted to give Rachel praiseworthy mention for her exemplary behavior for four years, but that she did not want to do the same for Mary's dog. Consequently, she mentioned neither dog.

Later, the pastor of the Reformed Church in town, mentioned earlier, wrote a note in which his humorous comment was that Rachel was the best-looking figure in the picture!

The date of commencement tied us to the war by being on June 6, 1944—the Normandy Invasion!

SIX

◇◇◇◇◇◇

AFTER COMMENCEMENT WHEN I was again in Clifton, I received a letter from an unknown gentleman inviting me to lunch with his Lions Club and to speak about how my dog guide helps me in my life. The club met at the Biltmore hotel in Manhattan in New York. To accept the invitation, I either wrote a letter or telephoned him—I don't remember that detail.

I do not know how he had obtained my name. It may have been from the American Foundation for the Blind (located in Manhattan).

On the designated day, I boarded an inter-city bus to Manhattan. At the New York terminal, I took a taxicab to the Biltmore Hotel where my host greeted me. After lunch, he introduced me to the club members as the speaker of the day.

Parenthetically, in 1939, Leader Dog, another school preparing dog guides, was founded with pledged financial support from the Lions Clubs International. Unfortunately, many members assumed that Leader Dog, in Rochester, Michigan, was the first and only school supplying dog guides.

Throughout my lifetime, when in an airport or hotel or restaurant, a member of a Lions Club has approached me to inquire whether I was satisfied with the dog that his club had given me. Each time, I explained that the Lions had not given me my dog, that my dog was not from Leader Dog but from The Seeing Eye in New Jersey, and that I had paid for my dog (because Leader Dog supplies its dogs free of charge).

At this luncheon, I made a point of explaining that difference plus a brief history of The Seeing Eye, Inc.

After my presentation, my host thanked me and allowed time for members to ask me questions. Then he presented me with a check with which to advance my education by earning my master's degree at New York University! God had used strangers to accomplish His plans for my life. Throughout my life, persons unknown to me have blessed me with recommendations for a fellowship, teaching position, etc.

At that time, I had not found employment except for the offer from the Piney Woods School in Mississippi. I will repeat a statement made in the previous chapter, namely, that the state of Mississippi at that time of segregation had provided no school for black blind children though it had a school for white blind children. At that time in history, black and whte children were segregated in separate facilities for education. This issue will rear its head again later.

Now I had a choice, either to accept that teaching position or earn a master's degree. The school in Mississippi would be there next year; the opportunity to earn a master's degree might not be available next year. I felt that I could not accept the check from the Lions and then not use it for a year.

You can imagine my surprise and elation in realizing how my life was being shaped and how I was walking on a path previously not on my road map! Because I had not found employment except in Mississippi under negative conditions, the money to pay for advancing my education seemed a godsend now.

At New York University, some women lived in The Judson in Washington Square downtown. Earlier, The Judson had been a hotel for sailors.

My room was anything but spacious, with only one window, a

noisy radiator, a small closet with a cloth drape to serve as its door, bed, chair, table, and a bathroom-type sink without a vanity under it. Communal showers and toilets were down the hall. The Judson served no meals; consequently, we ate at a variety of eateries in the area.

From The Judson, I was about a block from the building in which my classes were offered. In one of my classes was a male student from Mississippi. I engaged him in conversation about Piney Woods School. He knew of it. I explained my awareness of it because of the job offer to teach there.

He said it would be a poor choice for me because in addition to its poverty, the teachers and staff at the school might not accept me into their circle because of my being Caucasian. Furthermore, he was even more certain that white residents in the community would reject me as a white person because of working at a school for black children!

I had to wonder whether those same white church members contributed money to support white missionaries to spread the Gospel in Africa among black natives there.

My classmate, a black man himself, urged me not to consider teaching there.

(Much later, a married couple from my church congregation in their retirement went to Piney Woods School to work in food service or wherever else they could assist the school. When they returned to us, they were greatly disillusioned after their experiences there.)

I believe that God, knowing about the problems facing me at that school, purposefully redirected my life by using the Lions Club to award me a fellowship to continue my professional preparation by studying at New York University.

In another class, Jeannette was a classmate. At the end of that class, she and I left together, walking to her subway entrance; then I walked to The Judson.

After we had done this several times, another classmate whispered to me, "Jeannette is black. I thought you needed to know that!" (This was 1944 in the city of New York!)

This was a graduate-level class for teachers; nonetheless, skin color was an issue. I had to wonder how this white teacher treated black children in her classes.

When I was in Miss Taylor's class, we had a black girl in our group, but her skin color was never a matter of concern, if not by blind children, certainly not by parents who met Evelyn.

Determined not to change my behavior, I continued leaving with Jeannette as before. How could a white teacher reject a black teacher on so flimsy a reason as skin color? Jeannette, like her classmates, was also working to improve her professional skills. She already had a bachelor's degree. When educated white professionals demean an educated black professional, the reason has to be ignorance on the part of white individuals.

A parallel situation exists between seeing persons and blind individuals when the former exclude the latter based on ignorance about what some blind individuals *can* do but assume that all blind persons are stupid, even mentally retarded, inferior to seeing people.

I think the problems between white and black and also between seeing and blind reside in pride. White persons who attend or graduate from college or graduate school feel superior to individuals who do not; then when they encounter a black or blind person who has achieved the same level, their pride is injured and this poses the question: How can black or blind persons accomplish what I have done when they, to begin with, are inferior to me? Why did white teachers not admire Jeannette for improving her situation? Did they expect her to accept the roles of scrub woman or laundress or clerk in an all-black store? After all, Jeannette was already a teacher with a bachelor's degree.

Another of my courses was history of education. When I discovered that in this graduate course we were using the same textbook that I had used in a sophomore course at NJC, I approached my adviser to ask how we might negotiate this duplication. Was there another course that I might take in lieu of this history course? I was not asking to have my program shortened by the number of credits assigned to the history course; I was requesting another course.

My adviser was inflexible. His response was, "Just think how easy it will be to get an A in that course because of having used the textbook earlier!"

I told him that I had not come to graduate school to review what I had already learned but to add to what I already knew.

Then, to make matters worse, the instructor required graduate students to keep a notebook in which we wrote each question at the end of chapters and paired it with the sentence that answered each question from the related chapter! This was *graduate* education?

In another course, the woman instructor had come from a progressive school for children. (We know that progressive education had very little impact on the total field of education for children.) Relative to teaching children music notation, she claimed that she never forced anything on children but waited until a child requested it. If one child in a class of twenty asked for music notation, what did the teacher do with the other nineteen students while teaching the one, we wanted to know. Similarly, when children did not request reading, arithmetic, or spelling, what was the teacher teaching?

One male student, at that point, stood up, walked to the door and said, "You are a charlatan and have nothing to offer me." He opened the door and was gone.

Many of us agreed with him. How can any teacher wait until a child asks for spelling or fractions or American history or grammar, etc.?

This same woman instructor told us several times during the year that Morton Gould had been one of her students. She said it in such a way that she believed he was great because she had been his teacher rather than he was great even if she had never been his teacher.

All in all, I was not impressed with the quality of teaching at NYU.

I do not know whether the entire College of Education was this weak or whether only the Department of Music Education was inferior.

In reading Colin Powell's autobiography, I learned of the high academic standards of the City College of New York and its long list of distinguished graduates. In public media we seem to hear more about New York University.

Although I had started the academic year with Rachel, I ended the school year with a different dog guide. Between Thanksgiving and Christmas, Rachel was losing weight while her abdomen was enlarging. She drank water thirstily but soon vomited up the water just consumed.

When I returned to Clifton for the holidays, Daddy and I took Rachel to a Clifton veterinarian who diagnosed Rachel's problem as dropsy but suggested that we take her to a specific veterinarian located in Newark for a second opinion. In the meantime, he advised me to withdraw all drinking water usually available to Rachel and occasionally permit her to lick ice cubes.

In Newark, the veterinarian gave the same diagnosis. He informed us that Rachel's condition had no cure. He suggested that we leave Rachel with him to euthanize. We agreed to that.

Because many persons in the waiting room had recognized Rachel's harness as that of a dog guide, they inquired about her when we were exiting without her. Neither Daddy nor I could speak. Instead, we shook our heads, and I held up the empty harness, leash, and collar. The message was clear.

As we drove home, Daddy and I said not a word. At home, I wept for my sweet, lovable Rachel who had worked splendidly as my first dog guide but was now no longer present. She had introduced me to and immersed me in independence.

Mamma and Daddy grieved, too; they had grown to love her dearly.

After a few days, when I could talk without breaking down, I phoned The Seeing Eye to share my sad news. I was immediately scheduled into the January 2 class with the same instructor I had had when I first trained. He had accepted me as a ninth student in his class of January 1945.

Because of that, I phoned my adviser at NYU to explain what had happened and to say that I would be arriving late for classes.

As I trained with Circle, another German boxer, my instructor was confident that I could return to New York with Circle after only two weeks.

Circle adapted exceedingly well to life with me under metropolitan conditions.

I wish to share a few experiences from that year. In order to have reader service, I traveled to 59th Street to the New York Lighthouse for the Blind where volunteers were readers. This is a multipurpose agency with reader service as only one of its services.

One reader suggested that I come to her apartment for the reading. During one of those sessions, Circle was lying beside my chair as usual when the manager knocked to say that he had come to do a few repairs. He worked quietly while the reading continued.

Then suddenly, he said in alarm, "It's alive!"

We were surprised by his outburst. My reader asked, "What do you mean?"

He explained, "I thought that dog was just an ornament, you know, a big stuffed toy, but its eyes blinked. It's alive!" Apparently afraid of dogs, he backed out of the apartment with his ladder in front of him as protection against that big dog. He said he would return after the dog was gone. Circle, of course, never rose to her paws.

In order for me to reach the Lighthouse, I rode on the double-decker Fifth Avenue bus. However, I first had to convince the conductor that I was blind and that my dog was a guide. Eventually, he consented to admit us onto the vehicle.

Apparently, he was still persuaded that I was a fraud and watched me carefully to expose me.

One day Jane, a resident from The Judson, was a passenger at the same time I was but had a different destination. Because I had recently received proofs of photos from a studio for personnel purposes to accompany applications for teaching positions, I pulled them from my handbag and handed them to Jane for her opinion about which proof I should select.

We were sitting on the back seat bothering no one. Suddenly the conductor rushed back to me and charged, "I thought you said you are blind!" I assured him that I am. Then he challenged, "If you are blind, what are you doing with pictures?" He was convinced that I was an imposter.

I did not attend commencement in June; my diploma was mailed to me.

During the summer of 1945 in Clifton, I received a letter from Betty Ryder Strickland in Paoli, Pennsylvania. Betty had graduated with me from NJC. During the time when I was in New York, she married Howard Strickland, a graduate from Rutgers University. Howard was blind, though Betty was not.

The letter informed me of a teaching position available at Royer-Greaves School for Blind Children with multiple impairments: mental retardation, cerebral palsy, emotional disturbance, etc. Betty and Howard were teachers, not administrators. Howard was head teacher, though his university major had been in social service. Officially, Mrs. Jessie Royer-Greaves was the administrator; she was not a teacher by training.

On the basis of Betty's recommendation, I was hired without an application or interview!

I arrived at the school on Saturday of Labor Day weekend. My second-floor bedroom was small with space for only a single bed, desk (that served as a dresser), and one chair. The closet was inadequate for all-seasonal clothing.

My classroom was even smaller, containing a table and four chairs with no educational supplies. I was to teach Braille reading but had no reading readiness materials.

Besides teaching, I was to be a houseparent. Teaching was from eight o'clock in the morning until five in the afternoon with a morning and afternoon recess and an hour for lunch. My house parenting hours were Monday and Wednesday evenings from five in the evening until eight the next morning. Weekend duty was alternate weekends; the other team relieved my team. Weekend duty began at five on Friday evening and ended at eight on Monday morning! Two houseparent teams had already been determined. Betty, Howard, and Marion Genthner (a blind high school graduate) were one team. The other team would be Lucretia Thorpe (a former student at this school), Charles Napier (another new teacher who did not arrive until Labor Day) and I. This arrangement made for a strong and a weak team. Betty, Howard, and Marion knew much more about the school than Charles and I, both new. We could learn nothing from Lucretia to help us. A stronger arrangement would have been to have Marion with me or with Charles because she had already been at the school several years.

Six older teenage boys lived together in one room and were not part of my house parenting load. Most of those six had no home other than the school and were on campus when I arrived.

Instead, I was assigned to seventeen younger boys whose beds were in one large room on the third floor. The building had no fire escapes. I cannot understand how building codes could allow a school to sleep twenty-three children and three adults on the third floor with no fire escapes. I was learning rapidly that this school seemed comparable to Piney Woods School but without the issue of skin color.

I was assigned to make the seventeen beds for my boys who would be arriving on Monday. The older boys brought me linens. One by one, I made each.

As of that moment, I was the whole team for the third floor.

Royer-Greaves School was a private school, but several states paid for children to attend it. I surmise that employees of states that paid

Royer-Greaves had never visited the school to determine what state money did or did not provide for each child.

Mrs. Greaves had no respect for blind adults even though her school purported to educate blind children. Her mantra was, "You are lucky to be working here. Who else would hire a blind person?" I did not buy her philosophy; she wanted slave labor. I figured my total hours of work in a month and my wage of sixty dollars per month; the school was paying me twenty cents an hour with two university degrees! Seeing persons were paid more than blind employees. For instance, Betty, with one degree, received more than I. A few years later, a houseparent was hired in the person of a seeing high school graduate. One payday he was complaining about how little he was paid and expressing his belief that we teachers were rolling in money. I showed him my pay; he was receiving more than I was!

On Labor Day, Charles "Chuck" S. Napier arrived from Chicago. His room was on the third floor. When unpacked, he joined the rest of us. Each of us supplied information about his or her background and teacher preparation.

Chuck had had an accident when he was seventeen years old in 1931. Before that, he had dropped out of high school and worked for a furniture store. His job was to be in the body of the truck to alert the driver when the truck would not have sufficient clearance to pass under a bridge or railroad or in a tunnel. On one of the deliveries, telephone wires hit him across the face, injuring one eye.

He had undergone several eye surgeries. In one surgery, according to Chuck, the ophthalmologist operated on the wrong eye, causing blindness in the formerly uninjured eye. Consequently, he was blind in both eyes.

Chuck also shared that he had been engaged to marry Ila when the accident occurred. Afterward, when recovery of sight was unlikely, Ila jilted him.

Chuck was still very bitter about her treatment of him, even though he was then thirty-one years old. He failed to recognize the fact that

Ila was an adolescent at the time of the accident and that blindness was undoubtedly unnerving.

Meanwhile, rehabilitation services in Illinois sent Chuck to the state School for the Blind in Jacksonville to earn his high school diploma and then sent him to the University of Illinois where he earned two degrees in psychology.

I fear that rehabilitation personnel viewed college education as a solution to all problems, with little or no attention to the clients' adjustment to blindness or attitudes. After earning the two degrees, Chuck operated a concession stand in a public building where he sold coffee, sandwiches, candy bars, cigarettes, etc. Chuck did not work in psychology, however, perhaps because of the Great Depression.

I do not know how he had learned about Royer-Greaves School's vacancy. He had not been professionally prepared as a teacher, but that fact was of no concern to Mrs. Greaves. All that she wanted was blind persons with warm bodies and strong backs. Only Betty and I had been prepared as teachers.

I was not attracted to Chuck because of his cynical, sour personality. He was wallowing in self-pity, resentment, and bitterness. In the fourteen years since the accident, he had not achieved adjustment to blindness. In Chuck's case, college education had not resolved his problems. He was paranoid and suspicious, assuming that everyone had a hidden agenda and that what people said was not what they meant. He smoked cigarettes continuously and consumed coffee all hours while awake. He had not made a favorable first impression on anyone.

Chuck talked either about college experiences several years earlier or about what he was going to do "some day."

While in college, he lived with several other blind students. I think that this arrangement was a grave mistake on his part. He might have gained more by living with seeing male students if they could have tolerated his personality aside from his blindness.

I do not know how his family had treated him after the accident.

I assume that Chuck was demanding, expecting that someone should jump to serve him whenever he spoke and gave an order. Chuck had nine siblings; consequently, he had a ready-made cadre of slaves to manipulate.

My impressions of Chuck in those early weeks might seem harsh and severe, but that is how I viewed him initially. He definitely did not use even the basic principles of psychology in his interpersonal relationships. When he spoke, he sounded more like a high school dropout than a university graduate because of his frequent use of slang and crude language. I had the feeling that he had attended classes and completed courses but had not internalized the information, so that it was an integral part of him. By contrast, Betty and Howard were Phi Beta Kappa and polished without stuffiness. The courses had not been change agents in Chuck's life, the essence of education. Nothing in him had changed since the time when he worked on the furniture truck. That same Chuck was present fourteen years later with little evidence of a university education. Although he had graduated with two degrees in psychology, Chuck put forth no effort to establish himself in professional psychology as a therapist or practitioner.

Although Chuck was present in the evening to help give baths and put the boys to bed, frequently in the mornings when additional baths were necessary or help to dress some of the boys, part of his responsibilities, Chuck was absent. At breakfast, Mrs. Greaves asked me where Mr. Napier was. I answered that I had not seen him on duty. She then sent one of the big boys to go to Chuck's door to knock to wake him. This occurred countless times. I felt that Mrs. Greaves should have given me part of Chuck's wages for each time he had missed duty, forcing me to do his work in addition to my own.

Chuck claimed that his alarm clock failed to ring. We teachers contributed money to buy him a new Big Ben alarm clock. Chuck's absences continued, unaltered by a brand-new clock. Now what was his excuse?

Relative to the students assigned to me for reading, Mrs. Greaves gave me children who were not speaking, not toilet trained, did not comprehend simple language, such as, "Billy, sit down," etc. These children were not candidates for reading, but these were the ones I was expected to teach. When these children made no progress, Mrs. Greaves said I was not a qualified teacher! Not being a teacher, she understood nothing about readiness for reading, such as ability to speak, comprehension when spoken to, knowing comparisons of large/small, smooth/rough, round/not round, asking questions, eagerness to learn, etc. She knew nothing about teaching but set herself up as an expert and selected children based on their chronological ages, not their intellect or readiness for reading. Without seeing progress in the children assigned to me, teaching was without reward.

Off-duty weekends offered little in social options. Life off campus provided nothing. Townspeople assumed that the adults at the school were also multi-impaired. Even though I attended on alternate Sundays the Presbyterian church, farther from the school on the opposite side of Lincoln Highway, I experienced no real welcome there or invitation to attend Sunday school or the women's organization. Wanting to establish my own identity, I had chosen that church because the children of the school attended the Methodist church. Because town social options were so limited, on off-duty weekends we associated with the same few adults on the teaching staff.

Not infrequently, we were ordered to help with some "emergency" on evenings or weekends that were supposed to be our personal time.

When one of my boys was ill with measles, Dr. Jones examined Bobby and prescribed medications. He warned me not to give the tablet with citrus juice; the result would be explosive vomiting soon after. I was managing very well with the child.

Then Mrs. Greaves came to third floor just as I was giving Bobby a pill. Mrs. Greaves said that she had brought him orange juice. I told her what Dr. Jones had told me.

"Nonsense! He needs orange juice." The boy drank the juice and soon after erupted.

I expected that Mrs. Greaves would now order me to remake the boy's bed. Before she said a word, I walked out of the dormitory. *Clean up the bed yourself,* I thought. She never apologized for not following my advice.

The school had no isolation room for a child with a contagious condition. The boy who had measles was in his regular bed in the big room with sixteen other boys. I imagine that the others must have already had measles because we had no new cases afterward.

One recreational option was the playhouse behind the main building—a playhouse for children but large enough for adults to stand inside it. The two rooms had no furniture or toys to attract children. The four windows were broken. Chuck decided that he would replace the panes on our next off-duty Saturday. He ordered materials. On Saturday, he offered to teach me how to replace the glass. I think he had invited me primarily to be his guide to the playhouse that he could not find by himself.

After showing me how to do the work using glazer points and putty, he started on another window. Soon I heard glass shatter and profanity. I continued on my window. I did that window and two others while he could not complete one until he obtained more glass.

My success did not set well with him. He had a very low opinion of women's ability to do anything; my achievement with glass galled him. That is why he stayed away from me after he broke the pane. Yet, I was not going to pretend ineptitude and incompetence just to let him feel superior. Women were not ignoramuses merely because he thought they were.

About a month after I arrived, Mrs. Greaves suggested that Chuck and I take the children to the meadow to play on a huge log. The children pretended that the log was a horse or airplane or boat or whatever else their imaginations conjured up. Then the log began to roll because of the children's energetic activity. Jackie Neff rolled off, and the log pinned him to the ground. Children were ordered off the log, and Chuck succeeded in freeing Jackie. A child was sent to summon help for Jackie. Jackie was taken to the hospital, where he died a few days later.

I expected Mrs. Greaves to explode with charges against Chuck and me for negligence and carelessness. She never uttered a word. After all, she had sent two new teachers to the meadow. As new teachers, Chuck and I would not have gone there without instructions from Mrs. Greaves to do so.

We teachers were deeply grieved to lose Jackie. The Stricklands and Marion had known Jackie much longer than Chuck and I had had association with him.

One noon in the dining room, a boy was choking on food. I rushed to his chair, pulled it away from the table, lifted him off the chair, turned him upside down, and slapped his back several times. He coughed out the food that had obstructed his windpipe. Then I helped him to his chair again. Mrs. Greaves merely said, "Nice work." This was long before the Heimlich maneuver had been introduced.

When cold weather arrived, we issued our boys their one-piece winter underwear, provided by their parents and stored in drawers in the adjacent room.

In the following weeks, Chuck and I discovered that the boys had great difficulty putting on their underwear correctly. They had legs in sleeves and heads through the seat, etc.

At the next faculty meeting, I reported the boys' hassles with their winter underwear. Mrs. Greaves and the other teachers treated the matter lightly, with an air of "That's been true every winter."

I suggested, "Why can't the boys have two-piece underwear for the winter?" No one had ever thought of that!

Mrs. Greaves said she would write to the parents to send two-piece winter underwear.

I was truly surprised that she would accept a suggestion from me, a new teacher. The boys were able to manage this kind of clothing without the confusion experienced each winter before.

In late winter or early spring of that first year, Chuck went to Chicago for an interview about a rehabilitation counseling position. When he returned, he was noncommittal about the experience. I sensed that it had not gone well, though the final official decision had not yet been made.

Later, when the letter from Chicago arrived, I was present while someone read it to Chuck. The letter was not flattering or encouraging. In fact, it was quite negative about Chuck's responses to questions. The gist of the message was that Chuck had answered most questions with "I don't know whether I can do that" or "I'm not sure" or "Maybe not," etc. The writer—who had interviewed Chuck—wrote that he wondered why Chuck had come such a distance when he believed that he could not do the work of a rehabilitation counselor.

I thought much about that letter and wondered, too, why Chuck would go for an interview about a position he felt unqualified to perform. Did Chuck think that because he was an Illinois native he would automatically be accepted regardless of his negative attitudes, lack of self-confidence, and inadequacy to perform the job requirements?

In those days, a rehabilitation counselor was not required to earn a degree in counseling but be enthusiastic about being able to help blind clients find employment and persuade employers to accept qualified employees, etc. Even though Chuck had two degrees in psychology, he felt incapable to execute this job. What did he need to feel qualified?

In spite of Chuck's outer crust and rough edges, I saw potential in him. *How can he realize his potential*, I wondered. He seemed to dislike women because of Ila, but not all women were duplicates of Ila. Furthermore, Ila was an adolescent at the time of Chuck's accident. I can appreciate why she might have run away from a man who was then blind. Besides, if Chuck were then as pugnacious, cynical, embittered, angry, and resentful as he was when first I met him, he probably frightened Ila into thinking that when a man becomes blind, he also becomes incompatible as a friend or future spouse, yet I am certain that Chuck never considered how he might have contributed to Ila's withdrawal from him.

In my conversations with Chuck, I tried to convey friendship and appreciation of his potential. He seemed to soften a bit. In short, by late spring, he asked me to marry him. I saw this as a rebirth for him, adopting a more natural and healthy approach to life; maybe I had truly penetrated his shell to touch his need for companionship. Perhaps he had discovered that a relationship was preferable to the loneliness and isolation he had experienced since his accident.

Unfortunately, I was ill-equipped to judge Chuck's merit as a husband because of my own sheltered and over-protected life and lack of exposure to dating men, due to my mother's iron grip on me. Could my love for him permanently convert him into a responsible spouse? Was his love for me genuine or only a convenience? Would he view me as an equal or only as a second-class spouse to serve him with food, laundry, and other household chores befitting a wife?

Nevertheless, we planned our wedding for August 21 during our only vacation month from the school.

In early August, I accompanied Chuck to Chicago to meet his large family. En route, Chuck tutored me in all the names: Which sibling was married to whom, which child belonged to which couple.

The family warmly received me. Although at that time Chuck had nine siblings, at this writing only the youngest, a brother, is still alive.

When I returned home, my mother was taking full charge of the arrangements. She kept pushing for a church wedding, which I rejected vehemently because of the additional expense that my father could not afford.

We were married at home. The reception was conducted simply in Uncle Andrew's clubhouse. I had absolutely no input about anything related to the reception; Mamma shut me out of her plans. Mamma decided everything, even though it was my wedding. When was it ever different with her?

Chuck said that he wanted the honeymoon in New York City. I soon learned that he had saved no money for the honeymoon. Consequently, I paid for everything. Chuck told me while we were in New York that he wanted to go to a Broadway show. I asked whether he had money for tickets. No, he did not. After that response, I said, "In that case, we are leaving New York in the morning!" With my money rapidly disappearing, we returned to Clifton.

There, I would have two more surprises.

Chuck summoned an insurance agent for life insurance on himself, "to protect Grace." After Chuck had signed the application, the agent asked for the deposit. Chuck said, "Honey, I don't have it. You pay him." I did.

After the agent departed, Chuck said to me, "Now make sure that you pay the premium each time it's due!"

I reminded him that he was the one who had signed the policy, and that meant he should pay the premium.

His counter was, "When I die, you are the one who collects the money; so you should pay the premium!" The "protection" was for only three thousand dollars! How much protection was that amount? (On which planet had he been living to have such twisted thinking?) He was not protecting me. He was protecting himself. I had married a man who was already shirking his financial responsibilities!

That same month, he summoned another insurance agent for health insurance coverage. He did the same thing as before. He even refused to pay for his own policy. He expected me to pay for both health insurance policies even though I earned *exactly* the same amount as he.

Back in Paoli at the school in September, matters did not improve. When I was planning to go to town to buy groceries, he ordered me not to buy any store pies, "because they taste like paste on cardboard." I obeyed.

On one of our off-duty weekends, I began making potato salad and would chill it with permission in the refrigerator owned by the Stricklands.

Chuck told me that he did not use salad dressing on his potato salad.

I explained that dressing is added to potato salad in the preparation stage and not at the table during the meal. I thought he would accept that explanation.

He insisted that he took *no* dressing on potato salad.

I told him that he would not like potato salad without any dressing.

He became angry. "I know what I like. Get it through your thick head that I want no dressing—zilch! Can you understand that?"

I made two batches of potato salad: one for him without dressing, one for me with dressing.

When I served the meal, I was not surprised that he did not like his potato salad.

He said, "This is the worst potato salad that I have ever tasted. You can't even make a decent potato salad!" In his opinion, I was one of those inferior, incompetent, ignorant women who fit his preconceived thoughts of all women. It was a self-fulfilling prophecy. I was not considered special or loved or cherished by him. This was our first month of marriage!

One of the few times that Chuck bought groceries was when he had gone to town with someone. He never shopped alone or walked to town as I did. He brought home a store pie!

I said, "You told me never to bring home a store pie. Now you bought one."

His response was, "Well, if I want pie, I have to eat this junk. You don't make a pie for me!"

I said, "Then you teach me how to bake a pie on an electric hot plate." Silence was his reply. A hot plate was the only source of heat for cooking; it was primarily for making his coffee.

This man whom I had hoped would respond to my love was, instead, bullying me with verbal, emotional, and mental abuse.

I return to my hunch that his family took whatever bullying he handed out without correcting him, "because poor Chuck is blind!" Consequently, he had developed a pattern of bullying anyone who happened to be near.

I wanted to leave him but did not believe in divorce.

He had not changed after all. Why? I gave that question serious thought and arrived at two explanations: First, he might have had a distorted idea of marriage, namely, that when one marries, all his problems melt away. He recognized that he still had his problems; therefore, I was the wrong woman, he concluded. Second, because I am blind, I was an inferior wife, since he considered himself inferior as a man because of being blind. He might reason that if he had a wife with normal vision, he would then feel normal. According to him, my blindness reminded him of his own blindness and his own inadequacies. Only by having a wife with normal vision could he accept himself as successful and acceptable to others and himself.

I could do nothing about his perceptions. To him, they were his reality.

I am not a psychologist or psychoanalyst but knowing him as I did, no matter who his wife might have been, he would still have had his present personality anomalies.

I tried approaching him with tenderness and affection. His reaction was, "Okay, what do you want?" He interpreted tenderness and affection as maneuvers to get something from him. He was convinced that I had to have a hidden agenda.

He was emotionally cold and withdrawn. How could I reach him? He filled his days with chain smoking of cigarettes and consumption of coffee. Still later, I would discover another of his dependencies.

Because he was always broke but could not account for where his money had gone, I had to wonder where he was spending it and for what. In my mind, I compiled a list: gambling, alcohol, prostitution with women, prostitution with men, drugs. Which was it? He already had addictions to coffee and tobacco. My husband was some kind of pervert or criminal! Why was he deceiving me? Why had I been foolish enough to think he had salvageable qualities? What kind of marriage farce is this?

For our first Christmas break, Chuck wanted to go to Chicago to visit his family. Now he had train fare and was not broke. I had learned by observation that when he did not want to pay for something, he claimed being broke. On the other hand, when he wanted to do something, he had the money with which to purchase it.

On Christmas Eve, he called his mother an uncomplimentary name; she responded with anger but said nothing to put him in his proper place. I am inclined to believe that the whole family took Chuck's mean-spiritedness in silence, "because poor Chuck is blind!"

Chuck suggested to me that, because his mother had no telephone, we go to the corner store to phone my parents to wish them Merry Christmas.

Outside, he told me that he wanted to leave and return to Paoli. I informed him that, if he planned to leave, he must first buy a suitcase for his things or travel with a paper sack, because I was not leaving.

I reminded him that he had caused the problem by insulting his mother in her own home and that we were guests in her home. I was keeping the present suitcase for my return to the school later.

I urged him to apologize to his mother. I never heard an apology, if he ever offered one.

He still wanted me to pack our suitcase. I refused. I felt that while I was in the bedroom packing, he would whisper to the family that Grace was upset and wanted to go home, so he had to follow orders from her, thus making me the culprit. I was learning the tactics that he used, always to exonerate himself. I did not pack. Because of me, we stayed in Chicago as long as we had originally planned.

I think my hunch was correct. The family took whatever sassy tongue Chuck uttered and overlooked it "because poor Chuck is blind." Although Mrs. Napier was angry, she said nothing to put Chuck in his proper place. What Chuck needed from his family was a set of rules applied to him just as they apply to every other member of his family. Why was he an exception just because of blindness? His family had converted him into a social misfit who was a bully in the family and a wimp with extremely low self-esteem everywhere else. Bullies cannot do anything; that's why they are bullies. Chuck was lonely because of not knowing how to relate to other human beings. His lack of interpersonal skills created chasms instead of bridges between him and others. Being sarcastic and abusive exacerbated his problem.

Chuck responded to situations as an adolescent, incapable of maturing into manhood. Although he had a university education, he did not know how to use it, because little of his education had become internalized. He was irresponsible financially. He was untruthful and deceitful. Egocentric, he was unwilling to share and reciprocate. Addicted, paranoid, passive-aggressive in personality, he lacked familial loyalty. He felt accountable to no one. Even after only six months of marriage, I could write this thumbnail sketch to summarize his lack of character and maturity. I think that he stopped maturing after his accident at seventeen. So many of his responses were those of a seventeen-year-old boy, not those of a man in his thirties. Blindness is not a license to abuse others and be free of condemnation. He had learned that he might be a tyrant and everyone else would submit in silence to him. Blindness does not make abuse acceptable.

When his family permitted him to be a bully, he was not forced to find more appropriate methods for dealing with life's demands. Therefore, he had no reason to choose more effective strategies, leading to maturity. His family, in short, sanctioned his bullying and abusive behavior, causing him to be stuck at seventeen and unprepared for adult-level responsibilities.

Back at the school, he adopted a new scheme: He clapped his

hands twice and said, "Abdul, the coffee pot is empty" or (clap-clap) "Abdul, where's my lunch?" etc. If he had done it only once or twice and quit it, I might have accepted it as his attempt to be humorous. Instead, he continued it for several days. I had to nip it permanently. I said, "My name is Grace, not Abdul. I am your wife, not your slave, and 'Please' is appropriate!" He never did it again. If his family had treated him accordingly, he might have evolved into a decent human being. After all, he was not the first and only person to be blinded in an accident. I have known countless individuals whose lives have been changed by accidents, but they coped successfully to become individuals of note. I think that Chuck never began the process of coping. Instead, he took the easy route, namely, abusing persons closest to him, becoming a shriveled-up persona, wasting his life on chemical dependency and pushing away anyone who sought to be friend or spouse. In his perverted mind, he was the only Wise One; everyone else was a fraud.

For a university graduate, he had no interests or pursuits except cigarettes and coffee and what I discovered much later.

His Braille skills were woefully inept. When he had occasions to send me letters, I could neither read most of them nor understand the content because he invented his own Braille contractions but did not know the Braille Code well enough to use it correctly. Plus, he composed a letter using fragments, not sentences. He read almost no Braille books or magazines.

When he asked me to read to him, I did but soon discovered that he was asleep after the first or second paragraph. Reading books together could have been an activity to share as spouses. Instead, he deserted me in midstream.

Similarly, he suggested that "we" write a letter to a specific relative. I brought out the typewriter, inserted paper, and waited for Chuck to begin the letter. It was always a statement about the weather. Then he was asleep; deserted again, I was left to complete the letter. When he suggested that we write to his mother, I urged him to write it himself.

In protest, I reminded him that his mother might conclude that I was preventing him from writing to her, that I was opposed to his communicating with her through me. Still, he depended on me to write those letters.

Although he claimed that Dr. Brad Burson was his best friend, Chuck seldom wrote to Brad or phoned him. I think he was merely enjoying name-dropping. Brad had a national and international reputation as a scientist who happened to be blind.

Chuck also refused to discuss finances with me. His attitude was that *his* money was strictly his and that *my* money was also his. I have a feeling that when he proposed marriage, he saw marriage as a way to double his income. In the 1946-1947 academic year, each of us earned seventy dollars a month. After marrying me, he considered his income one hundred forty dollars a month. I did not hand him my monthly pay but had to struggle to maintain my ownership of it because of his usual excuse: "I'm broke." *Was he truly broke? How was he spending his money?* He refused to explain how he had spent his money. *Or did he have the money but claimed to be broke merely to force me to pay for this and that?* I wondered. Because of his refusal to explain, I had no answers to my own questions.

As a bride, I wanted harmony and tranquility and not feuding.

In July of 1947, my father died suddenly because of a massive heart attack. I had loved him dearly. I staggered from the blow. Chuck did nothing to comfort or support me. Instead, in an angry, condemning voice, he said, "You need to go to a psychiatrist. You're nuts!" This was only a few weeks after the funeral. He used his "knowledge" of psychology to belittle or label me but never to apply a diagnosis to himself.

In that same summer when my father had died in July, Circle was not eating well. She lacked appetite even for foods that she had previously particularly enjoyed: cottage cheese, sardines, boiled eggs, etc.

The veterinarian examined her for a variety of problems, each of which proved to be negative. Then he discovered she had tuberculosis of the digestive track, but the condition was too advanced to save her. This proved to be a summer of bereavement—silent and alone for me.

Late in 1947, my paternal grandfather died. The following spring, his will was processed. He left each of his surviving children eleven thousand dollars. Because my father was already deceased, my grandfather left my brother five thousand five hundred dollars and me the same amount, as my father's inheritance.

As soon as I had the check in hand, Chuck said that he wanted one thousand dollars to start a beekeeping project. He promised to repay it with three percent interest and also to turn his hobby into a small business by having merchants in town take jars of honey on consignment.

This scheme proved to be only hot air and empty words. Chuck did nothing to contact merchants. I have a hunch that he expected me to do the contacting of merchants and the leg work involved. I was learning about his schemes to avoid work and to have me do what he should be doing himself.

When the wood for hives arrived, I worked as hard as he did to assemble twenty-one hives with one or two supers each (compartments permitting the bees to expand the colony). Chuck did assume the responsibility of securing permission from a property owner to set the hives in his orchard. Because of Chuck's inactivity, no jars of honey became retail products. Instead, Chuck gave away most of the honey.

I worked as hard as he did with live bees. I wore all the protective gear except gloves. With bare hands, I could work more effectively. I had my share of bee stings.

I never took my dog, Esta (another German boxer), to the hives. I did not want her stung, especially on the nose, face, and eyes.

After only a few years and without discussing the matter with me, he gave away or sold all of our equipment to another apiarist. Because of his previous lies to me about other situations, I do not know whether he truly sold the equipment and pocketed the money but told me he had *given* the equipment to Walter Burkey. The money was not his to keep since he had borrowed it from me.

For nineteen years afterward, he repaid me not one dollar of the principal or interest! That issue will arise much later.

After the third year at the school, I resigned. Because of our evening and weekend duty and an eleven-month school year, I could not enroll in evening or Saturday or summer courses to advance my professional career. I could not stay at Royer-Greaves School any longer.

Chuck had said soon after we married that he would stay at this school only two or three years and then move on to higher and better jobs. Contrary to his word, he was doing nothing to find other employment.

I concluded that I had to be the leader in this family, that if I left the school first, Chuck would have the courage to leave. I had no job to go to when I resigned, but I believed in myself enough to know that other positions existed and that I could fill one because of my professional skills.

I believe that Chuck had accepted Mrs. Greaves's words about "No one else will hire you" that she repeated often. I never believed her.

As my first year had drawn to an end, I had resolved to stay at Royer-Greaves a second year to prove that I had been rehired when a different employer examined my record. When a new teacher stays only one year in the first position, a prospective employer has to wonder: Was she not rehired because of a problem? Was she offered a second-year contract but refused it? Even though Royer-Greaves was a very inferior school, a prospective employer might not have believed it and assumed that criticism of the school was an attempt to hide the applicant's real problem. So now, I had three years at Royer-Greaves to my credit.

I contacted the New Jersey State Commission for the Blind, specifically, Miss Josephine L. Taylor (no relative of Katharine Taylor) to let her know that I had left Royer-Greaves School and was unemployed.

Immediately, she had plans for me. At the Commission's expense, she was sending me to Ypsilanti, Michigan, to the college there for six weeks for summer session to gain basic skills in social work. No, she was not trying to change me from a teacher to a social worker. She had something else in mind, unknown to me at that moment.

This was 1948 when, at the end of our courses, I flew with Lillian Rosenbom from Michigan to Chicago where I visited the Napiers. This was my first airplane flight. I have flown countless times since then.

In November, Miss Taylor summoned me to her office whereupon she began telling me about the state's itinerant-teacher program for visually-impaired and blind children. For the reader to comprehend the significance of this, I must supply historical information here.

In the early 1940's, a new blinding condition was appearing throughout our country. Doctors were having greater success in keeping premature infants alive than heretofore. However, in a matter of weeks or months after such births, these babies were found to be blind though earlier their eyes were normal. But why?

Medical research ventured into countless aspects in attempts to unlock the reason why premature babies in epidemic numbers were blind. About fifteen years after the first cases, research revealed the secret: Premature babies had been placed in incubators to keep them alive. Unfortunately, infants were in incubators too long, and the concentration of oxygen was too high. As a consequence, blood vessels in the retina were damaged, leaving babies with impaired vision. The condition was first called retrolental fibroplasia. Later a more correct name came into use: retinopathy of prematurity.

How did those facts affect me in the field of education? Residential schools were full to capacity. How could other blind school-age children be educated when the residential schools could absorb no more children? Classes similar to Miss Katharine Taylor's class served relatively few children when compared with the number of children enrolled in residential schools. Besides, some children lived too far from such classes to make commuting feasible.

The Commission had begun its itinerant-teacher program by hiring seeing teachers to serve blind children in their homes as preschoolers and in local public, parochial, or private schools. These teachers moved throughout the day from one school with a blind child to other schools, usually with only one blind child in each school.

Miss Josephine Taylor wanted to perform an experiment, namely, could a teacher who was blind perform the tasks of an itinerant teacher? I was her first choice for this role.

She asked whether I thought I could perform this kind of teacher responsibility with all the traveling required.

My immediate response was, "Yes. When can I start?"

"On December 1st!" I was thrilled by this opportunity and challenge.

What did my basic training in social work have to do with itinerant teaching? I would be in contact with school principals, nurses, and teachers, as well as parents, ophthalmologists, well-baby clinics, public health nurses, other medical doctors, and community resources of many types as I encountered needs in families. My role for each family I served was to ferret out the services the family needed because of the blind child's membership in that constellation, services from financial aid to the other end of the spectrum.

I was grateful for my knowledge gained at Ypsilanti.

I would be paid one hundred fifty dollars per month plus reimbursement for transportation expenses.

SEVEN

PLANNING AHEAD IN LATE November 1948, I telephoned the YWCA in Camden to determine whether it was residential. If so, I might live there a few days until I found permanent accommodations. The woman with whom I spoke said "Yes," to my question "Is it residential?" Good! Camden was the most metropolitan city in the three counties (Camden, Gloucester, and Burlington) that I would be servicing. Bus connections in Camden radiated out in various directions to meet my needs for traveling to many towns in my territory.

Arriving at the Y with suitcase and typewriter, I learned that it was *not* residential! The person with whom I had talked by phone might not have known what *residential* meant but said yes anyway as some persons do when faced with an unfamiliar word. Now what was I to do? I could not afford to stay at a hotel.

The director or manager, whatever her title, said she had a list of homes where women might stay. She phoned Mrs. Ben Harvey. Afterward, she informed me that Mrs. Harvey would be eager to provide a room. Then the director summoned a taxicab to transport me to Empire Avenue.

When we pulled up in front of the Harvey house, the driver told me that he was going in alone to look the place over to make sure it was a safe place for me to live. When he returned, he assured me that the house was clean, that a middle-aged couple lived there, and that another single woman was a roomer.

My room was in back on the second floor. It had a double bed, table and chair, and closet. I would share the bathroom with the other roomer and with the Harveys. Because I would need to leave early many mornings and not be sure of when I would return home, I elected to eat my meals out rather than with the Harveys and Estelle.

To set my schedule, I phoned the families I would be visiting to learn how to reach each destination by bus: which bus to use, where to leave the bus, where to go from that bus stop to find the house. After I met with the mother and the preschool child, I asked directions to the school that the child would be attending. If the child was already in school, I learned the way to it to meet the principal and teacher. I did not ask the mother to walk with me to the school. I requested directions, instead, in terms of number of blocks, in which directions, on which side of the street, etc. I felt going alone with the information given me was a way to build the mother's confidence in my ability to work effectively with her child.

After I had demonstrated that I could manage a few children, my caseload began to grow. An infant was my youngest client, the oldest a twelfth-grader preparing to attend college.

To clarify, I must explain what I did with children in school. I did not teach everything, only those academic areas that the classroom teacher was not qualified to teach, such as Braille reading and writing, computation with specialized equipment, map reading, and typewriting.

For high school students, I did not teach foreign language but the Braille used in that language, not algebra but the unfamiliar Braille symbols, etc.

I met with teachers to discuss our separate roles and how I might supplement what they taught. I wanted to know about problems that they were encountering with my students. Possibly, I might be able to suggest a resolution or alternative approach. For instance, one boy did not turn to the announced page in a specific text book when the teacher told the class. She found that she had to say the boy's name before he sought the correct page.

I worked with the boy to explain that the teacher did not have time to tell each child and to use his or her name. I emphasized that when the teacher said, "Class," that was when she was talking to everyone in the room and that included him, so he should do what all the other children were doing. He adjusted; he fit into the group situation.

With preschool-age youngsters, I worked with the child while the mother observed. We might use a peg board or string beads or talk in order to develop vocabulary to speak in sentences, read a story aloud to the child and ask comprehension questions, etc. Some of the time was devoted directly to the mother, giving her opportunity to ask questions or mention concerns. Most of the time, I never met with fathers, who were working away from home.

In one situation, the wife wanted me to meet with her husband on a Saturday morning because of his inability to accept his child's blindness. After I arrived on Saturday, the wife called her husband from another room. He came into the room where his wife and I were. She introduced us. He said something like, "Glad to meet you" and turned to leave. The wife spoke up, almost in anger, to remind him that I had come on a Saturday to meet with him. With his attitude, I feel that I did not accomplish much with him.

At school, the principal found a place where my student and I might work: a landing in a staircase, a large closet with two doors for air circulation, the library, the lunchroom early in the morning or in the afternoon, a corridor, the teachers' room, etc. After all, we did not need a whole classroom for the two of us. The student had a desk and chair, and I had a chair. We worked very well wherever the designated site.

In some towns, I had to read my watch often, because the bus to my next school ran hourly. If I missed it, my schedule for the remainder of the day was shattered.

Sometimes I reached my first school in the morning only to learn that the child was absent. The mother had telephoned me, but I had already left the Harvey home to buy my breakfast and begin my bus connections. Because of child absences or school schedule changes, I left a copy of my itinerary everywhere I was expected so that I could be reached. In those days, of course, I had no cellular phone as I do now.

I noticed great differences in my acceptance among the many principals in whose schools I taught. In one, my name, address, and phone number were included in the school's directory distributed to all employees of the school and to me. When I first asked that principal for permission to do something special with my student, he said, "You are one of my teachers; you are not a guest in this building. If you feel that something will enhance the child's education but is unusual, you do not need my permission. I trust your professional judgment."

In other schools, I was not given a directory, nor was I included in one because no one asked for my home address, though my telephone number was on file and on my itinerary.

In some schools, teachers who did not teach my student knew what I was doing, suggesting that someone had done a thorough job of acquainting all teachers as to why I was in the building. In other schools only teachers who worked with my student seemed to know why I was there.

For instance, I met a teacher in the teachers' room where I kept my coat. She said, "I wish I had a job like yours." Curious, I asked her why, thinking that she was interested in becoming a special education teacher. "Well, here it is only eleven o'clock, and you are going home. What a soft job you have!" She knew nothing about my job. I explained that my day was not finished; I mentioned to which towns I would be going the rest of the day and that after school visits, I made home visits and would not reach home until after six. She had a new picture of my "soft" job.

A teacher in another school asked, "You didn't have to go to college to do your job, did you?" I clarified that I already had bachelor's and master's degrees. I said that I need to know methodology in teaching my student in her school just as she needs to use appropriate methodology in her classroom.

One day while David and I were working in the lunchroom, one of the food service women came to me to ask, "We need to write a note to the principal upstairs. How do you spell *principal*?" Earlier I had heard her and the other women discussing that question. Some maintained -*pal* while others wanted -*ple*. I spelled the word with the -*pal* ending. As she returned to the other women, I heard her say, "She doesn't know either." Apparently, she was advocating -*ple* and did not want me to prove her wrong.

Even some persons in town had ideas about me. One day I had just boarded a bus near one of my schools and walked down the aisle for a seat. As I passed two women on my left, I overheard their conversation:

"That blind woman goes to that school."

"What kind of school is it?"

"Elementary."

"Elementary? Isn't she rather old to be in elementary school?"

"You see, it takes her kind longer to learn."

I often wondered what my many bus drivers thought I was doing. I always carried a tote or briefcase. *What is she selling? Why does she go to so many schools to sell her wares?* Of course, some drivers took me to only one school and probably did not know about my other schools on different bus routes.

My third dog, Esta (another German boxer), thrived on an itinerant teacher's busy life. She was alert and keen. When we waited for a bus, she sat watching in the direction from whence it would appear. Other vehicles passed us with no interest on Esta's part. However, when the bus came into view, she stood up and shook. I am sure that the bus drivers noticed how she had recognized their vehicles.

On one of my routes, I was sitting next to a woman who wanted to talk. She was concerned about her mother who was very ill.

About six months later, I sat beside her again. I recognized her voice though I did not know her name. I inquired, "How is your mother? The last time we talked, she was very ill." She was surprised that I had remembered her. She told me that her mother had died.

One day, I was sitting directly behind the bus driver, and Esta was stretched out under the side windows, partly beside the driver. At one stop, a man asked from the curb, "What are you doing with a dog?"

The driver answered, "I'm delivering it for a friend." I smiled because of his neat, impromptu response.

On another ride, a man across the aisle from me asked, "Is your dog a male?"

I answered, "No, sir."

Then he asked, "Is it a female?" *What other choices do we have, I thought?*

The most dramatic fellow-passenger was a man who sat against the window. I sat beside him while Esta tucked herself in by my feet away from the aisle. We sat in silence for about twenty minutes before he began to speak with no preamble: "You're going to hell."

Because I knew I had a weirdo beside me and tried to lighten the mood, I said, "Really? I thought this bus was going to Riverton," I commented.

"Don't be fresh. You are going to hell."

"What makes you an authority about where I will spend eternity?" I asked.

"You are blind, aren't you?"

"Yes, I am."

"Well, either you or your parents have sinned against God. If you are still blind when you die, that means you are not forgiven and you are damned to go to hell!" I was very thankful that he was not my father.

On a very hot day in June in Williamstown, I had just left a home and was waiting on the corner for a bus to Camden. The pavement was scorching Esta's paws. A woman also waiting for the bus told me that my dog was standing on three paws with one in the air, and then the dog shifted to a different combination of three paws to bring up a different paw to cool off above the concrete. Of course, she was also panting very hard. When the bus arrived, we took an empty seat 2 or 3 seats behind the driver. Because the bus was not air-conditioned, Esta's panting continued vigorously.

About halfway to Camden, we drove into a garage, a stop I had not previously experienced on this route at this time of day.

The driver summoned mechanics to check the bus's compressor. "Something is wrong with it."

After examining it, the mechanics reported that the compressor was working just fine, no problem.

The driver insisted that something was wrong and ordered them to recheck it.

Surmising the problem, I spoke to the driver. "Your engine is turned off. Do you still hear the noise?"

In surprise he answered, "Yes, I do!"

I suggested that he come back to my seat. I pointed down to the dog. He chuckled in relief. We then went on our way to Camden.

As Esta and I were leaving the bus, the driver patted Esta and said, "Goodbye, Compressor!"

On another trip toward Camden on a different route, a policeman stopped our bus. He ordered the driver to go no further and to wait until given permission to continue his route, because a man ahead of us had gone berserk, randomly shooting multiple victims, even a two-year-old sitting in a barber's chair receiving a haircut!

In December, we were traveling in a sleet storm toward Philadelphia. When a bus ahead of ours skidded dangerously, our driver pulled over to the curb and stopped. A woman passenger asked how long the delay would be.

The driver said, "I'm not going any further until a sand truck comes to take care of the ice."

The woman complained, "But I'm going to Philadelphia to do Christmas shopping. This delay will shorten the time that I can shop."

The driver reminded her that if she were injured or killed in an accident, she could not go shopping at all.

Riding buses regularly is an education in human foibles.

One January, Esta developed a nasal problem when outdoors in the cold, damp weather of Camden, which is on the Delaware River. She gasped as if choking or having difficulty getting enough oxygen.

When the veterinarian examined her, he was less concerned than I, because he had a solution. He suggested that I purchase a bottle of whiskey and combine equal parts of whiskey, sugar, and water. I am now unsure but think each dose might have been a tablespoon of each. Then I should let Esta lap it up from her pan, so that the fumes from the whiskey would soothe the membranes of her nasal passages.

I already knew that my landlady, Mrs. Harvey, was president of the Women's Christian Temperance Union (WCTU) and that my having a bottle of whiskey in my bedroom would be viewed suspiciously.

Therefore, after I bought the whiskey and went home, I told Mrs. Harvey very directly that it was for the dog and how it was to be administered. She offered to supply the water and sugar.

At first, Esta was reluctant to taste this concoction. Once she dipped her tongue into it, she discovered that she liked it. After that, she eagerly consumed her medicine. Then Mrs. Harvey said matter-of-factly that she would keep the alcohol in her kitchen and that the dog might have it whenever I indicated.

I happily can recommend this remedy for a dog with the same problem. In time, Esta stopped making those frightening noises.

After four years, I moved away from the Harveys and into an apartment. I never thought about retrieving the bottle of whiskey.

Soon after my move, Mrs. Harvey died from a heart attack, I think. After her funeral, Mr. Harvey brought me the bottle of whiskey.

Now, using pseudonyms, I will introduce you to some of my students:

Amanda was born a normal child and was in first grade. She underwent what was to be a routine tonsillectomy when, during surgery, her heart stopped! Deprived of oxygen, she sank into a long-term coma. Doctors advised her parents to institutionalize their daughter because she would remain in this vegetative state permanently.

The mother refused that option. Instead, she set up the hospital room with a small phonograph and small library of children's books and recordings, all previously familiar to the child. While playing a record, she massaged the child's arms and legs. At other times, the mother read stories or poetry to Amanda. This became a full-time job for the mother, who talked to the girl as if she could hear and understand, though comatose. In fact, some medical personnel claim that comatose patients may be able to hear even when unable to respond.

In time, Amanda emerged slowly from the coma, though she would not be normal as she had been before surgery. The child had to relearn how to talk, walk, do routine tasks, etc. She was now a special education child because of impaired vision. Amanda's mother is to be admired for her determination to work diligently with her child in spite of advice given by medical personnel.

Melissa was four when I first met her. She was outgoing and charming. On my first visit, I needed to make some assessments of her abilities to comprehend and execute directions given. I asked her to show me the following: her hair, ear, face, sock, sweater, etc. She was one hundred percent correct.

Then I changed directions by letting her string beads and later clap her hands three times and five times and two times. She was again completely correct.

Then suddenly, she said, "And here's my panty and slip!"

The mother, observing from across the room, exploded, "You naughty girl! Apologize to the lady."

I rushed in to defend the child by explaining to the mother that Melissa was not naughty but that her mind was very active. After all, I had asked about her other clothes. In her thinking, I had not completed the list. It was only natural that she might include her panty and slip. I explained that she was only four and innocent, not fourteen. I am unsure that I had convinced the mother that Melissa was responding to me in spectacular ways, indicating a very keen mind. I assured the mother that she could be grateful that her child was highly intelligent.

I have to wonder even today what Melissa has developed into: a lawyer, a psychologist, a scientist, a linguist?

Gary had turned four in November. On my last visit before the Christmas break, I read to him, with great dramatic performance, the poem that begins: "'Twas the night before Christmas ..." When I finished reading, I exclaimed, "Wasn't that fun? It is a happy poem."

The boy's reaction was not what I had expected. He was sober, even somber. "It's not nice to laugh when someone is sick," he protested.

Surprised, I explained that no one was sick, that the poem is about Santa when he comes on Christmas Eve. Gary still insisted that someone was sick.

I asked him to tell me the words that he had heard about someone's being ill.

"Where you said, 'He threw up the sash!'"

At his age, he certainly knew what *threw up* meant even when he was unfamiliar with *sash*. That has become one of my favorite memories at Christmastime.

Michael was a twin with a sister. Her vision was much better than his but still within special education definition, and I never worked with her. Both had been premature and had impaired vision because of retinopathy of prematurity.

He was eight, if I recall correctly, but seemed much younger. He spoke in monosyllabic responses. I was in the process of teaching him to speak in sentences. He seemed retarded.

I worked with him in classifying objects. For example, I said four words, such as *apple, glove, grapes,* and *banana,* three of which went together as one classification; the other word was of a different category. The child might respond in one of two different ways: 1) "Glove doesn't belong there, because I can't eat a glove," or 2) "Apple, grapes, and banana go together, because I can eat them. I can't eat a glove."

We did countless variations of these. I felt it imperative each time he gave me an answer to ask him "why?" in order for me to analyze his reasoning process.

One day, I chose four names (and these are important): Mary, Susie, Tommy, Betty. He chose Susie. I concluded prematurely that he did not know the difference between girls' names and boys' names, but I asked, "Why?"

"Mary, Betty, and Tommy end with y. I don't know what Susie ends with!"

I was flabbergasted. He was not yet reading Braille, but he knew how to spell Mary, Betty, and Tommy! He was not retarded. Soon after that, the school year ended, and one of us moved, thus ending my contact with him.

Alan was in upper elementary grades and quite normal and desirous of becoming a priest in the church. I do not know whether he ever achieved that goal or what he is doing as an adult. This anecdote is more about his school than about Alan.

We were working in our room with the door closed when the air-raid alarm sounded. (Even after World War II, schools continued having air-raid practice.)

Obediently, Alan and I walked into the corridor and faced the wall.

When everyone was in proper place and position, the principal announced that she was displeased with the school's performance—being late and confused.

When we were dismissed, Alan and I returned to our room and resumed the lesson. Again the air-raid signal sounded. Again we entered the corridor and faced the wall.

The principal reported some improvement but still it was not what she fully expected.

After we were in our room again and working, the fire alarm sounded. Alan and I proceeded down the stairs and outside where we waited.

Though I did not hear any classes outdoors, I assumed that they had taken their stations on the other three sides of the building.

In time, the principal came to us to permit us to reenter the building.

When we reached our floor and were ready to enter our room, the principal stopped Alan and me and then spoke to everyone in the corridor: "Mrs. Napier and her student were the only two who differentiated between the air-raid and fire alarms. You should have gone outdoors as they did!" The principal was unhappy with her teachers.

In Brenda's school, she and I were working when the fire alarm sounded. When I opened the door and stepped into the corridor, I smelled smoke. That was a jolt when one expects it to be a rehearsal and not the real thing.

With Brenda's hand in mine, we went out the front door and waited on the main sidewalk by the street.

Actually, there proved to be no danger. A child had returned to school after having a contagious illness, and someone was attempting to sanitize the child's books by placing them in the kitchen oven. With the temperature too high, the books began to smoke. Making the most of the situation, the principal rang the fire alarm.

Doug read Braille well enough when alone with me but rejected braille when with his classmates who read print.

The teacher felt frustrated in trying to integrate Doug who would not participate in group reading.

I hatched a plan and shared it with the teacher. The next time that I visited Doug's school, I brought a children's book not of the basal reading series and read it dramatically to the class, never referring to Doug.

I gave Braille books status as I interacted with the group without referring to Doug. My goal was to give Braille books respectability with seeing persons, not merely with blind readers.

The teacher reported to me in the following days that Doug was participating with his books.

Of all my schools, only one PTA requested that I present a program for its organization. Maybe the explanation for that is that those who might have asked me were reluctant to have me make an extra long trip at night in order to give a program, which was what I had to do for that one school.

The same Gary mentioned earlier had a reputation for, when in other persons' homes, opening drawers and closets and examining contents therein. His parents thought this permissible because he was not able to see (a behavioral myth).

On a weekend, Gary and his parents came to my home to collect some equipment or books that I had brought on Friday for Gary from the New Jersey State Commission for the Blind office in Newark.

While we three adults were conversing in the living room, Gary was wandering around in my apartment. He found a suitcase in my bedroom and unsnapped it.

Although I knew it was empty, I made the most of the moment to teach all three a lesson. Rescuing my suitcase from the boy's hands, I said, "You may not look in my suitcase. That is personal and private territory that you may not invade and violate."

One of the parents said, "He is just looking with his hands. A blind child needs to do that."

I explained that a blind child has no more right to violate another person's privacy than does a seeing child. Yes, Gary may feel the outside; that is all that a seeing child sees, but he may not open suitcases, drawers, closets, handbags, or wallets that belong to other persons. If the parents did not like the lesson, it was one they had to learn in order to guide Gary through socially acceptable channels. He was not a toddler but ten or eleven years old at the time.

Because blind children cannot observe other children of the same or different age to know what is age-appropriate behavior, parents must make those decisions in order to shape the child's behavior. Practicing socially taboo habits in the homes of friends and acquaintances will result in exclusion and isolation of blind children by those persons who disapprove of behavior such as Gary's.

Terry was an eleven-year-old girl, though small for her age. In supermarkets, her parents permitted her to ride in the seat designed for toddlers. As I pointed out in an earlier chapter, just because a child wants to do something inappropriate is no reason to allow it. Parents must explain, for instance, that the seat in the grocery cart is for two- or three-year-olds so that the child can be safe while the adults are shopping. They need to tell their child, "You are not a baby and should walk as I am doing."

Older children who have been accustomed to riding in the grocery cart are likely to be humiliated and embarrassed when learning that only babies ride in the cart, not big kids. Such a child might challenge his parents with, "Why did you let me ride in the cart when I was too old to do that? People must have been staring at me. Don't let me do things that other kids my age should not do."

Larry was four years old, but unlike Gary or Melissa, he did not relate to me. He refused to sit on the sofa beside me. He refused to talk. The problem was not shyness but willful non-compliance.

The more I learned about the parenting skills—or lack of them— the more I began to understand Larry. He was permitted to do whatever he wanted to do whenever he wanted to do it. He would sit in the family car and blow the horn for long periods of time. In the middle of the night, while the rest of the family was sleeping, he went outdoors.

The mother told me that Larry was having trouble with his throat. I asked what the doctor had said. "I didn't take him to the doctor," she informed me. "But he can't swallow green beans and potatoes or meat."

I surmised that I had not heard the whole story. The mother said that he was very clever in that he pulled drawers out far enough to make steps to get on the counter to find cookies or pretzels. No, he did not have difficulty swallowing them! During one of my visits, the mother glanced into the kitchen and reported to me that Larry was on the counter eating cookies. She did nothing to stop him. I reminded her that the time was four forty-five, not long before his main meal. "Shouldn't you stop him so that he will be able to eat vegetables and meat?" "No, he likes cookies."

What chance for normality did Larry have with such lack of discipline?

On one of my visits, only the father was at home. He complained of a headache. I asked what seemed to cause his headaches. "Oh, I know what causes them. When I lie on the floor, Larry kicks me in the head!"

I assumed it had happened just once. When I asked when that one occasion was, the father said, "It wasn't just once. It happens many times. It makes the boy happy."

Here we have a very dysfunctional father who allows his child to kick him in the head because it gives the child pleasure! What chance does this boy have to develop normally when he is permitted to live with *no* discipline?

Larry had been born with buphthalmos, or only rudimentary eyes. He needed surgery to implant prostheses to fit the eye sockets. This would need to be repeated several times until he was an adult because of the changes in the sockets and his facial features.

The father refused to permit the surgery. "The surgery won't help him see. So why put him through surgery?"

Without the implants, the boy would experience social rejection and isolation. I explained the importance of the surgery. I think that the parents expected that the Commission for the Blind was about to force the issue.

One day when I went for a scheduled visit, the family was gone! Neighbors told me that they had moved to another state. I wonder what has become of Larry after all these years? I wonder, too, whether the family had moved to another state; or is that what they told neighbors but moved to another community in New Jersey. If so, sooner or later, the Commission would hear about this child and his family. The father might then be able to retain his same employment, whatever it was. With the child's bizarre behavior, neighbors would soon become aware of that family and its strange, blind son.

Donna was seven when I met her. She had developed hydrocephalis (what is commonly called "water on the brain" in lay terms, which causes pressure on areas of the brain. That pressure, in turn, causes specific problems for Donna, namely, cerebral palsy and blindness. Although she seemed to be a bright child, her life was perilously short. In a year or a bit longer after I had met her, she died.

I worked with Benjie (who had been another of the premature babies) in first and second grades. He was an extremely brilliant child and just lovable and sweet, unspoiled by his mother's wise rearing strategies.

He was a precocious Braille reader, reading twenty-four first-grade books to his class's five. Instead of taking him into second-grade books while in first grade, I used first-grade basal readers from other series. Much of the vocabulary was the same except for names of children and their pets.

I started a notebook with Benjie. Each page had a title of a category: days of the week, months, colors, helpers, fruits, vegetables, flowers, etc. I told him the title of the page and asked him for words that belong on that page. I wanted the book to be his words, not mine. One day he came to me quite excited. "I think I have something to add to the notebook. Isn't your dog a helper?"

"Yes, she is."

"Then we need to add her name to the Helpers page." And we added her name to the helpers already in the list: mother, teacher, fireman, policeman, librarian, nurse, doctor.

To make conversation with him one day, I asked, "What would you like to be when you grow up?"

His prompt answer was, "A teacher."

Curious, I wondered how many teachers he had already been exposed to as a first-grader. I asked, Music teacher? Gym? Science? Reading? To each he said, "No."

I told him that I did not know what kind of teacher he wanted to be.

Almost in exasperation, he blurted out, "Just an old teacher like you!"

In addition, I read third- and fourth-grade science books to Benjie. They would have been a bit difficult for him to read and derive meaning, but his listening comprehension level was high when someone read to him.

When the Commission assigned Wendy to my caseload, I contacted the family for my first visit. When I arrived, a woman said she was the baby-sitter for the youngest child, not my student. Because of what developed later, this woman might have been the mother claiming to be the baby-sitter. She told me that the mother was due back momentarily. I waited two hours, but mother and Wendy never appeared. I left.

Back at the Harvey home in the evening, I wrote a report about this bizarre absence of mother and child when I had made an appointment.

After several days, the Commission received word from the father to report that he did not want a blind teacher working with his daughter! The Commission representative explained that it could send another teacher but that he could not come so frequently as Mrs. Napier because that location was not in the male teacher's territory. The father preferred that arrangement.

Strange as it sounds, the father was a psychoanalyst!

When the Commission filled in the details for me, I had to be concerned about Wendy in that family when the father had such a psychological abhorrence to blindness. Why was the father having such difficulty in dealing with his child's impaired vision that having a "non-blind" teacher made the child's problem magically vanish?

This introduces the topic of how parents of young blind children may respond to blind adults. Some parents may feel that they can learn from blind adults, learning information that will help with rearing of their child. On the other hand, a different parent, with dreams of a surgery or medication or some kind of treatment that will remove impaired vision, realizes that here is an adult who was not cured of blindness and hates the thought that maybe his own child may not be so fortunate either. As long as Wendy's father can banish blind adults from his life, the better chance he has to focus on wishful thinking and fantasy about the day when his daughter will no longer be burdened with visual impairment but will have normal vision.

The father has solutions to problems for his patients but no solution for his own problem except for wishful thinking and denial: This present problem will dissipate and be a phantom from the past but no threat for the future.

What has become of Wendy in that kind of setting? Is the child forced to deny that she has a visual problem and forced to live in a make believe world where nothing is wrong?

That reminds me of another family where the adults refused to mention the word "blind" in their home, reasoning "The boy must not know he is blind!" With that attitude, nothing appropriate for the boy will be accepted that relates to the boy's blindness: Braille reading and writing, specialized equipment, long cane, dog guide, rehabilitation training, etc.

My youngest client, a blind infant, was born out of wedlock. His eye sockets needed to be cleaned daily. I arranged for a public health nurse to visit the mother to show her how to clean the baby's eye sockets. In turn, the public health nurse referred the mother to a well-baby clinic as a way to reduce medical expenses. I explored financial wherewithal and established eligibility for the two of them to receive support as needed.

Meanwhile, I was trying to work with the mother to establish a healthy emotional relationship between mother and son. As he developed, the mother needed to be aware of various stages of child growth and development.

After several months, the mother asked, "When is it going to happen?"

"When is what going to happen?" I asked.

"When is the state going to take my baby?"

I explained that the state does not collect blind babies and keep them for the rest of their lives. This son of hers was her baby, not the state's. She was his mother, and she was responsible for his care.

That was not what she wanted to hear. I have to wonder what has happened to this baby. Did she abandon him? Was he adopted? Was he institutionalized just to free the mother from responsibility? Special needs children often face dismal futures.

Why do I not have answers to my own questions about these children? One or both of the following might explain my lack of information: 1) A family moved to another part of New Jersey or even to another state, or 2) I moved away to do something different in my career. I did not spend the rest of my working life as an itinerant teacher. I was an itinerant teacher for twelve years.

The preceding examples of families with blind children illustrate the responsibility of all parents to prepare their children for adult life and not to prolong childhood needlessly.

During my first four years as an itinerant teacher, I spent weekends with Chuck in Paoli in one room. On Friday afternoon after my last school or home visit, I did not return to the Harvey home but went directly by bus to Philadelphia where I boarded a local train to Paoli and then walked from the station to the school. Because Chuck still had only the electric hot plate, our meals were usually soup and maybe a sandwich. On Saturday, I laundered Chuck's clothing and cleaned his room. On Sunday morning, I attended church without Chuck, who had no interest in spiritual matters. On Sunday evening, I returned to Camden.

Chuck had no grasp of my position as an itinerant teacher and what it involved, because his total life was spent on campus—no public transportation, three meals a day at predictable hours without paying for them, two recesses each day, an hour for lunch, no rent to pay.

I was usually already on the road each morning before he left his bed. Before that period of four years, Royer-Greaves School had hired a houseparent for the boys on third floor (for Chuck's boys). Consequently, Chuck no longer had those responsibilities. During Christmas or spring or August breaks, we usually visited his or my family.

During one of my visits to Clifton after my father had died, I discovered that my piano was no longer in the house! Mamma had never discussed with me the idea of getting rid of my piano, but it was gone! She probably figured that as a widow she needed money and that she could sell the piano for cash.

In addition, she might have reasoned that the piano had belonged to her father; therefore, it was now her property to do with whatever she decided to do, even to dispose of it if she wished. This was another of her ways to demonstrate that I was not a legitimate member of her family. So her reasoning lacked logic, as usual. In truth, my grandfather had given ME the piano, so that I might take lessons. My father was not present to protect my rights. *Where and when will end her disregard for me?* Even though I was an adult and a teacher, she treated me as a retarded child. Grace will never notice that the piano is gone, she would think.

This was a second insult after Mamma said that I had to pay ten dollars a month to store our wedding gifts in her attic; Mart stored things in her attic without charge, because, according to her, "Mart was too poor to pay." (I was earning only one hundred fifty dollars a month and had to pay rent, for my meals in restaurants, for everything I needed.

A few days after Daddy's death, Mamma was moaning about how poor she was and that she needed the two hundred and fifty-five dollars spent on my wedding! If I had paid her for the wedding, she would then figure out that I owed her for the typewriter, Braille writer, and whatever other old expense Daddy had spent on me. She was a manipulator, always scheming.

When I was ten years old and alone with Mamma, she told me several times that she should have married Ed Delaney, a policeman, or Jake Carrl, a letter carrier, instead of my father, because they earned more money than Daddy and had regular incomes all year round and not just seasonal work. I hated hearing what she said about Daddy. A mother who talks that way to her ten-year-old child is dysfunctional. Then when she becomes a widow, she bemoans the fact that her husband is gone!

Frankly, I have to wonder how Daddy was ever attracted to her. He was optimistic and positive, she pessimistic, negative, critical, griping, never happy, manipulating, scheming, and dysfunctional as an adult.

Happily, after four years as an experiment, I was declared a success as a blind itinerant teacher. After that, the Commission hired other blind teachers to do the same kind of work. I felt gratified that my efforts had succeeded in opening another source of employment for qualified individuals. According to the American Foundation for the Blind, the unemployment rate among working-age blind persons is seventy percent. In some job descriptions, the blind employee must know Braille. Tragically, about only ten percent of blind individuals can read Braille successfully.) I continued as an itinerant teacher for eight more years.

For the four years of the experiment, I lived with the Harveys. Once the experiment terminated, I received a substantial increase, a salary equivalent to that of seeing itinerant teachers working for the Commission. After the experiment, from 1952 to 1960, I rented an apartment in Collingswood, a suburb of Camden. The apartment was on the second floor of a home where the landlady lived on the first floor. We (Chuck and I) had a kitchen, a study or office that also served as dining room when we had guests, a living room, two bedrooms, and private bathroom for the first time since before being married!

Again, I bought most of the furniture.

Chuck did purchase a Magnavox phonograph. He surprised me by having that much money available when he always claimed to be broke but could not explain how he had spent his money.

My mother had been a widow since 1947 and lived with my brother and his family. However, she still regarded herself as the "woman of the house," even though my brother's wife was truly the manager and mother of two young sons. Because Mamma saw herself as alpha woman, she tried to take charge of everything including meals and rearing of the grandsons. Because she continued to live in HER house (because my brother had moved into our father's house), she saw herself as being in charge, even though she could contribute nothing financially to maintain the property. Her only income was a soldier's widow's pension of fifty-two dollars and forty cents per month. With that as her only income, either my brother or I had to support her.

With all of that as reality, I felt that my brother and his family deserved a respite from Mamma's attempts to domineer for five years. With that in mind, I invited Mamma to live with me, although I knew beforehand from the beginning this arrangement would be difficult.

For the first six years in our apartment with Chuck's visiting me only on weekends, Chuck did attend church with me. I overheard him one time telling someone that he went to church just to please Grace (an invalid reason for attending church).

Then suddenly, Ann Perry, Chuck's supervisor, became a widow. Several times Chuck said that Ann's husband had left her a "bundle" (a large sum of money). I doubt that Ann revealed the amount that Walt had left Ann and her young daughter; Chuck imagined that it was a huge amount. He smelled money!

From then on, Chuck developed Sundayitis. Each Sunday morning, he was up and ready for a robust breakfast. Then as I dressed for church, he sprawled across the bed because of some ailment or symptom. He was always well enough to eat a filling dinner when I returned from church when I found him no longer on the bed but with the radio on while he drank coffee waiting for me. One Sunday after I had left the house, I discovered that I had forgotten my gloves. When I reentered the house, the radio was on and he was already in the kitchen drinking coffee! That is how quickly he had recovered from his ailments!

From then on, Chuck's focus was on Ann. He was first in line to show his interest. He helped her any time she spoke, while he never responded to my requests for assistance. He used selective listening to his advantage when at home. This was how he so often exhibited his passive-aggressive personality. He would agree or volunteer to do something for me but then promptly dismiss it. An example will illustrate this: On a Saturday morning, we had enough bread for breakfast but none for lunch. I mentioned this fact to Chuck. I also said I was planning to serve grilled cheese sandwiches with tomato soup, Chuck's favorite lunch. He volunteered to go to the store for bread. I thanked him for his willingness.

I knew from past experience that when I reminded him later in the morning, he would balk because of my "nagging." So I said nothing as noon approached and he had made no effort to leave the house. The store was at the corner of our block but across the street, not a long distance.

At noon, I served tomato soup with crackers. Belligerently, he challenged me, "You said we would have grilled cheese sandwiches, but now you serve crackers!" (He could remember what I had said but seemed to have no recollection of what HE had promised to do.)

Calmly, I explained that he had offered to go to the store to buy bread but that I could not make grilled cheese sandwiches without bread. Therefore, I had to use crackers to accompany the soup. Then, predictably, he added, "You didn't remind me!" He was never wrong; I was never right.

Another example will suffice. The rod for hangers in the bedroom closet went from front to back of the closet, while, if it went from side to side, it would accommodate more garments. I pointed out that fact. Chuck offered to change the rod, stating, "That's an easy job to do." However, from week to week, he made no effort to make that change.

One weekend, while reviewing the events during Chuck's absence since the previous weekend, I mentioned that the landlady had a handyman do some chores for her downstairs and then offered his service to me, should I have any jobs to be done. I asked him to change the rod, which he did with no hassle.

Chuck's immediate reaction was, "I told you I would change that rod for you!"

My retort was, "Yes, you did, but that was six months ago!"

Some weekends, Chuck did not come home because of helping Ann with this or that. I truly believe that he firmly expected a chance to marry Ann, thinking that then all his problems would vanish because of having a wife with normal vision. In addition, he could claim her house, car, and bank account as his own.

Chuck also liked to argue about trivialities. For instance, he complained that I squeezed the toothpaste tube the wrong way. I gave him his own tube of toothpaste and bought another for my use.

He complained that the toilet paper was on the rod backward, that the loose end should be in front. I asked him what he did in a public bathroom when he found the roll going in the wrong direction. "Do you complain to the management of the restaurant or hotel?" I reminded him that he had my permission to reverse the roll, if it bothered him that much. I was not going to spend weekends bickering over trifles. *Why couldn't he find the end of the tissue when it was behind the roll,* I wondered. He did not want solutions but preferred something to gripe about; I refused to squabble about non-issues.

Meanwhile, I was attempting to advance my professional status. In the summer of 1953, I enrolled in a six-week session at George Peabody College for Teachers in Nashville, Tennessee. Three staff members of the American Foundation for the Blind (P. C. Potts, Pauline Moor, and Georgie Lee Abel) served as faculty. These were historic times. Segregation between white and black students still persisted in the South. When AFB first proposed the summer plan to the administration of Peabody, the college maintained that integration would not work in the South. AFB stated that it would have integration or take the summer session elsewhere. Peabody acquiesced but with grave misgivings.

I wish that Chuck had been there in Nashville to meet the young professionals to witness their enthusiasm. Because of his low-esteem problems, he might have gained something from my blind classmates to boost his self-confidence; not all classmates were blind. Tragically, Chuck could feel superior only when he was teaching retarded children.

The fact that I lived the greater portion of our married life alone registered not at all with him. Why did he marry when he preferred to live by himself? I believe that my summer experiences in Ypsilanti, Nashville, and later in Syracuse not only filled my need for professional development but also the emptiness in my life.

In Nashville during breaks throughout the day, many black teachers gathered around me to ask questions about agencies, other resources, techniques, and materials. For most of these women, this was

their first experience with integration. They knew that white teachers had many more advantages in the field of education. Now we
could share that wealth of knowledge with our deprived sisters. The
black teachers wanted to make the most of those six weeks to gather
a storehouse of information to take back to their respective schools in
September to aid other teachers and the students they taught. I felt
privileged to serve as a bridge from my experiences in the North to
theirs in the South.

Georgie Lee Abel complimented me on how I interacted with
black teachers in order to enrich their professional lives. "You could
have been one of the faculty here this summer," she said.

Kathern Gruber, who had taken such a great leadership role in
the rehabilitation of blinded veterans in World War II, was present.
She added so much with her genuine personal involvement in the
lives of veterans. Even a few blinded veterans were members of these
courses.

Nashville was where I first met Emma D. Rowe, who taught in
Dade County, Florida. Emma and I became dear friends through the
years since Nashville until her death in her retirement.

The process of integration worked very well in our group except
for one woman, blind and from Alabama. She brought with her a seeing companion and guide. On the first two days when all were becoming acquainted and introducing ourselves, she whispered to her
guide, "Is he black?" or "Is she black?" When the answer was in the
affirmative, she turned in rejection of the black individual. If I recall
correctly, she returned home during the first week.

I thought this was evidence of having been taught to discriminate even when she could not see differences in skin color. Parents or
teachers must surely have shaped her thinking.

She could have been less obvious in how she gained the information. She could have arranged early with her guide to squeeze her
arm in a certain code to let the blind woman know who was white

and who black, instead of asking each time someone introduced herself or himself.

In the summer of 1954 on a Saturday morning, Chuck's sister Margaret and brother-in-law and Gary, our eight-year-old nephew, appeared at our front door. Without my knowledge, Chuck had arranged with Margaret to have Gary stay with me for ten days! Because it was early July, Chuck was still teaching at Royer-Greaves. My mother had already left for Clifton to spend a few weeks with my brother and his family.

On Monday, of course, Chuck returned to school.

Even though Gary was subject to asthma attacks, Margaret entrusted her son into my care, after having lost her first son on the operating table during a routine tonsillectomy. She included in Gary's luggage his emergency medication with instructions for me to send him home promptly by airplane. (I question that as a solution in an emergency.) In doing so, she paid me a very high compliment.

Gary, I, and Esta visited Philadelphia. We toured the Franklin Institute to walk through a large, pulsating model of the heart. We visited the Liberty Bell. For lunch, we stopped at the Horn and Hardart Automat where Gary had his first experiences with choosing foods behind locked doors, dropping coins into slots, and retrieving food from its compartment. He offered to buy beverages; he chose milk for me and Coke for himself.

On another day, we joined friends in Collingswood to drive to a beach on the Atlantic Ocean. Gary had never been to any ocean. Although the surf was rough that day, Gary had no basis for comparison.

After lunch on the beach, I instructed him to stay out of the water until I had given him permission to reenter it.

He was obedient for a respectable period of time, but then my friends noticed that he was in the water again. I called him to come to the blanket and sit. He obeyed.

By then the surf was much worse. Lifeguards were trying to rescue a mother and child. Gary gave me a blow-by-blow account of the incident as it occurred.

Later I asked him, "Why did I call you out of the water after lunch?"

"Because you did not want me to drown. That woman and child almost drowned, but the lifeguards saved them."

On the Fourth of July weekend, we visited my brother's family in Clifton where Gary played with Billy and Bob.

On another day during Gary's vacation with me, we visited relatives in Baltimore and enjoyed the day on a relative's private boat to fish.

At home in my apartment, Gary was a little gentleman, obviously trained by his parents and older sister. He helped me with my chair at the table and held doors and said "Please" and "Thank you" at appropriate times.

One day he was standing by my chair and stroking my hair. "Your hair is," he said with feeling, "so—so—mousy!" I accepted it as a compliment. He was so sincere.

He told his mother after he had returned home, "Aunt Grace knew what I was doing all the time—even though she is blind!"

Later that summer, Esta became ill. We were walking home from prayer meeting and Bible study at church when she began walking in circles! I failed to have her walk straight ahead. A gentleman, noticing our problem, offered to walk us home. I hoped that a night's sleep would resolve the problem.

In the morning, I harnessed Esta and took her outside. From the front yard, I directed "Esta, left." She went about halfway past the neighbor's house but turned around, returning to our front yard.

Then I directed her to go right from our front yard. She went about halfway but returned home! She apparently realized that she could not work responsibly and must return me to safety at my house.

I phoned a cab and took her to the veterinarian who knew it was not from malnutrition and determined it was not from poison. He then concluded that it was brain infection! I took her home for a few days.

Then she lay in the kitchen against the wall. When I spoke to her to stand and go bye-bye, the only response she gave was to wiggle her stubby tail. Nothing else reacted to my words. It was as if she were signaling, "I hear you, but I can't do anything!" I was devastated. I summoned a cab and returned to the veterinarian. He said that death was imminent.

My majestic, responsible, intelligent, loving Esta was gone!

I think it was October when I returned to Headquarters to train with Vicki, another German boxer.

In the summer of 1955, I enrolled in courses at Temple University in Philadelphia. The New Jersey Commission for the Blind required us teachers to have certification in two areas but urged us to have it in three: special education, elementary, and secondary education. I thrived in the academic climate.

In the spring of 1956, one of my supervisors at the Commission, Dorothy L. Misbach, urged me to plan on attending Syracuse University's summer session. I had no plans to do so; I was expecting to return to Temple University. Dorothy told me that she would be teaching at Syracuse and needed me to help her with her courses. I knew that she needed no help from me. Why was she pushing me so hard to attend Syracuse?

When I learned that Beryl Nuzum, one of my cohorts at the Commission, was planning to attend Syracuse, I became somewhat more interested. Beryl and I drove there and were roommates in Sims Dormitory. I enrolled in a course with Dr. William M. Cruickshank, Director of Special Education, and in another course, Methods in Science Education.

I had met Dr. Cruickshank a few times at conventions and was favorably impressed.

I was extremely impressed with his teaching. Relative to research, he reported it by citing authors and giving sources—journal article with date or book with publisher. When students asked questions, he responded in various ways: "In my opinion ..." or "From my experience ..." or "I have had no experience with that but my educated hunch might be ..." or "Because that is out of my field, I cannot express an opinion." I have not had many professors who made those distinctions. Another reason that I respect him is that he spoke to me no matter how often we met in a day. His greeting might be as simple as, "Hi, Grace," but he acknowledged me. I had another department head who passed me by without a word. How did I know? My students told me, "Dr. Vaughan just passed but didn't even speak to you." Some individuals think this way: "If Grace can't see me, she doesn't know I am here; therefore, I don't have to acknowledge her." Dr. Cruickshank had a different philosophy and practiced it.

On Monday of the last week of summer session, Dr. Cruickshank met me as I exited the classroom to tell me to visit his secretary for an appointment. He gave no inkling what the appointment concerned. When I checked with his secretary, she informed me that the only opening in his schedule was on Friday afternoon. That was when Beryl and I had planned to start for home. I assumed that Dr. Cruickshank wanted to discuss the New Jersey Itinerant-teacher Plan, renowned throughout the country. Yet, with Dorothy Misbach on campus all summer, why would he ask me about the plan?

When we met on Friday afternoon, he explained that now that summer session was finished, he had to begin planning for next summer. In short, he invited me to return the next summer to serve as faculty! I had had absolutely no idea that this was his purpose for meeting with me. He said that he had been observing me all summer and liked the way that I had demonstrated independence with my dog, on and off campus.

Although another woman with a dog guide was teaching that summer, she went nowhere alone with her dog guide but relied for everything on a seeing person she had brought with her from home.

Dr. Cruickshank wanted his special education and rehabilitation students to witness how a dog guide really provides independence and mobility.

Apparently, Dorothy Misbach had known that Dr. Cruickshank was looking for a new faculty member. She could not tell me, however, that he would be observing me; yet she had wanted me on campus where he could evaluate my performance.

The summer session of 1957 was my first of ten summers to teach at Syracuse University. I thoroughly enjoyed my interaction with graduate students in that setting.

That first summer of teaching had not begun with promise for me. Less than a week before I was to leave for Syracuse, Mamma had asked me to open a kitchen window from the top for better circulation; I did so because she did not have the strength to do it herself. The next morning, before I went to work, she reminded me to close that window in case it rained later that day. In adjusting the inner and storm windows, the sash that I pushed up to close it came crashing down on both sets of fingertips! Mamma insisted that I go to our physician, because my fingertips were injured and bleeding. The doctor drilled a hole into each nail to relieve pressure. In a few days, my nails were black from injury.

A second blow came early on the morning I was scheduled to fly to Syracuse. Vicki woke me during the night. I took her outside to relieve herself; no, that was not the problem. I offered her water in the kitchen; no, that was rejected also. I led her back to her bed and sat by her.

Trying to determine what the problem was, I examined her head and neck, ran my hands down her spine, and examined each leg with no indication of trouble. Then I examined her torso. On her right side below the ribs, I must have found the painful area.

With no sound from her throat, her head swung around toward my hand; her teeth were on either side of my hand but with no pressure. The message was clear: You found the sore spot.

To convince myself of the truth, I repeated the entire examination from the top of her head. When my hand gently touched the painful area, her teeth were on either side of my hand but without pressure. Yes, that was the same location of pain.

At seven o'clock, I phoned the veterinarian to request that he come to the house, that my dog was in pain.

He said that he did not make home visits and that I should bring her to him at nine o'clock. I was displeased with his indifference. I had to be on the plane at nine o'clock. After harnessing Vicki, I added her muzzle, because I knew she was in pain. If anyone bumped that area, she might bite, although she usually threatened no one, but this was a dog in pain.

The third blow came in the form of tail winds after our most recent hurricane! Flight attendants would not leave their seats to help passengers. A sailor seated beside me said that in all his flights, this was the absolute worst! I sat with an emergency sack in my lap, ready to use it. So long as I faced forward with chin level, my stomach behaved. When I faced into my lap, my stomach did flip-flops, threatening the need for the bag. Was I not supposed to teach at Syracuse with these three omens?

After landing, I boarded a taxi. I asked the driver whether he knew an excellent veterinarian in town. Yes, he did. I had to hope that the doctor was really competent and capable of helping Vicki.

When we reached Dr. Wilson, he removed Vicki's muzzle without my knowing it. He lifted the dog to the table. She screamed in pain! He said, "I'd better put that muzzle on again."

That was when I told him that I knew she was in pain and indicated on her body the painful area.

He suggested that I leave her with him and that he would try to diagnose the problem. I had no other option. He summoned a taxi to take me to Haft's Dormitory on campus. The next day, he phoned me to report that blood study had not revealed the problem and that he felt he had to do exploratory surgery. Did he have my permission? Yes, of course. His next phone call was frightening and uncertain. He had found an abscess on Vicki's liver, but her prognosis was guarded; she might succumb and die.Several days of dismal reports followed. Of the social events on campus, I have a huge blur of that first week. Although I attended events, my mind and heart were elsewhere.

A fourth blow came when I discovered that my trunk had not arrived on time, as promised. The only supplies that I had access to were dresses and a raincoat in my suitcase. Everything else was in the trunk! I had arrived on Saturday, but the trunk arrived the next Thursday! When will this nightmare end? Then a report from Dr. Wilson was that he had a glimmer of optimism about Vicki's chance to recover! After several more days, he said that I might take her with me but not to work her until he saw her again. In time, Vicki recovered completely and was able to demonstrate to the student body, other faculty, and to Dr. Cruickshank that I had not let him down. During the previous spring to Vicki's surgery, she had had great flatulence with putrid odor. After her recovery, she never again had that problem. She lived the rest of her life on a special prescription diet because of her liver damage. The prescription diets are canned by Hill Brothers and are available from only veterinarians. I am truly grateful to Dr. Wilson for his excellent care of Vicki in bringing her back to health and energy.

I taught at Syracuse nine more summers until a full-time graduate teaching position came my way. Happily, Vicki's summers in Syracuse were uneventful, that is, without illness.

Each summer after the first in Syracuse, Vicki and I visited Dr. Wilson to show him how well Vicki was thriving and to buy dog food for six weeks.

On one of those visits, he discovered that he needed to extract one of Vicki's teeth. After he had pulled it, she locked her jaws shut and would not permit him to look inside again to determine whether she was bleeding.

After he tried and failed, I offered to help. He protested that he was a veterinarian and knew how to do it. I reminded him that Vicki was MY dog and not HIS. I touched her jowls and said soothingly, "Open up, sweetie," whereupon her jaws opened wide while Dr. Wilson looked inside.

Because I could no longer attend Temple University during summers, I enrolled in Friday evening and Saturday courses to complete a second master's degree in 1959. I thoroughly enjoyed those courses.

Then during late winter or early spring of 1960, I received a letter from the American Foundation for the Blind (AFB) offering me a fellowship to study at the University of Minnesota. I could not decide immediately to accept or decline the offer. I had a husband, an apartment, and furniture to consider, as well as a position with the New Jersey State Commission.

Some days I felt that this was an opportunity not to miss. On other days, I seemed unable to accept it.

One night I had a dream in which I saw writing on a chalkboard. The writing asked the question:

Do you own the furniture, or does the furniture own you?

With the issue framed in those words, I could answer that question. I accepted the fellowship to go to Minneapolis in September.

During that June, I cleaned my dresser drawers and Chuck's. When I examined his top drawer, I found many pills loose in the right front corner. I assumed that they were aspirin or cold pills that had fallen out of a bottle or box. I discarded them and continued with my cleaning of his drawers.

When Chuck came home on Friday evening, he went to his dresser and then exploded into a rage: "What have you been doing in my dresser?"

I explained that I had cleaned our dresser drawers. He was in a rage that truly frightened me. I feared that he was going to hit or choke me—he was that out of control. Then I realized that the pills were not innocent aspirin or cold tablets but illegal drugs! He continued yelling at me, exploding with expletives. I said aloud, "My husband is a junkie!"

He was standing on the far side of the bed while I was standing on the side closer to the door. If he had advanced toward me, I was prepared to run down the stairs and outside.

When I asked him who was supplying him with drugs, he refused an answer. I think I know the answer to that question. Chuck met Hank at his school, though Hank was not an employee there. How they first met I don't know. However, Chuck told me that Hank was a homosexual and had been in Eastern Pennsylvania Pennitentiary because of that. Later, I surmised that Chuck had manipulated the truth to throw me off guard. I believe that Hank had been in prison for selling drugs but was out again selling drugs again. Chuck had the audacity to invite Hank to our apartment and to eat with us!

Meanwhile, he was still exploding with vile language and orders for me to stay out of his dresser, that I had "no—business" in his dresser! Can you imagine a husband in his right mind ordering his wife never to go into his dresser again? Chuck was out of his mind!

When I refused to sleep with him and prepared the studio couch as my bed, he could not understand why. I told him that if I was not qualified to enter his dresser drawers, I was then not qualified to sleep in the same bed with him. He failed to comprehend my rationale.

At the same time, my mother was spending the summer with my brother as she did each summer while I taught at Syracuse. This summer, she was quite ill. Then on Labor Day, Mamma's physician told my brother to send for Grace. Against my protests, Chuck made arrangements with Ann to drive us to the hospital where my mother was a patient. I was ready to leave before nine in the morning, but Chuck kept saying, "Ann is coming."

She did not arrive until four in the afternoon. I am certain that Chuck knew her plans but deceived me about them.

He went into the hospital with me. After staying literally five minutes, he left to rejoin Ann.

About ten minutes later, Mamma was dead! I tried until midnight to reach Chuck to tell him about Mamma; he was not home. He never explained what he and Ann had done that evening.

When he phoned me in the morning, his reaction was, "Oh, I didn't know she was that sick," even though I had been sent for, and Mamma was in an oxygen tent and comatose. Mamma had lived with me eight years.

During that summer, I tried to counsel Chuck about seeking professional help to receive therapy because of his addictions. His response was, "I don't have any problems." Any time afterward, when I tried to help him, his defense was the same.

After the funeral, Chuck ordered me to engage an attorney who would evict my brother from his house and force him to sell it, giving me half of the selling price! Chuck smelled money when he had realized that Mamma's will had left her only possession jointly to Mart and me. Chuck was not really thinking about my welfare but about how soon he could get his hands on my money.

I refused to comply with Chuck's demands. I sold my half of the house to my brother for one dollar!

Chuck was furious with me for surrendering my inheritance, according to Mamma's will. He was concerned, in truth, about not being able to get my money into his hands; he was not protecting me but himself. I had contributed nothing to the maintenance of the house. Neither had Chuck. My brother's money and labor had done that. Chuck called me a fool and other names.

I departed for Minneapolis shortly after the funeral, after putting the furniture into storage and paying for it. I believe that Chuck was happy to have me out of state. He no longer had to visit me on weekends and had a legitimate reason for staying in Paoli on weekends to be near Ann.

In Minneapolis, my adviser, who taught part-time and was a student part-time, required me to carry twenty-two graduate credits! When another faculty member asked how many credits I was carry-

ing, he was outraged that my load was so heavy. He told me that when
he was a doctoral student, he never carried more than nine credits at
any one time. He went to my adviser to express his indignation about
her treatment of a doctoral student.

Of course, my adviser had assumed that I had complained behind
her back, when in reality I merely had answered the question: "How
many credits are you carrying?"

Because I was a full-time student, I believe that my adviser feared
that I would graduate before she did and that the university would
hire me to replace her. She need not have worried about that, because
the head of the department, Dr. Maynard Reynolds, had told me that
he maintained that a blind person should not be in the field of education! Notwithstanding, he had admitted me. Overloading me with
credits was one way my adviser could be rid of me. I would either
leave voluntarily or fail if I stayed for a second year. Either way, she
removed what she saw as competition. Even after I had received a
letter offering me the fellowship for a second year, I decided to return
to Philadelphia. I did not want to continue with the same adviser, but
Jeanne R. Kenmore was the only one on the faculty in my specialty
area. Besides, she was giving misinformation in classes. For instance,
when a student asked why a certain Braille writer was called Lavendar, my adviser had answered, "because it is colored lavender!" In
truth, a Mr. Lavendar designed the machine, and it carried his name.

I did not correct Kenmore when she offered incorrect information
because I knew she would resent me even more, but I lost respect for
her when I saw the gaps in her body of knowledge in her specialty
area.

While in Minneapolis, I resided on the second floor in a small
room in Pioneer Hall, a coeducational dormitory. The house director
was concerned about my living on the second floor as a blind student.
I don't know who had assigned me to the second floor. We had a demonstration of a fire drill. We were instructed to break the glass in order
to unlock the door because we were, in fact, locked inside Pioneer

Hall. Then when we had a "real" drill several days later, I was among the first five or ten women to reach that door. From behind the group, I instructed someone to break the glass. No one would. One or two kept repeating in panic, "We are locked in here to burn to death!"

I forced my way through the group to reach the door. With the heel of my slipper, I broke the glass and unlocked the door. Afterward, the house director said that she would not worry about me in another drill and complimented me for knowing what to do.

Another episode in Pioneer Hall is worthy of inclusion here. On a Saturday evening, I had shampooed my hair and had it in pins overnight. Then I settled down to study. The buzzer in Judy's room sounded repeatedly, indicating that she had a call on the phone in the corridor. I ignored it but did notice that someone seemed determined to reach Judy who was apparently not at home.

Then my buzzer sounded. I assumed it might be Chuck. No, it sounded like a teenage boy who said, "I'm looking for a blind date. Are you interested?" I lied by saying that I was studying for a big test and could not go with him. I figured that I was more blind date than he was looking for.

I imagine that when he could not reach Judy, he contacted the switchboard to explain his predicament, "I can't reach Judy. Can you recommend someone else?" Then the man on the switchboard might have said, "I know just the right blind date for you. Her name is Grace!"

Although Pioneer Hall was coeducational, it was unlike many coeducational dormitories today where men and women live on the same floor. Pioneer Hall was H shaped. One vertical bar was for women, the other vertical bar for men. The horizontal bar contained dining room, kitchen, lounge, and switchboard area.

When a male student entered our section to gather trash from wastebaskets, the male voice called out, "Man on first floor." "Man on second floor." Etc.

I enrolled in a doctoral program at Temple University immediately at my own expense and rented a large, furnished room as my home near the campus. Our furniture remained in storage for seven years. Not even once did Chuck offer to pay the storage charges.

I had no fellowship at Temple and used whatever savings I could from my employment at Syracuse University, my only income for a year. Whatever remained of my inheritance from my grandfather also helped to pay bills.

A gentleman was my adviser for a very short period when he was killed in an auto accident. Although I was very fond of Dr. Wilt, she had been my adviser in my master's program. I thought that I should not call on her again as adviser. I chose Dr. Sallie Rhue, who was my instructor in mathematics. She agreed.

Later I invited Dr. Wilt to be on the committee, though not as chairman. She declined. About two weeks later, she summoned me to her office to inform me that she would accept her place on my committee. She confided that she did not like being on the same committee with Dr. Rhue based on prior experience, but for my sake, Dr. Wilt agreed to serve on my committee. Dr. Wilt told me that when the faculty voted to accept or reject me as a doctoral applicant, all faculty except Dr. Rhue had approved me. Rhue's reaction was, "I don't know whether a blind candidate can be a doctoral student. I'm not going to vote for her when I don't know her potential." Nevertheless, without my knowing that background information, when I asked her to be chairman of my committee, she accepted, instead of being honest with me about her doubts and apprehensions. She had a conflict of interest. Instead of resolving to support a doctoral student, as a chairman should, she allowed herself the "pleasure" of trying to sink my ship. I have to wonder now whether she stayed at Temple as long as she wanted to be there or whether the university terminated her service after Dr. Kress had observed her treatment of me and Wilt's reports of previous problems.

As I discovered as I interacted with her, no matter how much I did on the dissertation, it was never enough. She would approve something and then want it rearranged or expanded. I could never achieve full approval. My dissertation grew to 502 pages! An unheard of length for a dissertation! I think that Dr. Rhue expected that her continuous dissatisfaction with my dissertation would cause me to quit and drop out of the doctoral program; then she could remind other faculty, "I told you I thought a blind person cannot be a doctoral candidate."

After having two unworthy advisers who wanted me to fail, I succeeded without their help! Such individuals have definite personal problems and should not be in positions of trust because they are sinister in their responsibilities to doctoral candidates. Apparently, I had sufficient determination to succeed in spite of both advisers.

When I arrived for my oral defense of the dissertation, Dr. Roy Kress was in charge of the committee and not Dr. Rhue. He was Dean of the Graduate School. Before the committee voted on my performance, I left the room as requested. When I returned, all excepted Dr. Rhue congratulated me. Dr. Kress asked Dr. Rhue, "Aren't you going to congratulate Dr. Napier?"

Her response, after a phoney cough, was, "I have a cold."

I think that Dr. Rhue had never met a blind student before and was truly ignorant about how some blind individuals are superior. Again, it is the demonstration of the saying, "My mind is made up. Don't confuse me with the facts. I am determined to prove that I am correct." I don't know how long Rhue had been at Temple before I met her. Neither do I know the behind-the-scenes functioning of faculty. Was every faculty member with a doctorate eligible to vote on a doctoral candidate, or must the voting faculty be tenured first?

I graduated in June 1968 among one hundred thirty-seven graduates receiving the same degree, Ed.D. (Doctor of Education).

At some universities, students have a choice between Ph.D. and Ed.D. Not so at Temple University. A doctoral student in education had to receive the Ed.D. I had inquired whether I might receive the Ph.D. when I began my program. I learned, "If you are in education, it has to be the Ed.D." At some other universities, a student may earn the Ph.D. by adding foreign language proficiency and statistics mastery to their programs. At Minnesota, I had completed a course in German proficiency for all Ph.D. candidates. Students in that course were in medicine, science, engineering, etc. as well as education. I met that requirement. I was adding statistics to my program. In fact, it was my statistics professor, Dr. Raymond Colyer, who had asked me how many credits I was carrying.

At commencement, before the processional, the person directing events instructed me to sit in the aisle seat. During ceremonies, reporters and photographers were interviewing me and taking pictures. By then, I was already teaching at Colorado State College for two years. (When Dr. Rhue learned that I had been hired to teach at Colorado State College even before I had received the doctorate, her reaction was, "Oh, I'd give my eye teeth to teach at Colorado State College!"

When I was reviewing the literature for my dissertation, I had come across many references to Colorado State College. It was nationally prominent in the field of education.

After commencement, Dr. Roy Kress initiated correspondence with me. We exchanged countless letters until his death. I had earlier enrolled in one of his courses. I treasure my association with him.

While in Philadelphia, I developed severe hyperthyroidism with weight loss and extreme exhaustion. I had two of the three causes: malnutrition and emotional stress. With little money, my diet was inadequate. Chuck was certainly causing me stress.

In January of 1966, I was rapidly running out of money. I told Chuck. I expected that he would repay his debt to me for his beekeeping project. Instead, in a harsh voice, he said, "Go on welfare!" Although I applied immediately, financial help was slow in arriving. In May, June, and July, I received eighty dollars a month designated for rent.

I was not the only one who had experienced physical stress since my story is so intertwined with those of my dog guides.

In 1963 and 1964, Vicki was battling osteoarthritis. A veterinarian learned from X-rays that the condition was in Vicki's neck and spine. Vicki had difficulty climbing a flight of stairs or boarding a bus. One day she skipped a meal. Sometimes a dog will do that when digestion is upset, so I was not really concerned. Then she skipped her second meal for that day and the two meals for the next day! This was not normal or of little consequence. I was now worried. In desperation, I picked up her pan of feed to encourage her to eat. She ate greedily. Encouraged, I placed the pan on the floor again. She stopped eating. I picked up the pan, and she ate hungrily. Ah-ha! She could not bend low enough to eat or drink! After that, I placed her pans on a box so that she could more easily consume feed and water.

I reported all this to our veterinarian and to The Seeing Eye. Both concurred that Vicki should be retired.

I agonized over whether to have her euthanized or to retire her with someone, but with whom? I even wrote a creative piece in the form of a letter from Vicki to another dog, explaining why Grace was troubled and what "going to sleep" would be like or what living with strangers would be like. My problem was how can I communicate with Vicki to have her understand that I was not abandoning her or that I had not stopped loving her? How could she know whatever I did was not a happy choice for me?

Then I learned that The Seeing Eye had an "old dogs' home" in one of the kennels. This is not one of the school's routine services. In 1964, the school had a few old dogs; adding one more was no problem.

I accepted this resource. On the day I arrived with Vicki for my new dog, two instructors met me at the front door. One took Vicki's leash from my hand and led the dog away, after a quick hug from me. That was the last I saw Vicki. Now I must concentrate on my new dog! The year 1964 was the last full year of classes in Whippany. The next year a brand-new building, designed as a school, arose on the opposite side of Washington Valley.

Vicki was quite a tomboy in personality, contrary to Esta, always a dignified lady in comportment. Nevertheless, Vicki proved to be one more excellent worker.

I recall a summer experience in Collingswood with Vicki. She and I had gone to my dentist. On our return, the skies opened with a torrential rain as we stepped off the bus, but we still had more than a block to walk.

When we reached the shelter of our front porch, Chuck called down, "Wait there." In a moment, he came to the screen door, opened it, and thrust a towel at me. For a nano second, I thought this was a warm fuzzy gesture. Then he said, "Dry off the dog." So much for warm fuzzies. I had been in the same downpour, but I had to slosh my way up the stairs, dripping as I went. In the bedroom, I removed all my clothes to replace them with dry garments.

Vicki was with me for the last six years when I was an itinerant teacher. She accompanied me to Minnesota and back to Philadelphia where I enrolled at Temple University and rented one of three furnished apartments. Urban renewal kept pursuing me so that I had to move to enable demolition of old buildings near the campus.

She was inclined to bark when the doorbell rang, though she was quiet at all other times. The driver for the dry cleaner came early; when he rang the bell, Vicki barked furiously. I felt that I had to handle this matter before answering the door. I corrected her with "Pfui!" for barking and led her to her bed, then opened the door. I hoped that I had at last impressed Vicki with the dissatisfaction I experienced with her barking.

Later that morning, my reader announced her presence by ringing the doorbell. Again, Vicki burst into sound but ran to her bed where she sat, still barking! She had learned the wrong lesson!

In Philadelphia, I usually took Vicki outdoors at ten o'clock in the evening, as her last time to relieve herself until morning. When we returned, she went to bed while I continued studying until midnight or later.

On one of these evenings, I was using my talking book machine (phonograph) with talking discs. I had the volume low so not to disturb my neighbors. An hour or so after Vicki had retired, she came to me and pushed the arm with the needle off the disc. Then she returned to her bed.

The message was clear: "I'm trying to sleep. Shut it off!" Although I did not shut it off, I resorted to using headphones after that.

One of my professors told me a week later about his experience in class in Physiological Psychology. We were in an evening course. The professor kept hearing heavy breathing, even snoring. He looked across each row of students, trying to find the graduate student who dared to fall asleep in his class. All students were attentive, busily writing notes. Where was the sleepy student?

Belatedly, he realized that the disrespectful sounds were coming from the dog at my feet in the front row—and close to his feet!

One summer a friend, Vera Brady, my mother, Chuck, Vicki, and I drove to Maine to spend a week at One Mile Lake. Vicki tested the water with one paw but withdrew it promptly; she never ventured into it again. I was the only one who entered the lake each day; the water was chilly.

We wore sweaters until noon.

Of course, the nights were wintry by New Jersey standards for August. We used two or three blankets. I bedded down Vicki each night on a thick throw rug, covered her with a warm blanket folded to make several layers over her.

I awoke in the wee hours and heard things in the room vibrating! What was happening? *That sounds like the dresser shaking. Are we experiencing an earthquake? The chair was making a noise. Is someone else in this room? The highway is too far away for heavy vehicles to cause vibrations here. What is it?*

Curious, I left my bed to investigate. I felt the floor shaking, yet I was the only person moving.

The greatest vibrations were near Vicki. I put my hand on Vicki's blanket. She was still on her rug and under the several layers of blanket, but she was shivering violently. Her shivering was strong enough to cause furniture to rattle!

I uncovered her and guided her to my side of the bed. I urged her to jump onto the bed. She was reluctant to do that. That was a no-no. I lifted her up there, crawled in beside her, and covered both of us. (Chuck slept peacefully on during all this.) Eventually Vicki fell asleep and produced her grandfatherly snores. I hoped that she would not catch a cold and be ill because of her earlier experience being cold and shivering so violently. Her thin, smooth hair did not provide much protection in this extreme cold.

When it was time for us to wake up and leave the bed, Vicki was the first one out, acting very sheepish. I made no notice of the fact that she had been in the bed.

One day at home, I was shelling fresh peas. One flew to the floor. Vicki pounced on it, but she did not eat it or even chew it. Instead, she played "ball" with it! She tossed it, ran after it, tossed it again for a surprisingly long play time. Can you picture a boxer playing ball with one pea?

Vicki's successor was Dola, a German shepherd. When Vicki could no longer stand, The Seeing Eye had her euthanized and wrote a letter to tell me so.

Although for my first year as faculty at Syracuse University I taught in Crouse Hall, the remaining nine summers were in one of the city's elementary schools where many special education classes and classes for normal children were conducted. Vicki was there for the second through seventh summer, Dola for the last three summers.

We had to walk farther to that school (off campus) than to Crouse Hall. Dola and I enjoyed those walks to and from Hafts Dormitory where I resided with some of the other summer guest faculty.

In the school building, I had my own classroom all day. I could set up table displays or bulletin-board displays, assured that no one would disturb my efforts.

One summer I placed a Braille copy of the final examination on the bulletin-board. I urged students in my Braille course to examine anything in Braille on the bulletin-board. Few students did so. After the final examination, I told the class that their final examination was on the bulletin-board and showed them which pages it involved. I heard groans! Those summers were very happy and gratifying for me. Because neither dog wandered away from me, I did not tie them. When class was in session, either chose a spot and settled down unobtrusively. When I visited the ladies' room next to my classroom, no one had to wonder where I was. Each dog had stationed herself in the corridor, pointing to the door where I was.

One summer before I left for Syracuse, I instructed Chuck to take my typewriter to a specific repair shop to have specific repairs done. I wrote this information in braille for Chuck's benefit. Later, he telephoned me in Syracuse to inform me that he had "bought" me a new typewriter. I could not believe his words; he would not spend *his* money to purchase me a new typewriter. I had to wait until I returned home to learn more.

At home, I asked to see my new typewriter. "Where did you put it, Chuck?"

"It's still in the store."

"Why didn't you bring it home?"

His answer was, "Because you have to pay for it!" That was how he bought me a new typewriter. He could not even use English to express the truth correctly.

As I reconstructed the situation, he carried my typewriter into the store and asked, "How much will you give me for this typewriter?" and pocketed that money, and then said, "My wife wants me to select a new typewriter that she will pay for when she returns home." He completely ignored the fact that I wanted my typewriter *repaired*. Drug addicts will steal other persons' property and sell it to use the cash to buy more drugs. Chuck fit the profile of a drug addict. What next will he steal from me? One December while I still resided in Philadelphia,

I had a severe cold. Chuck said he had a cold pill to help me. I took it. I soon learned that it was not a cold pill but apparently one of his illegal drugs! It put me to sleep immediately; a cold pill had never done that. The next thing I experienced was Chuck's slapping my face to waken me. Later, he offered me another "cold pill" which I refused.

Frankly, I had to wonder whether Chuck was trying to kill me with his drugs! If I had not responded to his face slapping, he probably would have disposed of his pills by flushing them down the toilet and be completely innocent when the police arrived. Chuck would probably have reported that I had been using illegal drugs.

Then I recalled that on the evening after my father died, Chuck had given my brother a pill "to help you sleep." The next morning, my brother asked Chuck, "What was that pill? It knocked me out immediately." Chuck never answered the question.

How many other times did Chuck dispense his illegal drugs to innocent persons whose well-being might have been jeopardized?

For the next several months, my hearing was troublesome. I could not localize a sound. Although I could hear a bus coming, for instance, I could not determine whether it was approaching from my left or from my right across the street. For a seeing person, this might not be a problem, because vision would supply the truth. For a blind individual, this was a definite danger.

I went to the university's Audiology Clinic where Dr. Rosenberg, one of my professors, examined me. I was under his care until the problem dissipated. He immediately understood the problem as it affected a blind patient. I cannot be sure whether Chuck's pill had caused the problem, but I resolved never again to accept a pill from Chuck, regardless of what he called it. I was married to a fiend!

Whenever I tried to encourage Chuck to seek therapy and detoxification, his only response was, "I don't have any problems," evidence of denial. I had no hope that Chuck would ever be normal again.

During another summer, Chuck bought himself a new suit from a Paoli store but had the store send me the bill in Philadelphia; my mail was forwarded to Syracuse. He must have assumed that I would pay for his suit from my Syracuse salary, even though that money had to support me for a year. Without comment, I sent the bill to Chuck in Paoli.

At another time, Chuck said he was giving me a new wristwatch for my birthday. He directed me to select one from the AFB catalog. I did, and wrote the letter, addressed the envelope, and affixed a stamp. I gave him the envelope for his check. He refused it. I enclosed my check. He never reimbursed me.

However, after the watch arrived and I was wearing it, Chuck said, when we were with friends, "Grace, show them the watch that I gave you for your birthday!"

At the end of one of those summers in Syracuse, Chuck urged me to return home on Friday evening rather than on Saturday as I usually did, because Ann Perry's daughter was being married on Saturday afternoon. I encouraged him to attend the wedding without me. No, he insisted, I should return home on Friday evening.

When I returned to my apartment in Philadelphia on Friday evening, Chuck was not waiting there for me! The air inside the apartment was stale because of being uncirculated for six weeks. I had no food for supper.

Chuck phoned from Paoli to say that he and Ann had driven to the airport but could not find me! I said, "How could you find me when you did not know which airline I was using or the time of my arrival in Philadelphia? Furthermore, why would Ann be chauffeuring you to Philadelphia when her daughter is having a wedding rehearsal this evening? You lie through your teeth. Are you in the bridal party?" No, he was not.

"Then why was it more important for you to be with Ann than to be here with me?" His parting words were, "Don't forget to bring a wedding gift tomorrow!" Ann was his friend, but he could not spend his money for a wedding gift for Martha!

Before I had breakfast the next morning, I had to go to the grocery store for food. I had no desire to attend the wedding after the way Chuck had treated me.

Chuck seemed to be losing his ability to reason logically. Also, his lies were so outrageous, yet he thought I believed everything he said. What was happening to his brain? Were the illegal drugs destroying his brain? He seemed unable to differentiate between truth and falsehood.

Earlier, I recognized that he had problems. When I thought he was unhappy in our marriage, I tried to guide him to seek marriage counseling in order to help both of us. "No, I don't have any problems."

Later when I surmised that he was experiencing clinical depression, I again tried to have him see a mental health therapist. "No, I don't have any problems."

Still later, when I knew he was using illegal drugs and alcohol in addition to dependence on coffee and chain-smoking of cigarettes, I had no success in helping him to acknowledge his problems. He was in denial about his condition. Drugs deceive the user. Chuck was truly mentally ill!

What is the name of his condition other than drug addiction? Was an illness driving him to drug addiction, or was drug addiction causing other problems?

He was also a hypochondriac. He enjoyed poor health. He had to have symptoms to nurse. When he lost a symptom, he gained two others. Or was his "hypochondriasis" a screen to convince me that he was sick (perfectly respectable to be sick) when, in reality, addictions were throwing him into a stupor? In his thinking, if Grace thought he was sick, she would not be suspicious when he fell into a stupor (attributing his sleepiness to being sick). "Poor Chuck is sick again!" He spent his life trying to deceive other people when, in fact, he was completely deceiving himself. His passive-aggressive personality reduced his interpersonal skills to non-existence. He was truly mentally ill.

Because Chuck's behavior had not really changed except to intensify from our first month of marriage, I am now convinced that he was using drugs even before we married!

My initial reaction to Chuck's addiction was shame for him and shame on myself that I felt others would ascribe to me, once they knew the truth about Chuck. Others might even surmise that I, too, was a drug addict or that I condoned drug addiction in my husband. Over time, my view changed drastically about drug addiction in my husband.

EIGHT

In March 1966, while still living in Philadelphia and working on my dissertation, I received a phone call from Colorado State College (CSC) in Greeley to inform me that the Department of Special Education and Rehabilitation wanted me to teach there full-time and urged me not to accept any other offer. Dr. Dick Wolfe, a faculty member, was relaying a message from the department chairman, Dr. Tony Vaughan. I had nothing in writing to rely on should other attractive offers come my way. How had CSC heard of me? I knew no one in Colorado.

About once a month, I continued to receive phone calls from Greeley, insisting that I not accept another position. Thinking about this vocal offer, I wondered whether it was something that would really materialize into employment or whether the phone calls would stop when the department had found someone considered better qualified to fill the post. I had questions in my mind and heart: Did God really want me to go to Colorado? Should I stay on the east coast? How would I be accepted in Colorado? If the job was offered, where would I live once I arrived there? How did they obtain my name when I knew no one there? I prayed about the matter. Searching in my Bible for answers to my own questions, I came upon Joshua 1:9, which reads, "Have not I commanded thee? Be strong and of a good courage; be not afraid, neither be thou dismayed: for the Lord thy God is with thee whithersoever thou goest." And Isaiah 50:7 "For the Lord God will help me; therefore shall I not be confounded: therefore have I set my face like a flint, and I know that I shall not be ashamed." And Deuteronomy 31:6 "Be strong and of a good courage, fear not, nor be afraid of them: for the Lord thy God, he it is that doth go with thee, he will not fail thee, nor forsake thee." and Matthew 6:8 "For your Father knoweth what things ye have need of, before ye ask him." and Psalms 27:1 "The Lord is my light and my salvation; whom shall I fear? The Lord is the strength of my life; of whom shall I be afraid?" Yes, of course, I was not going to Colorado alone; God would be going with me. In fact, He would go ahead of me to lead the way and to remove stumbling-blocks to make my path safe. *If this is where He wants me, He will be there with me. I will not be going alone or living there without Him.* In one of those calls, I was informed that, because Dr. Stan Bourgeault was resigning from CSC, I would be succeeding him—but still nothing in writing. Now I saw the connection previously missing from my understanding, relative to who in Greeley knew me! Who was this Dr. Bourgeault? I knew immediately. The academic year I was in Minneapolis, Stan was a doctoral student in special education, with prior professional preparation and experience in the education of blind and visually-impaired children. He had worked at the Minnesota School for the Blind. We were in some of the same courses. He was the only one I could think of who might recommend me for the position that he was vacating at CSC, where he was on the faculty but planning to move to Lebanon with his family to work for the American Foundation for Overseas Blind. I am truly indebted to Stan for his confidence in me.

As I review my career, each position was offered to me before I had heard of the opening or could apply for it. Betty Ryder Strickland wrote to me about the teaching position at Royer-Greaves. Miss Josephine Taylor offered me the position as itinerant teacher. Dr.

William Cruickshank offered me the position on summer faculty at Syracuse University before I even knew that he was not inviting my predecessor to return. AFB sent me a letter offering me a fellowship to study at the University of Minnesota; I had not inquired about fellowship funds. Stan Bourgeault recommended me to the faculty at CSC. I do not know how Maurice Olsen (to be heard of soon) obtained my name, possibly from AFB or the New Jersey Commission for the Blind or Bill Cruickshank.

In early June, before I had anything in writing assuring me of the Greeley position, I received a phone call from Maurice Olsen, superintendent of the Missouri School for the Blind in St. Louis. He was offering both Chuck and me teaching positions. At last I would succeed in moving Chuck away from Royer-Greaves and the drug dealer, I thought. I asked Mr. Olsen whether we were required to live on campus. "No, I prefer that faculty live off campus," he said. That was exactly what I wanted to hear. He said he would be sending two applications.

When Chuck arrived in Philadelphia on Friday evening, I told him of Mr. Olsen's call. Chuck's reaction was, "He wants you; he doesn't want me." I assured him that Mr. Olsen had included both of us. "No, when he didn't mention my name, you asked whether he had a position for your husband." Chuck was not going to leave Paoli after all! Another disappointment. Still, I hoped that being closer to his family in Chicago might entice Chuck away from Paoli in order to live in St. Louis.

When the applications arrived in the mail, I completed mine with the help of a reader. (I did not yet have electronic or computerized equipment that would enable me to complete that task by myself.)

The next time Chuck came, I gave him his application. He took it reluctantly. I had a strong feeling he would not complete it and return it to Mr. Olsen.

Although I received a contract promptly, none came for Chuck. I surmised the explanation for that fact, though Chuck claimed that he had returned his application.

To jump ahead to complete this part of the story, I accepted my contract but later wrote to reject it. If I worked in St. Louis and Chuck stayed at Paoli, we would be seeing each other even less often than weekends. I assume that Mr. Olsen was negatively impressed with my acceptance of his contract and then my breaking it when I learned that Chuck had no contract from Olsen.

Later, in October, I attended a conference in Louisville, Kentucky, where I met Mr. Olsen. I asked him why he had not sent my husband a contract. He said, "I can't send a contract when a person does not apply!" I was right; Chuck had not returned his completed application.

After Olsen's phone call in June, I received a phone call from Greeley from Dr. Tony Vaughan. He asked whether I might meet him for an interview in Washington, DC, at the National Education Association (NEA) Building. Yes, I would be happy to do that. He set the date and gave me directions to meet him on a specific floor at noon.

The day before, by prearrangement, I went to the home of Jack Napier, one of Chuck's younger brothers, who lived in the DC area. On Thursday morning, I went to the NEA Building and to the designated floor. Yes, Dr. Vaughan was there. He immediately suggested that we go to the basement cafeteria. He said, "I have never gone through a cafeteria line with a blind person. How do we do it?"

I explained that he might go ahead of me and tell me what our choices are and then place on my tray the items that I choose. (I did not select soup, lest it slosh all over my tray.) That process worked smoothly. After paying for both lunches, he then said, "Follow me."

"Keep talking so that I can follow you," I urged, with a prayer arrow soaring upward. I could foresee spilling my lunch on the back of his jacket! With relief, I arrived safely at our table without incident. Because of carrying a tray with both hands, I could not use my Dola to guide me.

The interview proceeded throughout lunch. It seemed to go favorably and without obstacles, though one can never be entirely sure about interview outcomes.

He was leaving that day to return to Greeley but promised to phone me on Friday evening. I supplied him with Jack's phone number.

Chuck came to Jack's home before Dr. Vaughan phoned. Chuck gave no encouragement but poured cold water on the whole experience. "He probably will not phone. That will be his easy way out. He will have some reason why he wanted you but his superiors rejected his choice of candidate. He'll find ways not to hire you. Be prepared. You won't get the job."

Jack was present to hear Chuck's wet-blanket spiel. I think that Chuck was reacting to his not getting the rehabilitation counselor position in Illinois, saying, not that he had failed the interview but that the interviewer was capricious and playing games with a blind applicant, as Chuck preferred to interpret the outcome. This thinking reflects two aspects of Chuck's personality: 1) low self-esteem ("nobody wants me") and 2) "You can't trust seeing people."

Before Chuck arrived, I had told Jack that I was unsure whether Chuck would go with me to Colorado.

Jack encouraged me to go without Chuck. "You have done a great deal with your life while Chuck just talks big but does nothing. So go without him. Don't throw away this opportunity to teach at a college."

I said nothing to Jack about Chuck's addictions. Jack said nothing about his surmise relative to Chuck's appearance, namely, the look of a junkie, if he had such a thought.

I am reminded here of a sage quotation as it applies to Chuck who expected to be chosen, though he lacked demonstrated abilities. It reads: "Begin somewhere; you cannot build a reputation on what you intend to do," attributed to Liz Smith, columnist. Chuck talked big about what he intended to do some day but never achieved anything. Then when someone else was selected, Chuck sulked and pouted in self-pity. Frequently, when he had heard of a woman's appointment or promotion, he said, "She probably gave sexual favors; that's how she got ahead."

The phone rang. It was Dr. Vaughan; Jack handed the phone to me. Dr. Vaughan had gained clearance from all levels to hire me. He would be putting the contract into the mail in the morning. I was elated! I would be starting as assistant professor at eleven thousand two hundred dollars per year! That was more money than I had ever seen! In fact, I had never earned that much in my life and especially not at Royer-Greaves School where my three yearly wages were seven hundred twenty dollars, eight hundred forty dollars, and nine hundred sixty dollars. Chuck was silent. Jack expressed his happiness for me and offered congratulations, whereas Chuck said not a word! Chuck said absolutely nothing; his predictions fell to the floor in ruins.

Already, I felt wealthy after the poverty I had been experiencing for several years and without Chuck's repaying the thousand dollars that he owed me. God was taking very good care of me!

After Chuck and I returned to Pennsylvania, I asked whether he was going with me to Colorado.

"No, I'm never going to leave Paoli. I want to stay near Ann!" I could have added for him, "I never want to leave Hank." At last, Chuck was being honest. He wanted to stay where his drug dealer could supply him and where he could be close to Ann.

In that summer (1966), Chuck and Ann were planning to attend a convention in Miami, Florida. Chuck told me that the car was reserved for only employees and that, if I was planning to attend the convention, I must go on my own power, not with him and Ann (another lie). Actually, I could not afford air fare and hotel bills.

When he returned, he had a slip of the tongue, revealing that a couple from Providence, Rhode Island, (who had been teachers at Royer-Greaves even before Chuck and I were employees there) had been passengers in the back seat of the car. (How cozy to have a couple both of whom were blind in the back seat and a couple in the front!) The next time I met Bill Dietrich, the school's business manager, he asked me why I had not gone in the car to the convention. (So I would have been allowed to travel in the car!) I told Bill that I had not been invited.

He could think that through. He might ask Chuck why Grace had not accompanied him; of course, Chuck would have a lie ready to explain my absence. Dietrich might also wonder about the relationship between Ann and Chuck and diligently watch the two of them.

Some of my friends attending the convention volunteered information to me that Chuck had not been acting as a married man. (Chuck probably assumed that no one at the convention knew him because he had attended only one other convention in his life, as far as I knew, unless he had gone secretly to conventions with Ann while I was in Syracuse summers.)

With all these pieces coming together, I wrote a letter of explanation to Mr. Olsen about why I had to break the contract. The college contract was more attractive, and without Chuck, I had no real reason for going to St. Louis.

Although I would have enjoyed using my furniture in Colorado, I did not have the money to withdraw the furniture from storage to be transported to Greeley. I refer to the furniture as *mine* because I had paid the storage fee for seven years; Chuck had never offered to pay the charge. Furthermore, I wanted a second-year contract before moving the furniture to Greeley. My only option was to send ahead only whatever belongings I had used in my three apartments in Philadelphia. (I had lived in a ghetto beside the campus. In addition, urban renewal was demolishing buildings, thus forcing residents to move elsewhere.) I engaged a freight truck to transport those few items to Greeley. Frankly, I had only a few dollars in my wallet, dollars remaining from my Syracuse paycheck after paying all other bills. The three eighty-dollar checks from welfare paid only for my rent for May, June, and July in Philadelphia.

As part of my educational research reported in my dissertation, children had been administered many short tests related to their listening comprehension based on prerecorded material produced at ever-increasing word-per-minute speeds. To keep written documentation of children's scores, I hired a doctoral student to retain the data in a notebook as the basis for my statistical calculations. He agreed to wait for payment (twelve hundred dollars) until I was employed and earning money. My Syracuse earnings were now unavailable for paying him. So I had to wait until I received money from CSC on the first of October.

Even though Chuck owed me one thousand dollars for his beekeeping hobby, he had paid me nothing thus far. If he had, then I would owe only two hundred dollars more, a manageable amount. However, without Chuck's repaid debt to me, a twelve hundred dollar debt was burdensome when I was all but broke already. Chuck's unethical character was destroying me financially, yet he claimed vehemently, "I don't have any problems."

Earlier that summer while at Syracuse, I wrote a letter to Emma Rowe in Miami, Florida, to tell her that I had a full-time teaching position in September at Colorado State College. Then I received a letter from her saying that she was in Greeley for summer session! Serendipity! No, God was keeping His promise. I now had God going to Colorado with me, and Stan and Emma already there to greet me! She urged me to arrive in Greeley as early as I could so that we might spend time together in order for her to orient me to the town and the campus.

Emma and I had spent several summer sessions together at Syracuse. Now, this summer in 1966 was to be my last to teach at Syracuse after ten summers. The summer of 1967 would be consumed by teaching in Greeley, because my contract involved four quarters of teaching. That same summer, Dr. Cruickshank was leaving Syracuse to move to the University of Michigan, Ann Arbor.

Emma phoned me in Syracuse to say that she had found a furnished house but that I had to decide immediately whether I wanted it. I asked about the source of heat in winter, because I did not want a coal-burning furnace. No, it had a gas space heater. I also stated that I wanted a clean house. Emma promised that it would be clean.

After my summer session in Syracuse, I returned to my apartment only long enough to empty it and tie up loose ends there in Philadelphia.

En route to Colorado by train, I stopped in Chicago to visit the Napiers. In my better days financially, I had stated in a letter to Chuck's sister Sue that I hoped to help her oldest child, Howard, with college expenses. He was a bright student and deserved to attend college. Sue's husband had deserted her, leaving her to rear four children without child support from the scoundrel.

Unhappily, my economics had deteriorated drastically, yet I could not bring myself to tell Sue that I was on welfare, that our marriage was ending, and that I was destitute financially until I could free myself from her brother. Without knowing those facts, she was angry that my words to help Howard were now not materializing. Ever since then, I have been Enemy No. One on Sue's list. (To Sue's credit, all four of her children are college graduates.)

Then I traveled by train to Colorado, where Emma met me in Denver on August 13.

When we reached Greeley, I was excited to become acquainted with my new residence. Inside, I moved gingerly in order to avoid the boxes that the freight truck had delivered. I found none. Not only had Emma hired a cleaning woman, but Emma also had helped her scrub down the entire interior of the house. In addition, Emma had unpacked the boxes, putting each item in a logical place: kitchen, bedroom, study, or bathroom! What a friend!

Between her final examinations, Emma and I walked, so that she might orient me to stores, bank, streets and avenues (like a grid with numbered avenues going north/south and numbered streets running east/west) and campus.

Emma and another teacher friend from Syracuse summers, Lisa Stokes, knew my financial status. Each gave me a check to meet my immediate needs; accordingly, I could repay them after the college had begun paying me on October first. I also had borrowed money from my brother. I would not ask Chuck for money. He refused me once; I would not now give him a second opportunity to demonstrate his lack of concern for me.

When Emma left Greeley to drive to Miami, I was truly indebted to her for the care she had displayed. Now I felt confident and oriented enough to start expanding my mental map.

Early, I became acquainted with my neighbors, Betty and Cecil Foster, who lived across the street.

I needed to rebuild my wardrobe, now depleted after years of poverty when I had purchased textbooks instead of shoes or adequate groceries. Betty offered to shop with me. I explained that I had little money but needed to find appropriate clothes for my teaching position. She knew of thrift shops which we frequented. Judging from compliments that I received later, Betty was a discriminating buyer as she selected clothes for me. She and Cecil extended warm hospitality.

Even before I began teaching, two women doctoral students and I went out to dinner one evening. After we settled ourselves at a table, a waitress requested that I leave the dog in the car.

I explained that the dog was a guide dog and that she stays with me.

Then, after the waitress left us, she returned to say that my dog might bite children if they came.

I assured her that my dog was disciplined and manageable. Meanwhile, no one came to take our orders.

Then a third time the same waitress came to the table to say that the management wanted us to leave the premises!

We did. We went to another restaurant without incident.

At home, I phoned no one about the episode but returned to working on my dissertation. The next morning, Dick Wolfe greeted me at the office with, "I heard that you were treated badly at the restaurant last evening!" He explained that the two students who had been with me made many phone calls to alert persons at the college about how badly I had been treated. Many of those persons no longer went to that restaurant. About six months later, someone from the restaurant phoned to apologize and to invite me to return. The management had been told by many individuals that the woman they had refused to serve was a faculty member at the college. This restaurant had been popular with department heads and others in authority at the college who had entertained official guests there. All that business stopped when they had learned about the management's shabby treatment of a faculty member. (The loss of dollars when former patrons refused to eat there forced management to apologize in the hope of restoring former relationships in the community.)

Meanwhile, back in Pennsylvania, instead of repaying me, Chuck arranged for a loan from Ann of twelve hundred dollars for me to repay within eighteen months at three percent interest! He was still protecting *his* money. Now it was Ann's money on the table, not Chuck's. Those were the only terms I had been given by Chuck or Ann.

With my pay for September, I began monthly payments of one hundred dollars. I continued this for seven months in addition to repaying Emma, Lisa, and my brother.

Then, because I was writing my dissertation, I needed to replace my old Brailler, the one my parents had purchased, with a new Perkins Brailler that cost one hundred and fifteen dollars. I skipped payment to Ann that month.

Chuck phoned me. His first words were, "Why are you reneging on your debt to poor Ann?" He infuriated me with the word *reneging*. Of all persons, he was not the one to use it. He did not ask, "Are you having financial problems?" or "Did you already send the check? Maybe it's lost or delayed." Because Chuck had reneged on his debt to me, he was assuming that I was retaliating by reneging on my debt to "poor Ann." No, I was a villain, according to Chuck. No one ever said that one of the terms of the loan was to pay something *every* month. I still had eleven months in which to repay five hundred dollars. My intention was to continue one hundred dollar payments after my purchase of the Brailler. I was angry!

I went to the bank for a loan of five hundred dollars plus interest of fifty-four dollars and sent the check pronto to Ann. She returned a check for her unearned interest. I returned that check to "poor Ann." I did not want "poor Ann" to suffer any hardship because of me! Now I was free of debt and free of Chuck and Ann forever!

At this point, I had resolved to divorce Chuck. He had made his feelings for me abundantly clear—or rather his lack of caring for me. Although I had been married to him for twenty years by 1966, I had nothing to show for it; I was married but had no husband. He lied and cheated. He had no family loyalty, no ambition, no credibility, no integrity, no future.

When I first found Chuck's cache of drugs, I thought that, if I divorced him, he might be shocked into reality about the severity of his drug addiction and might seek help from some therapist or some agency. If the divorce was effective in that direction, it was worth my separating myself from him. I might have to lose him in order to save him from himself.

Consulting an attorney, I learned that I must first meet a year's residency in Colorado. After that, I could file for divorce and wait the necessary ninety days for the divorce to become official.

To complete the story about Chuck, in December 1966 (after my first few months in Colorado), Chuck phoned to say that he was coming to visit me for Christmas! Because I had previously resolved to divorce him, I said, "No, you may not come." I think he was stunned that I spoke so forcefully. I surmised that Ann was leaving Paoli for the holidays, possibly visiting her father in Massachusetts. With that in the offing, Chuck decided, I concluded, that he would visit Grace for the holidays. I added, "I don't want my new friends here in Greeley to learn that my husband is a drug addict. Just looking at you, they will know that you are a junkie. Once they learn that, they might wonder whether I, too, am a drug user. You are not welcome here. Find another place at which to spend your holidays. Besides, I have only one bed here and refuse to share it with you. I have not had a husband for many years because of your infidelity."

I envisioned his coming to Greeley with a one-way ticket and whining, "I'm broke," and expecting me to provide his return fare. No more of that! Whatever money he might save with his ploy, he would spend on drugs and alcohol. I do not know where he spent the holidays but assume probably in Chicago, pouting about how his wife had treated him, now that she teaches at a college, trying to gain sympathy from whichever relatives might believe him.

Meanwhile, going in a different direction from Chuck, on campus during my first quarter of teaching, I discovered that two of my courses were back-to-back but diagonally across the campus from each other, nine city blocks apart with only fifteen minutes between classes! The first was in Kepner Hall, the second in Ross Hall. Because of that fact, I had to rush away and not linger to interact with my students.

Sometime in November when in conversation with my department chairman, I mentioned, without sounding complaining, that I had to rush between my first and second classes because of the distance between them.

He said, "I arranged those classes that way to see whether you can hack it!"

I asked, "Did I hack it?"

He assured me that I had.

In retrospect, I imagine that he parked his car somewhere to observe me after my first class to determine whether I reached my second class on time. I daresay he never challenged seeing faculty that way to determine whether they could "hack it." The assumption in common use is that seeing faculty can do anything and do not have to be evaluated on whether they arrive on time or stay the full class hour. Parking a car can be time consuming. Some faculty may allow themselves to be engaged in conversation, causing a late arrival at class. Some dismiss class early when they reach the end of prepared notes, having nothing further to contribute to the content of the session. After some faculty arrive in the classroom, they wait until more students arrive before beginning the class session; students soon learn that they need not rush because the instructor will wait for students to arrive late.

Those things are not checked, but a blind faculty member is deliberately given a problematic schedule as a hurdle to surmount to the satisfaction of administrators.

The same chairman reminded me frequently that I did not have enough students to justify my salary! I, as a first-year faculty member, was not responsible for the number of students assigned to me! He had hired me knowing how few students I would have. Why make it sound that I was guilty of incompetence for not having more students? I was learning rapidly that Dr. Tony Vaughan was completely different from Dr. Bill Cruickshank and lacked the latter's finesse.

I learned from a colleague that Dr. Vaughan had much unanswered mail on his desk. I spoke with his administrative assistant, offering to answer mail dealing directly with my program in order to relieve Dr. Vaughan of that pressure. She said that I could not answer mail addressed to Dr. Vaughan, so the accumulation of unanswered mail grew! Still, he considered me responsible for small enrollment in my program!

During my second year, because my name was in the catalog, prospective students wrote directly to me, and I answered all letters with multipage responses written personally to each. Later I learned that many of those students had enrolled in my program because of receiving personal letters rather than impersonal forms from other institutions. My summer enrollment from experienced teachers who sought additional professional preparation was much larger than in the academic year from beginning teachers in special education.

Because of the shortage of special education teachers, the federal government was encouraging teachers to enter this field by allocating thousands of dollars to colleges that offered certifiable special education degrees in turn to qualified summer-only or academic-year students, enabling them by awarding stipends to attend programs to earn certification or graduate degrees in specific areas of special education, such as education of blind and visually-impaired children.

I noticed early that CSC's Department of Special Education and Rehabilitation Counseling had little in uniformity in its terminology among areas within the same department. Each area used a different term from among the following: "handicap," "disability," "impairment," "pathology," "disorder," "problem," "dysfunction," "developmental delay," "limitation," "disturbance," etc. Anyone studying the college catalog might wonder why blindness is a handicap while deafness is an impairment; why speech disorders are caused by pathology—which virus or bacterium; why mental retardation is called developmental delay when the child so labeled will never catch up and have normal or superior intellect; etc. I interpreted this as a weakness and lack of communication among areas within the department. I also saw this nomenclature verbal soup as a disadvantage for students in the department. Students from one area might say "disorder" when the preferred word in another area was pathology or "disability" when "impairment" was considered more correct in still another area. Why have such disparity within one department?

As I conversed with faculty within our department, I discovered that I knew more about their specialties than they knew about mine. I feared that some of them had never taken a course or read a textbook about blindness or visual limitations. Their understanding of "blindness" meant total blindness. Although some faculty were able to apply "individual differences" to their own field, they could not comprehend individual differences in blindness but seemed to assume that every individual with "blindness" was exactly like every other individual with blindness. Consequently, I saw my responsibility not only to teach students but also faculty.

An additional negative was my being a woman faculty in my department where men were the majority. Like other women faculty in departments where men outnumbered women (in most departments at that time), we were not considered contributing members of the faculty; the men saw themselves as the brains of the department. The men felt that they could do everything better than their female counterparts and that women should respectfully surrender whatever authority they held to the more capable hands and heads of men. Men and women were not truly colleagues. Instead, men seemed determined to prove their own superiority by trying to embarrass female peers.

When this was the atmosphere between men and women faculty, you can imagine the greater lack of acceptance and respect when a woman is blind among seeing men!

For five years, I was denied use of state cars assigned to the college. When I requested a car and explained that I had a licensed driver, the answer was always, "No, that is unacceptable!"

In the summer of 1967, I wrote a letter to Chuck demanding the money he owed me because his thinking was that he could borrow money, make promises to repay with interest, and then abandon his responsibilities. If Chuck had been trying to repay me but had legitimate financial setbacks, I probably would have cancelled his debt to me. However, a person with Chuck's warped attitudes needs to face the reality of his obligations. Actually, I figured that if I wrote a Braille letter to him, he would tear it up and dismiss the matter with an attitude of "Go to h—-" with expletives. Therefore, I typed my letter to Chuck. When he received it in the school office, he would ask, "What's the return address?" and learn it was from his wife. Then he would most likely take it to Ann for her to read it to him.

Then she might initiate conversation such as this:

"How much do you owe Grace?"

"A thousand dollars."

"How much have you already repaid?"

"Nothing."

"Why did you borrow the money?"

"For my beekeeping hobby."

"Oh, Grace paid for that. I had assumed you were using your own money. How long have you owed her the money?"

"Eighteen years." Actually, it was more than nineteen.

This exposé might protect Ann (provided Chuck answered questions honestly) by cautioning her not to lend him money.

Chuck paid me but miscalculated the interest by thinking eighteen years instead of nineteen years, which fact I ignored. My strategy of sending Chuck a print letter instead of Braille proved successful in having him repay me.

I wonder whether he borrowed that money from Ann. If so, did he ever repay her in full?

We were legally divorced in December 1967 after more than twenty-one years of "marriage." Weld County in Colorado sent the divorce papers via a Chester County, Pennsylvania, process server who delivered the document to Chuck at the school.

How did Chuck react when served with the document? I do not know but can imagine his primary emotion was anger with expletives comparable to "That S.O.B!" Afterward, did he experience any remorse about losing his wife? I doubt it. He would see nothing wrong in his behavior toward me because of being out of touch with reality and his claim "I have no problems."

I wonder how he explained to his family the reason for Grace's divorcing him. There might be more lies that some of his family could see through as unfounded.

When his family learned of the divorce, several of them phoned or wrote to say that I was still welcome in their homes and that they hoped I would continue to write, phone, and visit them.

To comprehend why I had stayed married to Chuck twenty-one years, readers must consider the following factors:

1) Divorce was not as common in the 1940-1960 period as it is today.

2) Abused wives at that time lacked resources to assist them to escape abuse from spouses.

3) I had been reared at home and at church to believe that divorce is wrong. The idea was that once married, you are stuck with that spouse regardless of spousal mistreatment. Even when I became divorced in 1967, my church in Greeley had no ministry for divorced persons except talking privately with the pastor, which avenue I never took. The subject of divorce was avoided by never mentioning the word.

4) Perhaps, I might have divorced Chuck sooner if he had been

living with me every day. Because I was without him Monday through Friday, I was experiencing respite between weekends With him.

5) Divorce was viewed as failure on the part of the spouse who filed for it. One spouse cannot save a marriage when the other spouse makes no effort to save it but goes in opposite directions. Outsiders do not know the details of the problem, though some persons may assume that they know the truth about which spouse is guilty and which innocent.

I daresay that Chuck welcomed the divorce when it materialized, but "let Grace spend her money for it," he would gloat. He would reason, "I received divorce without having to spend any of my money."

Not until writing this did the thought of a legal separation occur to me. I could have used that vehicle, because I was not leaving Chuck for another man. Furthermore, Chuck was in Pennsylvania and I in Colorado, a comfortable distance apart for a legal separation. I have never dated another man since 1946 when we were married and no one since the divorce.

Much later, family members told me that when Chuck was thinking of retiring, he hoped to live with his sister, Sue, referred to earlier in this chapter and whom Chuck did not like but whom he was eager to use as a source of shelter in his old age.

However, she would not take him into her home because of his use of alcohol. Nevertheless, she was still angry with me for divorcing her brother! Perhaps, Chuck gave a sad story about how he had never used alcohol until after the divorce, making Grace the villain.

Sometime between 1976 (when I bought my home on Eighth Avenue) and 1981 (when Chuck died), Chuck's friend, Brad Burson (mentioned earlier in this volume), phoned to ask whether he might visit me. He was in Colorado, visiting his son in Boulder. I agreed to meet with him.

Late during his visit, Brad began to refer to Chuck and how his sister would not provide him accommodation in her home to enable him to retire. It was obvious to me that Brad served as Chuck's intermediary to test the waters, namely, whether Grace would be receptive to inviting Chuck, ill with emphysema and a heart condition, into her home for his last years on earth. I was unresponsive and silent as he spoke, completely uncommunicative, except to convey lack of interest in Brad's not-so-subtle proposal. I said nothing negative to Brad about Chuck. He could draw his own conclusions and relay them to Chuck.

I had long, busy days on campus, with no time to serve as Chuck's home health care provider as his health deteriorated. Chuck probably had no medical insurance except Medicaid. Nor did I wish to renew our former relationship, knowing full well his inclination to lie and to use people for his own convenience.

He had nowhere to go now except to stay at the school. I am surprised that the school administration permitted Chuck to live on campus without working for the school. Let Ann take care of Chuck. If Bill Dietrich was still at the school, he could draw his own conclusions when Chuck's sister (Sue) and his brother (Bud) and his former wife would not invite Chuck into their homes when Chuck was sick and dying. Not surprising to me was the fact that Chuck lacked the courage to contact me himself but relied on Brad to determine my position in the matter.

Chuck's total behavior indicates that he stopped maturing after his accident, remaining an adolescent for the remainder of his life, with adolescent reactions to every experience in life. I am convinced that he was a drug addict even before I married him, though I did not know that reality then.

We were divorced for fourteen years when, on February 1, 1981, Chuck succumbed to a massive heart attack, fell to the floor, and died alone before Ann found his body. He left his niece and his nephew, our two godchildren on his side of the family, each approximately fifteen thousand dollars! How did he accumulate so much money when he was always "broke?" Was he also a drug dealer as well as a drug user to earn money with which to pay for his own drug habit? He was, indeed, a boy in a man's body, using the money for excessive amounts of coffee, chain-smoking of cigarettes, and illegal use of drugs and alcohol. Caffeine, tobacco, drugs, alcohol, and money destroyed his character and life. Before the heart attack, he had been diagnosed with emphysema. He truly was a pathetic figure who alienated himself from everyone.

According to relatives, if Chuck ever asked Ann to marry him, she wisely declined the offer. In the end, Chuck had neither Grace nor Ann. His world of delusion crumbled in shards around him.

In 1970 he received his doctorate from Temple University but never used it in his career. I had begun my doctorate before Chuck ever talked about beginning his. When he was ready to have his dissertation typed, he asked me to type it for him. I said a firm, blunt "no" for two valid reasons:

1) He did not use the Braille Code correctly but invented his own contractions, the meanings of which were known to him alone.

2) His composition skills were abominable! He did not compose in sentences but in fragments. If I had agreed to type his dissertation from his Braille copy and asked him, "What does this mean?" his typical response would have been, "You know what I mean. Just type what you think I mean." Besides, I was involved already with typing my own dissertation. *Let him use his money to pay someone to type for him from his typewritten rough copy.*

While I was an unemployed doctoral student except for teaching at Syracuse University in summers, Chuck told me that he was going to buy a house in Paoli, a house handled by HUD at a low down payment. I refused to visit the house. I was afraid because of past experiences he would sign the dotted line at the closing and then tell me when we were alone later, "Now be sure to make the mortgage payment every month." Besides, how much of the the information from Chuck was truthful? I had been down that road before with life insurance, health insurance, "I'm buying you a watch for your birthday," and "I bought you a new typewriter." (Relative to life insurance, in my poverty I could not pay the annual premium in the nineteenth or twentieth year of its payment period; the policy lapsed, though the company never wrote to tell me so. The company had been receiving money from me for nineteen years without obligation to pay me anything. The policy was for only three thousand dollars. So when Chuck died, I could not submit a claim.)

Chuck died at age sixty-six after his thirty-five years at the school, living in one room all those years!

I attended his memorial service in the Chicago area. Thus ended the tragic life of a man who was afraid to live as an individual who accidentally had become blind. *Father God, be merciful to him and forgive him. He was sick but rejected You Who could provide the strength that he desperately needed. Amen.*

Because of my experiences with Chuck, I have had no desire to remarry. I have calculated that, except for the first two years of our marriage when we were together every day at Royer-Greaves School, I have been alone the greater part of the following nineteen years. Even when we were together on weekends, the time was unhappy. I had not chosen well my first husband; I probably would do no better in selecting a second husband. I know what I have in being single; I know not what I might have with a second husband.

Intellectually, I know that not all men are like Chuck; however, emotionally, I do not dare trust another husband. Instead, I would wonder when deception, falsehoods, accusations, abuse, marital infidelity, and emotional coldness would arise to remind me that the second husband was little different from Chuck.

I think of all that Chuck missed in his lifetime because of extremely low self-esteem and lack of confidence to venture forth into unknown but exciting realms of life. Rather, he settled for the predictability of daily routine year after monotonous year. I know he owned a microwave oven and a talking clock. (Even though I had my Braille writer when we married—the one my parents had bought—Chuck never asked me to teach him how to operate it. He knew only the slate and stylus as a way to write Braille.) Other than those, I surmise that he never experienced any other services or products available.

When he pursued and received a doctorate, was it to have children at the school address him as "Dr. Napier" instead of "Mr. Napier" or to impress Ann? If so, was the degree worth the labor expended? In short, he squandered a lifetime of opportunities awaiting him. He failed to step forward but cringed in the shadows.

Although I had tried to find the name of Chuck's psychiatric illness (if there is one other than low self-esteem and addiction) by reading whatever I could find, I was unable to identify his specific disturbance until the autumn of 2004 when I read material that described Chuck's condition as ATTENTION DEFICIT DISORDER/ ATTENTION HYPERACTIVITY DISORDER (ADD/ADHD). It is known to be hereditary and not limited to children. It can be treated, but Chuck consulted no one, preferring to live in denial. I have not described Chuck's behaviors and characteristics merely to expose him. On the contrary, I have done so in order to acquaint readers with the behaviors and symptoms of an illness, should readers have a relative or friend who manifests similar histories. I hope that others will be more successful than I in guiding your loved one to appropriate medical help. The condition can be treated.

I have heard or read that the condition is like watching a TV screen but with no control over what the screen shows or how long or brief the scene. For example, he sees a man fishing in a stream for two minutes. Then the scene jumps to a soap opera for seven minutes, followed by a commercial for a skin moisturizer. Then TV presents eight minutes of a professional football game, followed by a chef making a gourmet sauce for lamb. The next picture is a four-minute presentation about the correct way to plant tulip bulbs, with a sudden switch to the evening news. Chuck mentally wants to return to the football game but is incapable of stopping the screen from its wild, ongoing frenzy to return to the channel with the football game. With that being true, how does a victim of this disorder control and direct his life? He may conclude that people are as weird as the crazy screen.

Do Chuck's five brothers also have the condition or the gene for it?

Bear in mind, I am not a physician or psychiatrist. As a teacher, I have revealed Chuck's behaviors and characteristics, but maybe matching these to the disease is not the way to identify the condition. According to the article, "A Lifetime of Distractions" from *Harvard Health Letter*, October 2004, Vol. 29, No. 12., the condition is called Attention Deficit Disorder/Hyperactivity. A book that comes highly recommended is *Driven to Distraction* by Edward Hallowell and John Ratey. Their writings strongly suggest that my husband was afflicted with this disorder.

Meanwhile, back in Colorado, before leaving Greeley, Stan Bourgeault oriented me to my position's responsibilities. He had created a new course that I would be teaching about multi-impaired children plus the traditional courses. I rode with him in his car while he went to the post office and bank and made other necessary contacts to close matters in Greeley and pave the way for his exit from the United States. Between stops, we talked about my obligations at the college. I am very appreciative of his time and input to prepare me for my new role.

My new address, 1600 Sixth Avenue, was an old house whose furnace had been removed from under the house. For heat, I had the space heater in the dining room. I had a kitchen, living room, two bedrooms and bath, in addition to the dining room. One bedroom served as my study. My landlady expected me to gather leaves in autumn, shovel snow on Sixth Avenue and Sixteenth Street, burn trash in the large barrel in the yard, and water the lawn from spring through autumn.

Although I had completed all course work and my educational experiment in Philadelphia, I still had to continue working on my dissertation. Because any free time was devoted to this, I had little social life.

With my house in order, my class schedule determined, and Dola as my trusty guide, my full-time college faculty career was launched.

Dola, my German shepherd, encountered oscillating lawn sprinklers on campus. She stood still observing the moving spray of water. Once she figured out where the spray was going, she rushed me ahead before the water hit us in the back. She has been my only dog to cope so knowingly with those sprinklers. Her successors, Ruthie and Nannett, were less successful with sprinklers on campus. I wonder how my Waffle and Esma would have performed. I have a hunch they might be as skillful as Dola.

President Darrel Holmes was hosting a reception in the College Center for new faculty. Although I knew where the College Center was, I did not know the location in it of the Panorama Lounge. When I entered the building, a security person approached to ask where I was going. (I think he had been posted there to direct new faculty to the scheduled reception.) I explained that I was going to the Panorama Lounge but did not know where it is.

He said, "I think you are mistaken because there is an important meeting in that room this afternoon." (*So I am not eligible to attend an important meeting,* I mused.) In his thinking a blind woman could not be a new faculty member.

I insisted that the Panorama Lounge was my destination and requested that he guide me to it. He did so, though reluctantly.

When we reached the lounge on the top floor, he asked me to wait outside for a moment. I overheard him tell President Holmes that a woman with a dog guide insisted that she needed to come to this room. "I told her she was mistaken and that an important meeting is in this room. What should I do? She's just outside the door there."

"By all means, bring her in!" President Holmes directed. "She is one of our new faculty." I must admit that I enjoyed the interaction with the security person!

Because the college had hired several new faculty in Special Education and Rehabilitation that fall quarter of 1966, we were short of office space. Baker House had been bought for that purpose. I chose my office to be on the second floor in front.

When a teacher of children in the Laboratory School saw me heading to Baker House, she tried to stop me from going in. "This is not the Lab School, honey. I'll show you where it is."

When I informed her that my office was inside Baker House, she said I was mistaken. "You will be teaching children, honey, and they are in the Lab School." I assured her that I was hired to teach graduate courses in Special Education. "I'm sure you are mistaken. You will be teaching blind children, not seeing graduate students."

She assumed that I did not comprehend why I was employed by the college and that she, without seeing my contract, knew exactly what I would be doing!

One of my goals was to recognize voices of faculty and clerical staff in my department. In my first few weeks, I learned that the office staff included Dorothy and Dotty. I assumed this was one person with two names. When I asked for Dotty, I was sent to Dorothy and vice versa.

As I listened to comments, I discovered that the faculty knew less about blindness and visual impairment than I did about their specialties. Comments ranged from surprise that I could find my mailbox to concern that my office was on the second floor, a definite hazard for Grace, a blind person having to maneuver stairs! To their amazement

I could operate a paper-cutter without amputating my fingers. So I needed to educate faculty as well as students.

To bear out my claim about ignorance regarding blindness and visual impairment, I must relate an experience that occurred several years later. Two or three of the students preparing to teach children with visual disorders enrolled in an elective course dealing with another disability. After a specific class session, the students referred to came to my office and closed the door. "You won't believe what just happened in Dr. — —'s class!" In short, that faculty member informed his whole class that Grace Napier's dog was not well trained. He knew that, he claimed, because he had heard Grace give the dog a command! After the students left my office, I phoned the faculty member in question to tell him that he was in error to pass judgment on my dog's preparedness for guiding, that the dog is not my brain, that the training is based on my giving commands, and that he should not pass judgment when he knew so little about dog guides.

Another example occurred after Dr. Dean W. Tuttle arrived in our department. Dean was visually impaired and used a cane some of the time but not in every situation because he had some useful vision. I heard faculty comparing Dean and me. The speakers assumed that Dean was also totally blind but was better adjusted because he could put his hand right on the doorknob or find an empty chair without assistance at a faculty meeting or could walk outside even without his cane. These same persons thought that less well-adjusted blind individuals use dogs while the well-adjusted could travel outdoors without cane or dog. I wonder what those same faculty members thought when, perhaps ten or twelve years later, Dean trained with a Seeing Eye dog because his residual vision had deteriorated markedly. Those faculty should have known about individual differences and that in any disability group no two persons experience that disability in exactly the same amount or type of loss.

These attitudes remind me of an earlier experience in New Jersey. I had been a member of the American Association of University

Women (AAUW) for several months already, when at one meeting a member of the branch approached me belligerently. At that time, a non-member might attend only three meetings. This member challenged me with, "You have been here for more than three meetings; this is an organization for university graduates. So don't come any more."

I informed her that I was a member of this branch of AAUW. "You can't be, because blind persons don't go to college."

I assured her that I had graduated from Douglass College (formerly NJC) in New Brunswick. I inquired whether she had a master's degree. No, she did not. I revealed that I did, from New York University. She slinked away without an apology. She probably checked with the membership chairperson to verify my statements. She can be forgiven for her ignorance; after all, she was not a college faculty member in special education.

One of my Braille magazines, *Dialogue,* has a section called ABAP-ITA. Those letters stand for "Ain't Blindness a Pain in the Anatomy?" Readers submit personal embarrassing experiences that fit ABAPI-TA.

To illustrate an appropriate submission, I am including a true experience that I have had:

In the retirement community where I now reside, a warm-water pool and physical therapy are available. At one point I was receiving physical therapy in that pool on a scheduled basis. On a Sunday evening, I went to bed as usual, knowing that I had an appointment the next morning for physical therapy. Later I awakened, went to the bathroom, and then checked the time before returning to bed. Ten-fifty! *I'm going to be late for my appointment! I overslept!*

I threw off my night clothes, put on my swimsuit and a robe over it, unleashed Waffle who was sound asleep, harnessed her, and grabbed my tote with related items in it. I remembered to take my key with me and rushed to the pool!

At the building containing the pool, I found the pair of outside doors unlocked, as usual, but the inner pair of doors was locked. Why? I had never encountered those doors locked. I began knocking and then pounding on the door.

A woman came and spoke to me without unlocking the doors. "What do you want?" she asked. I explained that I needed to go to the pool for therapy; my therapist was expecting me!

She said, "The time is going toward midnight. Your therapist is not here. Go home."

Because of being totally blind, I was unaware that it was dark outside and not daylight. Besides, I had heard cars coming and going and people outdoors talking—just like daytime activities. Later, someone reminded me that shifts were changing for employees and summer evenings were pleasant enough for people to be outside to visit with others. ABAPITA!

My experiences with the arrogance and ignorance of supposedly learned individuals may inspire *Dialogue* to initiate an additional section called ARAPITA—"Ain't Rudeness a Pain in the Anatomy?"— where we readers can record tidbits expressed by foolish seeing persons.

I also notice that when I am called "Honey" by the ignorant, they are at the same time demeaning me. This reminds me of a veterinarian in New Jersey who, when he was ready to work with my dog and me, called out, "You're next, blind lady!" I would tell him my name each time, but next time I was "blind lady" again even though he addressed by name all other clients! I sought a different veterinarian.

Of course, some individuals reveal their ignorance about matters not pertaining to blindness. For instance, in early September of my first month in Greeley, a woman came to my door to urge me to vote in the upcoming primary election. She asked, "You will be voting, won't you?" I said that I would not, whereupon she launched her unpatriotic citizen speech.

When she finally finished, I said, "It would be illegal for me to vote." Again she erupted with her speech about how voting is *not* illegal.

When I could squeeze in a word, I explained that I had lived in Colorado less than a month and would not be permitted to vote. With an "Oh," she turned and departed.

Shifting now, in October of that quarter, I flew to Louisville, Kentucky to the American Printing House for the Blind (APH). This is a federally-sponsored agency to manufacture educational materials, books, and equipment for visually-impaired and blind students from preschool age through twelfth grade, doled out by the quota system. Once a year, every educational program has to name students officially enrolled and send the information to a state office that forwards it to APH. Those numbers are then totaled for the whole country and divided into the budget for that fiscal year. It might then indicate that APH could provide, say, $147 per student in materials, books, and equipment. This becomes the "Federal Quota" for that year. Some school programs might exist on only that much money per student. For instance, if a Braille class had ten students, the program could order (without paying currency) ten times $147 worth of materials, books, and equipment that year. A residential program having 139 students could spend 139 times $147 that year. Happily, some programs had their own money with which to purchase additional materials, books, and equipment. APH accepts orders for additional items beyond the quota allocation so long as currency covers the additional order.

At this two- or three-day conference, APH displays its new products and has discussions about educational trends and needs. APH conducts tours of the entire plant where most products are constructed by hand, such as three-dimensional maps and globes, devices for computational purposes, Braille books with masters on zinc plates, binding procedures, large-print books with heavy enough paper not to bleed ink from the opposite side and with no glossy surface to produce glare, etc.

It was at this meeting that I met Maurice Olsen, to whom I referred earlier.

In another year, my new department head suggested I attend a federally-sponsored meeting in Washington, DC, relative to employment of adults with disabilities. Each of us wore a badge showing our name and home location. We listened to speeches but had no opportunity for feedback.

When I returned home, I wrote a letter to the chairman of that event, suggesting that in the future badges indicate the type of work each attendee performs. After all, the conference was about employment, because we had never learned the range and variety of employment positions represented by the attendees. His response in a letter to me was, in essence, "We have always done it this way. We see no reason to change procedures." I never attended it again. It was obvious that the leaders had no desire to hear from *us*; instead, they wanted us to be impressed with appreciation of what the federal government was doing for us.

Other early professional trips included conventions of the Council for Exceptional Children (CEC) and the American Association of Instructors of the Blind (AAIB) and a newer organization, Association for Education and Rehabilitation for the Blind and Visually Impaired (AER). During one of CEC's conventions, I had previously heard the same speakers several times before who were now lined up to fill the section about blind students, so I decided to attend another specialty section, namely, learning disabilities. On the last day I met someone in the blindness field. She was surprised to see me because she had not seen me earlier in the week. She wanted to know why I had been absent. I explained my rationale for attending a section on learning disabilities. She acted as if I were a traitor to my own specialty. I explained that one specialty can learn from another specialty, and I was open to receive new information that might be practicable with blind children. I don't think I converted her to my approach.

Some years, I was a presenter at these conventions. Too often, I think, the same few speakers constitute the "speakers' bureau" for the blindness field.

Frequently, I fear, convention attendees abuse the privilege of attending conventions at employers' expense by attending very few or none of the sessions, instead indulging in parties or bull sessions, shopping, or sight-seeing. When I was employed by the New Jersey State Commission for the Blind, those who had attended conventions were required afterward to share with colleagues what they had learned; this did not mean a three-minute review of the whole convention but presentations in depth to benefit those who had not attended. I think that colleges and universities should have the same requirement. After all, not every faculty member can attend every convention. Some faculty need to stay on campus to cover classes for students.

I remember one faculty meeting much later when the chairperson of the department needed to know who planned to attend a convention and who would be available to cover more classes than usual.

I raised my hand to indicate that I was planning to attend the convention. At that moment the male faculty member sitting beside me leaned heavily against me to whisper, "We can share a room!" In afterthought at that moment, I should have said in a very loud voice for all to hear, "You want to share a room with me, sir! Sit somewhere else, scumball!"

Instead, I said nothing but pulled away from him. Rather than attend the convention, I chose to stay on campus. I did not want that man to think I was interested in any rendezvous with him.

However, I had timely opportunity to report the episode sometime later. Because this same male faculty was being charged with some offense, the institution was conducting a hearing. He had contacted me to come to the hearing to speak in his behalf. I had no intention to do so. I stayed away from the proceedings.

The chairman of our department visited each of his faculty members to ask whether he or she planned to speak for or against the man in question. I said that I had no intention to speak on his behalf and related my reason. The chairman then summoned someone from the dean's office and asked me to repeat what I had just revealed. I never knew the nature of the charges brought against him. I was not interested in knowing the specific offense with which he was being charged. At the end of the academic year, he left, not to return.

Another male faculty member (younger than I and also married) rode a bicycle much of the time. More than once, when I was walking on Tenth Avenue, he called out loudly, "Grace Napier, Miss Sex-Pot of CSC!" I had given him no encouragement to relate to me that way. Many students and homeowners in their front yards or on front porches might have wondered what was happening between him and me.

Because males were more numerous than females on the college faculty, I would venture to imagine that other women faculty had to contend with similar offenses from other males. Reporting him would have been only a matter of he said/she said with males protecting other males. (This was before federal legislation addressing gender harassment.)

During my vacation at the end of my first twelve-month contract, I underwent thyroid surgery for hyperthyroidism in which condition the surgeon suspected cancer. Consequently, he did extensive exploration in my neck.

Soon after being returned to my hospital room after thyroidectomy, I realized that my former roommate, Mary (actual names have been forgotten), had been moved to a different floor and that Betty was now my roommate but not very communicative, for whatever reason.

Then a technician came into the room and went directly to the other bed. Addressing Betty as Mary, he said, "I need to draw blood." Betty did not protest that she was Betty and not Mary.

I felt that I had to intervene before a dreadful medical mistake was permitted to occur, namely, using Mary's name but Betty's blood for analysis, and possible misdiagnosis of condition.

With my very sore and hoarse throat, I tried to communicate with the technician by squawking my words of caution. Annoyed with my noise, the technician came to my bed and asked, "What do you want?"

I explained hoarsely, "That woman is not Mary. Mary was moved to a different floor. This woman is Betty. Read her ID bracelet."

He thanked me and left without drawing Betty's blood.

OF course, for awhile as I recuperated from this surgery, my neck and throat were extremely tender. The first time I walked on campus to check my mail during my recuperation, I encountered the same man (who rode a bicycle referred to earlier) in the corridor. He slapped me on the back of my neck. I winced and almost collapsed from pain. I protested that I had had thyroid surgery. He never apologized but said, "Your thyroid is in the front, not the back," as if I did not know that fact. Not much later, he was gone, without my knowing whether his contract had not been renewed or whether he had chosen to leave for "greener pastures."

That year the announcement was made that faculty would receive an eight percent increase in salary. When my first check containing the increase arrived, I calculated the difference from my preceding check. Mine was an eleven percent increase. Assuming that a calculation error had occurred, I went to my chairman to point out this discrepancy. That is when he told me that I had been underpaid by my first department chairman who had died since I had arrived on campus, four years earlier. Although I appreciated his correcting the problem, I never received compensation for the shortages of the preceding years.

Financial errors remind me of another incident. Several years later, our administrative assistant directed me to sign my summer contract. I reminded her that I did not have a summer contract, that I was on a twelve-month contract. She insisted that I sign it, because a new system was being instituted. I signed, still with reluctance.

Later in the summer, I received a pay envelope containing two checks. I phoned the payroll office to report that a mistake had been made, that I had received two checks. The woman with whom I spoke referred to my records and assured me that no mistake had been made, that I was scheduled to receive two checks. I did not understand the reasoning but accepted her word.

A day or so later, the head of the payroll office phoned me in an obviously angry mood. "Why are you trying to cheat the university by keeping two checks when you know you are not eligible for two checks?" I tried to explain that I had reported receiving two checks on payday. "What was the woman's name?" she challenged me.

"I don't know her name. She did not say; I did not ask." I suggested that she ask each of the women in her office whether Grace Napier had phoned on payday to report receiving two checks.

She said that because one of those checks was an error, she was going to deduct so much each month from my pay until the amount had been repaid by me. She never phoned again to apologize about having learned from a woman in her office that I had, indeed, reported the matter. In truth, I was not supposed to sign a summer contract; the administrative assistant in our department was in error in requiring me to sign a summer contract.

Relative to equipment I needed for my students and prospective teachers in the beginning Braille course, I routinely prepared worksheets to use in class. Of course, each was an original. I requested a Thermoform Duplicator that produces each copy in a matter of seconds. I heard nothing in the way of a response to my requisition. I repeated that memorandum several times, emphasizing that seeing faculty had options by which to make print copies without having each sheet as an original. Why then did I have to make each sheet an original, requiring much time, unnecessary now that the Thermoform Duplicator was available? Eventually, I received the machine and supplies for it.

During my first five years, I was denied use of college (state-owned) cars to transport me to sites where my students were enrolled in practicum experience as graduate student teachers. I explained that I would engage a licensed driver each time. No, that was unacceptable. When I visited students in Colorado, I used either buses or drivers' vehicles.

In 1971, when Dr. Dean W. Tuttle, also legally blind, was hired, both of us were then permitted access to state cars with our selection of licensed drivers. (Why was my right to use state cars denied? Because I am a woman and not a man?)

Related to this topic is another experience worth recording here. Bob Crouse and I were scheduled to drive to Colorado Springs to supervise various students. I offered to make the phone call to reserve a car for the designated day. When I phoned the garage and stated our need for a car, Dick Weinmeister (who has since died) seemed to be taking notes relative to the car requisition. Afterward, he phoned our Special Education office and spoke with one of the secretaries. He said, in essence, "I have a car request from Grace Napier. I have a question. Can her dog really drive a car?"

The secretary said, "Yes, of course. Didn't you know that?" at which time she began to giggle. He asked, "What's so funny?"

She became serious and said, "No, the dog can't drive a car. Grace is going with Bob Crouse who will be driving!"

Earlier, when I arrived on campus, I was designated area director. With the additional professional expertise of Mel Weishahn, who taught legally blind children during the day in the Laboratory School plus one graduate course per quarter in the field of visual impairment and blindness, the two of us were the area faculty.

The enrollment in the summer quarter was larger than any of the other three quarters. Because of that fact, I felt that another faculty during the summer would be beneficial to students. With that in mind, I spoke to Dr. Tony Vaughan, Department Chairman, about my hiring someone for the coming summer; I had Dr. Frank Andrews in mind. He had recently retired as superintendent of the Maryland School for the Blind. I anticipated that he would teach a course on history in the blindness field. Dr. Vaughan agreed to the proposal. "When you have someone who agrees to do this, come to me, so that we can draw up a contract," he approved.

After I wrote to Dr. Andrews, he responded with eagerness to be involved with us in teacher preparation. When I returned to Tony to have a contract that could be mailed to Dr. Andrews, Tony said, "I never gave you permission to hire anyone!" I asked Tony to write to Dr. Andrews to explain that he (Tony) had changed his mind. Tony refused to do this. Consequently, I had to write to Dr. Andrews to break the news to him, after he had already compiled a reading list and course outline for students.

The next spring, I still felt the need for another faculty member during the forthcoming summer quarter. Assuming that Tony would be too embarrassed to let this happen again, I approached him about hiring a faculty member to teach calculation by means of the modified abacus during the summer. Again, he said, when I had found some-one who had agreed to do it I should let him know so that a contract might be sent. I had Dr. Tim Cramner in mind to contact. Tim agreed with enthusiasm. When I returned to Tony about the contract, he did exactly the same thing to me! Again, I had the unhappiness of hav-ing to contact Tim to notify him that my department head had with-drawn his approval. I imagine that both Frank and Tim think that I had been playing games with them or that I had hired others whom I considered more qualified. Not so! In 1970, Dr. Vaughan succumbed to a massive stroke and died; he had not been to a medical doctor in ten years! I have to wonder whether the forthcoming stroke had al-ready damaged his memory so that he had no recollection of my two visits with him requesting permission to engage one faculty each of those two summers with his verbal agreements. I learned later that other faculty had noticed lapses in his memory also.

Shifting gears now, agonizing, I knew many blind children who were not permitted outside their yards alone. In reality, they had graduated from twelfth grade but could not walk to the nearest mailbox to deposit a letter or go around the block to buy a loaf of bread or a quart of milk. I remembered my childhood when I mailed letters but had to walk two and a half blocks around our five-sided block to do so. I also went to buy basics for Mamma from Glover's store. Going in another direction, I crossed a side street to buy groceries from Schwartz's store a block away on another street. Yet, on the contrary, I knew about other blind children who had been denied similar opportunities.

I conjured up in my mind teachers who could teach both academics and orientation and mobility (O&M). An O&M instructor is trained to teach blind individuals (adults) to travel on foot safely, effectively, and smoothly with a long cane with techniques designed by Dr. Richard Hoover. His techniques have become known as the Hoover Method with the Hoover cane. Orientation, as a term, refers to knowing where one is in relation to other objects such as knowing where the mailbox at the corner is in relation to oneself when on one's own front porch, for example, or being able to explain how to reach the bus stop at a different corner. Mobility is being able to walk to that mailbox or to that bus stop elsewhere.

Because I was concerned about these blind children and adolescents, I wrote a grant proposal to the federal government describing my suggested program and the need for funds to hire a qualified O&M instructor who could plan that part of the curriculum and add it to the existing courses that prepared teachers to teach academics: Braille reading and writing, typewriting, mathematical calculation on a variety of devices, reading embossed or three-dimensional maps and globes, skills of daily living, organizational skills, study habits, signature writing, listening skills, etc.

My grant emphasized the fact that a school district with only a few blind or visually-impaired students could not afford to hire two teachers—one for academics and one for O&M. My proposal would solve that problem by enabling a school district to hire one teacher who possessed both sets of skills.

My proposal was approved and funded by the federal government agency where Josephine L. Taylor, the same one formerly at the New Jersey State commission for the Blind, then worked.

We were extremely fortunate to employ Robert Crouse who later earned the doctorate. At the end of his first year, we hired David Kappan to implement Crouse's curriculum, integrating it with the existing academic sequence, for students working for the master's degree in education of visually-impaired or blind children and youth. This prototype has been adopted by many universities.

When the new design of our program became known throughout the country, I received both criticism and commendation. Some persons thought that I was setting myself up to teach O&M; wrong! Others encouraged me to pursue my goal, saying that this kind of program was needed.

The year after we hired David Kappan, we hired Dean Tuttle. Kappan, Tuttle, and I were paid from state money. All other faculty in this area of specialty were paid from federal funds gained from approved grant applications. When Crouse moved on, we hired additional faculty so that at any one time we numbered six as the maximum.

Soon after that proposal was funded by the federal government, I wrote another proposal. Tony Vaughan phoned me after I had submitted it to him, who then was expected to approve it and send it to the appropriate office on campus for further approval and forward it to Washington, according to protocol. Instead, he told me that he was not reading it or signing it because he knew that that Washington office had already decided whose proposals it would fund! Writing a grant proposal is a major undertaking; sometimes the finished product is the thickness of a metropolitan telephone directory, yet my department head would not read it or approve it, even though my previous proposal had been approved for funding! What was wrong with that man?

I related the incident to Josephine L. Taylor who became very angry, "We do NOT decide beforehand which institution will receive the money. We read and study the proposals after the submission deadline before we make those important decisions." However, without Vaughan's approval, my proposal could go nowhere!

Another phase of the program was preparing teachers to work with blind or visually-impaired, multi-impaired children. Some of our students chose to be certified in all three disciplines; others selected academic/O&M or academic/multi-impaired.

In the summer of 1973, as a blind consumer, I trained at Telesensory Systems, Inc. (TSI) in California to read print material with a machine called the Optacon. Later I enrolled in TSI's teacher-preparation course, both at my own expense.

The next year, the University of Pittsburgh, through the efforts of Dr. Mary Moore, extended invitations to one faculty member at each of nine other universities to come to Pittsburgh for a five-day conference to accomplish three tasks:

1) To write a grant proposal to the federal government proposing to teach blind children to read print materials with Optacons;

2) To prepare a manual containing print materials suitable for children and adolescents; and

3) To become acquainted with the operation of the Optacon. I was fortunate to be already trained by TSI in the Optacon's use and to have previous experience of more than a year.

During the ensuing year, Dr. Moore sent us materials to read and critique in the first two objectives above, which feedback information she incorporated into the final proposal document.

Then we learned the exciting news that the federal government had approved our proposal. Each of the ten universities involved in the National Optacon Dissemination Program represented would be receiving five Optacon stations. Each university would educate at least ten teachers per year to enable them to teach children. Each teacher so trained would receive an Optacon station to use with his or her blind pupils. Each teacher would also receive a stipend to enable him or her to live in Greeley for a week of training.

Although this was originally planned as a three-year undertaking, it was extended for a fourth year, amounting to millions of dollars in equipment and actual cash.

I took my role seriously, probably teaching more teachers than anyone except perhaps Dr. Moore. For four years, I used a week in March between quarters, a week in June between quarters, a week in August (part of my official vacation), and a week in December between quarters to teach ten teachers at each session. In addition, during summer quarter, I taught Optacon to students on campus for ten weeks. Altogether I taught approximately 170 teachers in four years while our obligation was to teach ten teachers a year for four years. Many years later, I am still using my own Optacon. Sadly, I fear that most of the Optacons disseminated during the four years of the official National Optacon Dissemination Program are now gathering dust or locked away in closets unused because of the introduction of talking computers. Later, when retired, I was asked to give Optacon demonstrations or brief instructional sessions on campus, but much of the equipment was missing from the cabinet where I had stored each item.

The government grant also provided a stipend for each of the ten university faculty members involved in the National Optacon Dissemination Program. My employer, however, the University of Northern Colorado (formerly Colorado State College), would not permit me to receive the money, "because you already receive full salary." I explained that each of the training sessions that I scheduled between quarters was above and beyond my regular full load of courses. I contacted other faculty throughout the country to inquire whether their employers had permitted them to accept the money for their involvement in the Optacon program. Each had received the stipend of $2,000. This was for four years of work (sixteen weeks of teaching or equivalent to a semester of teaching each day from eight in the morning to five in the afternoon five days a week); this stipend was only once for four years, not once for each year. I had not written this stipend into the program. Josephine L. Taylor in Washington, DC, had seen fit to include stipends to university faculty to reward them for the extra time and effort each faculty member had invested in the program above and beyond normal course loads assigned by the university. In addition to the actual teaching in class, responsibilities included much correspondence with prospective students coming from all over the United States, correspondence with Washington, DC, with transporting equipment, manuals, and supplies to the classroom in the same building or to a different building before the first day of teaching, arranging to have the classroom locked overnight each time to protect the equipment, and returning the equipment, books, and supplies from the classroom at the end of the week back to the storage area. Apparently, the university valued my work above and beyond my regular load a year not worth even $500 to acknowledge my involvement in a national program funded by the federal government. That stipend to university faculty came from federal funds, not from the university or the State of Colorado.

Do you see a definite pattern of discrimination in several areas where I have been involved in legitimate college/university work? This is a sad commentary on an institution that prided itself on having a Department and a School of Special Education and Rehabilitation. These included placement of my first and second classes of the day at opposite ends of the campus with no time after the first class to help students after each session during my first quarter, shortage in salary for four years, no access to state cars for five years, and denial of the stipend written into the federal National Optacon Dissemination Program. Since when is working above and beyond assigned course loads not recognized and rewarded? Aside from the Optacon Program, I usually taught four or five courses each quarter. I had eight o'clock courses in the morning and also evening classes every quarter while some of our faculty never taught before nine or ten in the morning and never an evening class. Even more comes later.

To keep my "stipend" in our Greeley program rather than have it returned to Washington, I engaged a teacher from TSI to co-teach with me. She was paid an honorarium plus money for transportation and living per diem while here in Greeley. She came several times until my "stipend" was depleted.

During my twenty years at the university, I taught a wide variety of courses. My previous experience at Royer-Greaves School helped me tremendously in teaching "Multi-Impaired Blind Children." Other courses included "Beginning Literary Braille" with a weekly laboratory session, "Survey of the Blindness Field," "Agencies in the Field of Special Education and Rehabilitation," "Structure and Function of the Eye" in collaboration with ophthalmologists, "Introduction to Special Education" with large enrollments, "Techniques of Daily Living," "Reading with the Optacon," "Career Education for Elementary-level Children" (not vocational education), "Improving Listening Skills for Living and Learning," "Supervision of Practicum Students," and "Supervision of Doctoral Candidates." I had tried introducing two new courses, one in calculating with the modified Abacus and one reading biography and autobiography in special education and rehabilitation to gain information not supplied in textbooks, but both requests were denied. The second of these would apply to the entire student body in special education and rehabilitation, perhaps as an elective.

When Dr. Sloat was head of Special Education and Rehabilitation, he complained to me that we faculty who taught evening courses in the Denver metropolitan area were getting rich while the department needed some of that money. He said that he would confiscate my check at the end of the quarter and use it to meet needs elsewhere. I knew that legally he could not do so. At the end of the quarter, I took my check to show him the amount, $108.00. He was surprised that it was so little for teaching ten weeks; he did not take the check. What he failed to take into consideration was that my course had small enrollment because the population of blind children is much smaller than other special needs groups, such as the retarded or hearing impaired. Therefore, I had fewer teachers needing my course than other special education teachers in the metropolitan area. I had not offered to teach that evening course expecting to have a huge amount in my check but rather to render a service to teachers in the metropolitan area, those who could not commute to Greeley for the same course. The sum of $108.00 was puny remuneration for teaching thirty hours!

In the 1980-1981 academic year, the university was between presidents. Instead of a president, we had someone whose major job, it seemed, was to reduce the number of individuals on the faculty. We were offered one of three options:

1) a twenty-five percent reduction in work and salary,

2) no increase in salary for an indefinite period of time, or

3) retirement no later than the summer of 1986.

These choices affected faculty with the greatest number of years of service. Those persons with approximately fourteen years' service or fewer were not involved. I had fifteen years at that time. I chose to retire by August 1986. This option would give me exactly twenty years of service and a pension of fifty percent of earnings. Being a person of high energy, I had not planned to retire at age 64. Now some faculty are seventy-five or older and still working on the faculty. Some faculty who had approximately seventeen years chose option one or two above, trying to help the institution. They were retained for only one year and then terminated, left high and dry without a pension! Some of the faculty affected by the options grouped together and engaged one or more attorneys. The outcome of their unification in litigation was that the university was found to be in the wrong by forcing some faculty to retire with option three above. The legal decision was that an employer may not tell employees when to retire. Those in the group who had legal counsel were awarded a handsome amount paid by the university and reinstated.

After a legal decision had been reached, many of the faculty who had chosen retirement received attractive severance pay. I received not a dime!

I authored *A Manual for Teaching Braille Reading to Adventitiously-Blinded Adults*, which uses a different approach from previous manuals, namely, postponing the teaching of Braille contractions as long as possible to be sure that students really knew letters of the alphabet in words and sentences before introducing contractions. I must insert here that before contractions are presented, every uncontracted word in Braille has been selected carefully in order to use only those words that do not ever have contractions. For instance, instead of using *street* that uses the *ST* sign *(before the st sign was introduced)*, I used *road* or *lane* or *drive* in order to present only correct Braille throughout the entire text. *When contractions are introduced before the alphabet has been mastered, students are confronted with confusing symbols: Is this an e or an en sign, a g or a gg sign, an a or an ea sign, etc.?* The book contains a Student's Manual and a Teacher's Manual.

I never received even partial credit from my department chairperson in my annual review for my effort because the book had not been published before the annual assessment, though I had completed the text merely days before. Furthermore, the department chairperson was not qualified to pass judgment on the quality of the manual. He would not have understood the difference between a composition sign and a termination sign! (He did not stay on campus for twenty years as I had but moved frequently from one institution to another.) Some faculty like to build a long resume of courses taught, membership on committees, committees chaired, conventions attended, presentations made where, etc. Unfortunately, such a compilation has no rating sheet to indicate the quality of the work performed.

On a lighter note, I recall teaching an evening course on campus in McKee Hall on the fourth floor in a windowless classroom. About halfway through the session, the lights went out. Assuming that this was a temporary outage, I continued the class, saying, "You can still listen to me and participate in discussion. This is what totally blind individuals experience all of the time.

When the room was still dark, a male student volunteered to leave the classroom and find a window through which to evaluate the situation. When he returned, he reported that he saw no lights anywhere on or off the campus. Therefore, the problem was outside our building.

At that point, I decided to dismiss class, but I had to organize the students for what would be a frightening experience for some. I went to the closed classroom door and spoke to the students in a calm voice, assuring them that I could lead them safely out of the building. Without the elevator ability to operate, we had to use the stairs. I directed them to put on their wraps and gather up their notebooks and briefcases. I said, "Come toward my voice here at the door." Then I instructed them to make a human chain by holding someone's hand.

Then with my dog and I at the head of the line, we led the procession to the top of the stairs. Halting there, I said, "I am at the first step down. My partner is aware of this fact. As each of you is told about this step down, tell the person immediately behind you. We don't want anyone to fall." We proceeded down the first flight and turned where I stopped again to alert the person behind me of the next step down. We continued this process until we were on ground level, and all fifteen or twenty students were ready to exit the building with no further steps down. Outside the building, students were on their own to find their respective vehicles, while my dog and I walked home. I learned the next day that an auto accident crashed a car into a pole, damaging the transformer causing the widespread outage.

When I was about to retire, Dr. Tuttle encouraged me to consider teaching one course a quarter in retirement. I said that as long as I did that, the administration might be very slow to fill the position I was vacating. However, if I were completely out of the picture, perhaps Tuttle would see the vacancy filled sooner. That position was not filled for a year or two. (Secretly, I surmised that I would be paid less to teach in retirement than male faculty in retirement. I had my fill of discrimination.)

I suggested earlier that other women faculty were probably also harassed as I had been. I will relate an incident as an example: I overheard the Dean of the College of Education confront in a stairwell the Chair of the Department of Elementary Education, a woman! He reprimanded her, with other faculty and students moving up and down the stairs during this abusive tirade! I heard him yelling, "You do it my way or be fired!" Why didn't he request that she meet with him in his office, close the door, and then discuss the matter quietly as two professionals? His behavior revealed what he thought of a female colleague, Elaine! How did he become Dean in the first place? Was this problem of discrimination against women rampant throughout most universities then or uniquely pervasive at our institution?

Shortly before I retired, federal funding of our area's program ended. Tuttle taught during his retirement to keep the program operating with only two state-funded positions in our program. Although the third was funded, that person worked in the office of the College of Education, not assisting our program to survive. What is passing as a "program" now is a mere shadow of its former self. The three of us—Tuttle, Kappan, and Napier – had devoted more than seventy years to the program with a national and international reputation, only to see administrators permit it to disintegrate. Because of its international prominence, we had students from Germany, Spain, New Zealand, Taiwan, Sri Lanka, Iraq, Saudi Arabia, and Canada.

My annual evaluations were by faculty who never visited in my classroom during class sessions. I remember one year when a man from another area of special education evaluated me; his complaint was that I am too strict with students! He probably listened to student opinions but never bothered to learn the other side of the report. The next year, Dan McAlees evaluated me. He asked about the minus points on my previous evaluation. I explained that the evaluator said I was too strict with students. McAlees said, "Don't change. Continue to be strict; you are on the graduate level." He turned the minus points into plus points.

Teacher preparation, as I view it, is equivalent to law school or medical school or engineering. This is professional preparation, not freshman year. This reminds me of a graduate student who complained that misspellings should not enter into grades because this is not an English class. I asked her, "What language are you speaking or writing if not English?" I reminded her that as a special education teacher, she would be writing letters or reports to supervisors, principals, nurses, medical doctors, psychologists, therapists, and parents. "If they find misspelled words written by you, they will wonder where you received your degree and question whether you are qualified to work with the student about whom you are writing." I fear that I had not convinced her of the importance of correct grammar and spelling, especially of words in her professional vocabulary. I remember having one or more students write "advantageous" for "adventitious."

Before moving on, I wish to record here three episodes:

1)   While in an elevator on campus, only a man and I were passengers. He said in a very loud voice, "How are you today?"
     I responded in a quiet voice, "I am very well, thank you.

And incidentally, I am blind, not deaf. You don't have to shout at me to make me hear. I have very keen hearing!"

2) Another experience on an elevator occurred at Temple University Medical Center. As the door opened on seventh floor, I stepped out when a man said, "Ophthalmology is to the left."

I turned right and said, "I'm going to Audiology."

Hearing my words, he clicked his tongue and said, "First her eyes; now her ears!"

Hearing his tone of tragedy, I turned on my heel to say, "Sir, may I speak with you a moment?" When I had his attention, I added, "Sir, you have misinterpreted my heading for Audiology. I am a doctoral student at Temple University. One of my courses is in audiology. I have a specific number of hours to complete in the Audiology Clinic. I am not losing my hearing as you had assumed. Have a great day." I don't know who he was, whether a medical student, a doctor on staff, a patient going to one of the clinics, or someone visiting a patient in the hospital.

3) This next incident did not involve me directly, but I have read about it and use the anecdote in my introductory survey sections: An American had been invited to sit at the head table at a state dinner in Washington, DC. Arriving early, he sat at his assigned place, enjoying his status at the head table.

Later an Asian gentleman arrived, seating himself beside the American. The American wondered why this foreigner was at the head table. He must have made a mistake and surely someone will come and escort the Asian man to his assigned seat out there where he would not be so conspicuous as an outsider.

No one came to take him away. Soon the first course arrived. Both men began to eat in silence. Then the American thought, "I should show this outsider that we Americans are friendly and outgoing," whereupon he said to the Asian man, "Likey soupy!"

Although the Asian man smiled, he said nothing. The American concluded, "Just as I thought. He doesn't understand a word of English. Well, I tried to interact with him. There's nothing else I can do. I don't understand why he is at this head table with the rest of us celebrities."

The master of ceremonies assumed his responsibilities, telling a few jokes, recognizing American distinguished personages present. When ready, he introduced the persons at the head table and referred to the speaker of the evening, listing his many enviable accomplishments as Diplomat from China to the United States. "It gives me great pleasure to introduce to you Dr. Wellington Koo."

The Asian gentleman stood and delivered his speech in flawless English. When he finished, he sat down during thunderous applause. Dr. Koo whispered to the American, "Likey speechy?"

I think that this account holds a weighty and timely message for students entering the field of special education or rehabilitation. It is this: Don't judge anyone by the color of his or her skin or other difference, such as sitting in a wheelchair, using a person to sign for the deaf, using a dog guide, having a speech impediment, etc. He or she is probably not below your station in life. He or she may have many more accomplishments than you do. If you wonder, how can he or she do such-and-such when deaf (or blind, physically disabled, having impaired speech, etc.), just because you now could not do those tasks without your hearing or vision or ability to move physically, etc., remember that those individuals have undergone much indepth therapy or education to overcome each disability and to compensate by developing other competencies. In short, the pompous American in the anecdote was much less successful than Dr. Koo, put down by the American.

I enjoyed teaching and interacting with students. Some students regarded me as too strict and too demanding of their performances. So be it! I wanted each graduate to be like a Miss Katharine Taylor in the life of each child who is blind, as she had been in my life in elementary grades and throughout my life! These teachers were likely to be the first positive influence in the lives of blind and/or visually-impaired students, as Miss Taylor had been in mine. That goal is achievable only when graduate students realize their high calling in the profession of teaching.

One student tried frequently to finagle a different requirement from the one I had set. When a term paper was assigned, he preferred to do a project; when a test was scheduled, he'd prefer to give an oral report; etc. What would he do on the job when required to do a specific assignment? All of us have preferences, but when a superior on the faculty at a school designates a task to be completed, we comply rather than try to negotiate something more to our liking. Instead, the employee should strive to be proficient in writing reports, in oral presentations, and in research to gather facts. This kind of employee is more valuable to a school system than one who tries to change requirements.

I recall a student who usually came shuffling into my eight a.m. class five or ten minutes late. After one more tardiness, I took him aside to explain that this class begins at eight a.m. and that I expect him to be in his seat ready to begin before that. His response was, "On the job, I won't have to begin until nine o'clock."

I asked, "From which planet did you come? Teachers do not walk into the building when children do. Teachers are given a specific time to report for duty, well ahead of students' arrival."

After he graduated and began teaching, he sent me a letter. In essence, he wrote, "I have to begin teaching at seven-thirty. You were right!" I treasure his letter and his willingness to acknowledge the fact.

On the first day of each course, students received course objectives. Some students wanted to eliminate this objective or that objective as unimportant. I asked, "How much teaching have you done in the field of blindness?" The answer was usually none. Yet, with no teaching experience, novices wanted to determine what course content should be omitted. That's akin to an apprentice asking the construction contractor, "Can we build this house without nails or messy concrete?"

As an experiment at the opening of a course, I asked the class, "What questions do you have relative to the field of blindness that you are entering?" They had none, even though this was the first of their graduate studies in the field of education of children with visual disorders. Hadn't they any curiosity about this field they were entering? Some questions might be: How many blind children are in our country? What causes blindness in children? What help is available for parents when they learn that their child is blind? When blind children reach maturity, do they have any chance of being employed and supporting themselves? How many blind students am I likely to be teaching? Does Greeley have a library for the blind that I can visit?

Some students may assume that because the teacher is blind, he or she is also deaf and unaware of inappropriate behavior. Two women were whispering for a long time after class had begun and obviously were not listening to class proceedings. Very annoyed with this behavior, I looked in their direction and said, "Either complete your conversation in the corridor if it is that important, or terminate it now and begin paying attention to what is happening in this room." They were angry with me for embarrassing them in a group situation! Their behavior embarrassed them, not the teacher. This was graduate school, not kindergarten.

In a large introductory class of approximately 240 or more undergraduate students, I heard a student turning pages in a newspaper, probably the campus paper that was available that morning. Before class officially begins, reading a newspaper is acceptable, but when the instructor begins, students are expected to be ready to start as well. After class opened, I continued to hear the student turn pages in the newspaper. (Newspaper has a distinct sound, different from pages in a book or magazine.) After several minutes of this, I was aware that the student's attention was elsewhere than on the class topic of the day.

I stopped speaking in mid-sentence, looked in the student's direction, and said firmly, "Put that newspaper away!" I never heard that noise for the remainder of the session.

After class, a male student came to me. He identified himself without name as the one who had been reading the newspaper. He said, "I thought you are blind."

I explained that I am blind – "But I am not deaf!"

In a much smaller class, students were writing answers to a test. After class, a student reported to me that a specific student had been cheating by copying from other students' papers but had already left the room. I explained that at that point, I could do nothing; he was gone. "Let's see how well he did on the test," I said. Because the test was objective in type, the answers were either right or wrong, and my personal feelings did not enter into the scoring, as some might wonder. Of all the students, the alleged cheater received the lowest grade, low enough to be failing. So the situation solved itself.

Even though I was present in big classes during tests, I used our graduate students on stipends to monitor the students, one monitor going up the steps to the highest level while the other started from the top and came down to the lowest level. The two coordinated their watchfulness.

After tests in big classes, my assistant, a student receiving a stipend, scored the papers with a key from me. Afterward, he or she read to me the name of each student and his/her number of answers correct, which information I Brailled for my official record. I then established the range for A, B, C, and D, along with mode and median. For an individual test, I typed that information. In class, I had a student write all of that on the chalkboard. Then each student, after receiving his or her paper, knew the corresponding grade.

In these big classes, lecture was the primary mode of delivery. Nevertheless, I encouraged students to ask questions, and I succeeded in having some discussion. Maybe only fifty students participated during the ten weeks, but the remainder of more than two hundred benefited from listening.

On the first day of a course, I announced, "In this course, do not raise your hand to get my attention. I won't see your hand. Instead, speak up; interrupt me, if necessary." True, in a large class, I did not really become acquainted with students because of blindness. Seeing faculty, however, did not do much better than I in such large enrollments.

During a fall quarter, a young man came to my office. He was a freshman in my Introduction to Special Education course, he informed me. He had difficulty clarifying why he had come. I was patient and encouraged him to talk. Finally, he was able to say that he thought I might be angry with him but that he had discovered that he did not want to be a special education major and wanted to drop the course. I assured him that I was not angry and that freshman year especially was a great opportunity to discover his preferences and to pursue them. Knowing which fields of study were of less interest to him was important information in his search for a major. How sad it would be to make this discovery in his senior year. He departed with a lighter heart than when he had arrived, I am sure.

A student enrolled in my beginning Braille course. Because his major was not in my field, I asked why he was enrolled in this course. There might have been a variety of answers: My grandmother is going blind; my five-year-old nephew is blind; etc. Instead, he told me that he planned to be a medical doctor and needed to know Braille in order to communicate with his blind patients!

I explained that he can talk to and with his blind patients. Furthermore, by the time he was ready to open his practice, he would have forgotten whatever Braille he had learned in class. He insisted on staying. About two weeks later when we were involved in the technical rules for using or not using contractions, he dropped the course. He may have been among those persons who think "If a blind person can do it, it can't be very difficult. This will be an easy way to earn an A." I have heard professionals say something similar to me! When I was a graduate student in a methods class at Temple University and brought my typewriter to class for a scheduled test, the professor said that I did not need to type the test, that I might write it in Braille. I was surprised that he knew Braille and said so. He said that he did not know Braille but could figure it out; after all, he was a mathematician! I protested that this was not likely. He insisted. I decided to take him up on his dare. After class, I gave him my pages and hurried away. In a day, he phoned me to request that I come to his office to read my test to him. He said, "I thought that, if a blind person can do it, it can't be all that difficult."

After presenting a beginning course in Optacon for teachers, I followed it with an advanced one. In the first hour of the advanced course, I reviewed certain information. Afterward, a student said, "I wish you had given us that information in the first course I was in."

Another student, Chuck Wright, spoke up, "She did tell us that. Today's presentation was only a quick review. Look here. I brought along my notes from that former course. See, here is that information!" This points up the fact that not every student is equally attentive, yet one student in talking with another will vehemently declare, "She never told us that. Why, then, is there a question about it on the test?" With that in mind, I have great reservations about the validity of student evaluation sheets of faculty at the end of a course. I have read opposite statements on such papers. One student will add, "I like the fact that she sticks to her outline and does not digress as so many faculty do," while another paper reads, "I prefer a teacher who does not use an outline and is willing to talk about other things as some of my instructors do."

Some students regard an instructor as great who is easily distracted from the course content. Some students like an instructor who obviously aims to entertain rather than teach. Some students like a faculty member who dismisses students early frequently throughout the quarter or semester. As I think back to my student days, I preferred instructors who began promptly and dismissed us at the last official minute, who taught us much each session, who did not try to be cute or entertaining, who expected much growth from their students. Such instructors are true change agents. I like instructors who can make "Aha!" happen. At such moments students can say, "I understand that now" or "So that's what it means" or "I've been wondering about that for a long time" or "That side of the argument had never occurred to me before," etc.

As suggested earlier, the second course that I tried to introduce was devoted to biography and autobiography in special education and rehabilitation. These books provide information not available in textbooks only. Life stories reveal adjustment—or the lack of it— and attitudes not only of the writer but also of his or her family and persons in the general public toward individuals with specific disabilities, as revealed by their words and interactions with the person writing or written about. These books are especially helpful to novices in the field of special education and rehabilitation who may need to evaluate their own attitudes and motives for their chosen career.

Besides attitudes, these books illustrate problems to be solved, depending on which disability is present. A newly blind adult might explore several ways to keep paper currency organized and identifiable by him. A deaf person might struggle to find a way to know when someone is at her door. A person with an orthopedic disability may experiment to find a solution for cutting food with only one hand. The story of a child with a disability may reveal the parent's acceptance or rejection of the child, as well as how other children in the neighborhood or in school relate to him or her.

A "normal" individual may be naïve enough to think that every problem in the life of a person with a disability is easily solved. Or the "normal" person may lack creativity and imagination to suggest solutions to either the student/client or family member. We need special education teachers and rehabilitation counselors/teachers who are encyclopedias of information and appropriate techniques. Not every technique will be presented in university courses; the graduate professional must be a resource unto himself or herself rather than having to contact a former professor to seek a solution to a specific problem. The child or adult client may be surprisingly helpful in solving his or her own problem.

These children and clients need more than a treasury of techniques. Positive and negative attitudes are present. The child, for instance, may be highly motivated and demonstrate positive attitudes, but parents may be very negative, seeing only the disability and not the child. They may lack ingenuity and problem-solving ability.

My proposal for this course was denied.

The Library of Congress, National Library Service for the Blind and Physically Handicapped, provides a multiple-page list of these biographies and autobiographies. Armed with this resource, university students and professionals (and parents) can steer their reading in order to learn from these books. Some readers might prefer to read books only about their major focus, such as blindness, while others might prefer to read about as many disabilities as time permits. My proposal acknowledged that in most courses, students use textbooks but that in this course reading would be in biographies/autobiographies.

Similarly, those who had rejected the idea of introducing a course to accomplish skill in calculating with the modified abacus apparently underestimated the time necessary for students to gain proficiency and correct fingering. These skills are not mastered in one or two class demonstrations by the instructor. Furthermore, more than addition can be computed with the abacus. Each vertical rod has one bead (worth five) above the horizontal bar and four beads below that bar, with each being worth one. Because we believed in the value of the modified abacus, we included it in another course.

One faculty member had been making noises to indicate that he would like to be Area Director. I offered him the Area Directorship without resistance. He must have thought that being Area Director brought more money into his paycheck or brought more status or glory. Neither is true. Area Director receives no extra remuneration or glory. After only nine months, he said I could have back the Area Directorship! I suggested that we discuss this with the Department Chairman who agreed with me that we cannot toss these responsibilities about every nine months and that the person who had it presently must keep it for at least three years.

When Dean Tuttle became Area Director, he assigned me to continue writing the unhappy letters to students about failing comprehensive examinations or having too low a GPA to continue in Graduate School. I reminded him that he was now Area Director and that writing those unhappy and unpopular letters is part of being Area Director and that I had never assigned anyone to write those letters but wrote them myself as Area Director. I had not chosen to write those letters because of enjoying the role of ogre but rather those letters were an integral part of my position as Area Director. I reminded him that being Area Director can sometimes be a lonely chair and that whatever decision he makes will probably make students or faculty unhappy. "You won't always be popular."

Another faculty member said, even before the examination, he was going to flunk an international student on the oral comprehensive examination. With those words burning in my ears, I invited the Department Chairman to be present when the student came for his oral comprehensive examination. I wanted fairness in the process and not premeditated mean-spiritedness. In actuality, the student did fail because his answers were incomplete and unclearly expressed, indicating lack of mastery of the content of the master's degree program and not through unethical designs by an individual faculty member. With the Department Chairman present, that faculty member would not dare display his mean streak of character.

While Dean Tuttle was off campus on sabbatical, two faculty on federal funding from which their salaries were paid tried to unseat me by having me fired. They went to the dean with false reports about me. They wanted to be paid from state money with more security in their positions. When I knew what was afoot, I visited the dean of the College of Education (not the one who had yelled at Elaine in the stairwell), but Dr. Orvel Trainer, who assured me that I was secure in my position. He expressed his view of the two faculty thusly: "When you work with cannibals, you have to expect that they will try to eat you!"

Of our six faculty members, Dean Tuttle and I were the only two with doctorates. One of those two causing trouble said that he did not need a doctor's degree, that a doctoral program could not teach him anything that he did not already know. (What about humility and modesty?)

I picked up the phone in my office to make an outside call only to hear one of the two faculty talking negatively about me to a student in his office. Apparently, his phone was misaligned in the cradle, thus permitting me to hear the tirade.

What he does not know is that his students came to me to complain about him. Every one of his students was required to write a letter of commendation for his file. Students did not want to praise his teaching techniques or personal qualities but knew that if they did not comply, he would be punitive. I did not tell these students what to do. Instead, I asked them to weigh the two sides: If you do write that letter and if you do not. What are the consequences that you are willing to accept? That faculty member was not professionally qualified to serve on a university's faculty. If he had been successful in having me fired, his next attack would be against Dr. Tuttle, so that one of our graduates on the faculty would also have a state-funded position. The two of them were vicious and sinister.

When Miss Josephine L. Taylor came to campus, I hosted a reception for her in the evening at my home. Nevertheless, the two men were not savvy enough to attend when Jo was in control of federal funding that paid their salaries. Jo would certainly notice such disregard of her influence. Shortly before I was scheduled to retire, federal funding to our area terminated.

According to students who told me, one of the men proclaimed in class that there are no truly bright or gifted or genius blind individuals; they are of mediocre intelligence but over-achievers.

On a much brighter note, students as a total group were a joy! Most of them arrived with very limited knowledge about the field of blindness: its history and leaders in the field, resources and agencies, teaching methodologies, etc. but graduated as competent professionals who will serve blind and/or visually-impaired individuals with dispatch and sensitivity with honed skills, shaped not only by their education at UNC but also by their years of teaching experience , making positive impacts on many lives.

NINE

I DID NOT PREVIOUSLY own a home before coming to Greeley; I lacked cash from selling a house to use to purchase one here. As preceding chapters reveal, I was destitute when I arrived in Greeley (as are many doctoral graduates when they assume their first position). My finances would not permit me to consider buying a house until I had saved enough for a down payment on a reasonably-priced house. Consequently, I was a renter in Greeley for ten years, at the mercy — or lack thereof—of landlords.

My first residence was a furnished house at 1600 Sixth Avenue with a space heater in the dining room as the only source of heat. In winter, the floor was cold. When I notified the landlady after a year that I was planning to move, her reaction was, "Why would you want to move when every house looks the same to a blind person?"

Then I moved into Aspen Arms at 1624 Ninth Avenue where I had an apartment on the third floor and later the penthouse on the same floor. After I had lived in that building for six years, without warning the landlord—or his representative—ordered me to be moved out within ten days! Because I feared that he might move my belongings outside if I were not gone after ten days, I had locks changed on the two doors and my closet that opened onto the corridor.

Then I moved into a newly completed house at 802 Twentieth

Street. The landlord and I had agreed on the rent of $175 before I moved in. He waited outdoors until the moving van left and then informed me that he had to raise my rent to clear expenses. He said, "You professors are rich and can afford whatever I charge!" I hated the idea of finding another location and moving again. He was treacherous and unreliable as revealed by other deceptions.

After I had lived there for three years, he informed me that he was giving me first choice to buy his house because he said he knew I would rather buy it than move! I assured him that I had no plans to buy his house or do further business with him because of my past dealings with him. He would cheat me if he could in any business arrangement. For instance, his married son lived downstairs. When I moved out, I turned off the electric and gas meters mounted in my kitchen. Later I learned that the son was complaining about cold water. At that point I learned that I had been paying utilities for both apartments! Furthermore, when he was building the house himself, he made a hole in the wall of each room for a telephone connection. I chose to have a phone on the wall in the kitchen and in my bedroom. He said I should have the other holes closed by having the phone company repairman come in to make the necessary provisions so a phone could be installed in each room at my expense. I told him that if the holes were bothering him, he should call the phone company and pay the bill for such service. He refused to provide screen doors so that the other doors could be open without letting insects enter. He felt that the tenant should buy the doors, even though the doors stayed with the house when the tenant moved. No, I wanted no further business with him!

A neighbor informed me that a house around the corner had a FOR SALE sign on it. I asked that neighbor, Bill Cozbey, to visit the house and walk through it to determine its need of repair and improvement. He later reported that the house seemed to be in excellent condition, having been well maintained.

Then Bill and I visited it. I was pleased with this brick house's floor plan: a large sunny kitchen, a large sunny dining room, a huge living room with fireplace, two bedrooms and bathroom on the main floor, enclosed back porch, open front porch, and a finished second floor that I could use as a study and storage for my books. The basement had a laundry room and an apartment to rent for extra income. The backyard was large, but the lawn needed tender, loving care, what with the four children of a doctoral student who lived there romping on it. I would want to fence the backyard for the safety of my dog. A brick, detached, one-car garage was part of the property. Although the driveway was steep and narrow, I had no car to maneuver it.

I negotiated with the realtor, bringing down the price and including yard furniture. Then I went to Columbia Savings and Loan to apply for a mortgage. After the hard times my bank had given me when I needed to borrow money to pay the mover when my furniture came from storage in New Jersey and when I wanted to pay off Ann Perry in Pennsylvania, I refused to consider the bank for a mortgage. I wouldn't let the bank earn any interest from *my* mortgage after having told me that my request for a small loan had been denied because of not having a man to manage my affairs.

When the appointment for the closing arrived, I was apprehensive. I took along my most recent contract from the university. I wondered whether my blindness would pose a problem to the manager. Would she consider me a poor risk as an investment, "without a man to manage your affairs," as the loan officers at the bank had said to me? The closing went smoothly and without a hitch. The question of my blindness never arose. After all legal matters had been completed, the manager told me that she had a blind daughter-in-law and had no qualms about my ability to be a responsible homeowner.

Then in June 1976, I began moving into my house—mine and the S&L's, that is. Many of the items I transported myself from my former house around the corner to my house at 2011 Eighth Avenue. A moving van moved the big and heavy items.

After I was reasonably settled, my department faculty and staff surprised me with a housewarming party with a candlestick phone as their gift to me.

As I mentioned earlier, Dola came to Greeley with me from Philadelphia and lived in my first three residences. Then she developed hip dysplasia. I could not believe the diagnosis because I knew that The Seeing Eye checks each dog for that condition. I wrote to the school's headquarters for clarification. The school's veterinarian had used a scale of gradations. I think that the scale has nine steps on it, and Dola's possibility of having hip dysplasia was in the middle of the scale. True, she was nine years old before the condition presented itself. I took her to Fort Collins to the College of Veterinary Science at Colorado State University (CSU), where Dr. Harry Gorman performed surgery, not to correct the problem but to make Dola more comfortable with it. About a year later, she died.

Ruthie, a German shepherd, came to Greeley in 1974, living with me on Twentieth Street until we moved to Eighth Avenue. Later she developed a malignancy on her right hind leg, but after two surgeries, she was completely well at age six. She lived to be fourteen.

Ruthie was a quiet dog but knew when to use her voice. If I was on the main floor when the doorbell sounded, Ruthie made not a sound. When, however, I was upstairs when the doorbell rang, Ruthie barked to alert me to come down. She was another sweetheart.

She was with me when I taught an evening class from seven to ten o'clock. After class one evening, a student offered to drive me home. I accepted. When I started to tell her where I lived, she said, "I know where you live." We chatted until she pulled up to the curb. Ruthie and I exited her car, thanked her, and said goodnight.

After the car drove away, I discovered that I was not in front of my house. Where was I? We began walking north (I learned the direction later), hoping to find something familiar, but noted nothing. I then directed Ruthie to turn around; we walked past the house where I had been delivered and proceeded south for one or two more blocks.

I wasn't even sure that we were on Eighth Avenue, though it seemed to be a busy road.

After a specific crossing with the main street on our right, Ruthie made a decisive turn to the right to the curb. I did not know whether I had a traffic light at this intersection. I stood there listening to traffic flow. After being convinced that a traffic light was, in fact, operating, we crossed, whereupon Ruthie made a decisive turn to the left once on the sidewalk. *She knows something.* "Good girl," I encouraged. Partway up this block, she turned confidently to the right. There I found steps up, but I was still not convinced. We moved forward until we came to more steps. Yes, this was my front porch! "Good girl, Ruthie!" She received many pats and warm hugs.

Ruthie lived with me until 1985. She was becoming deaf and incontinent at age fourteen, a very old age for a shepherd. I hated losing this queen of a dog guide.

Nannett was my next guide, also a German shepherd. She seemed aloof, even with me. I had to wonder whether we were mismatched, though her work performance was excellent. In the house, however, she withdrew once the harness was removed. This lasted about six months. Then she fully accepted me and enjoyed playing ball and other recreational activities with me. Apparently the adjustment had to be at her own pace, not mine. After that, I never questioned again whether we had been mismatched. We were right for each other.

Nannett and I had a unique system of communication between us. When she wanted something, she came to me and "talked." I would name words she was familiar with, such as *play ball, cookie, drink, go outside, supper, go bye-bye.* She listened intently as I pronounced each, and I waited for a reaction. When I said the "right" word, she danced in delight, and I granted her request. The two of us had a genuine communication system. She was unique in being able to convey her ideas and needs in this way.

She was a grazer in her eating habits, eating small amounts all day long rather than consuming the whole meal greedily when it was presented. Later she developed some symptoms which I now have forgotten. I took her to the College of Veterinary Science where a surgeon could not diagnose her problem related to her stomach. He operated and found a large rock in her stomach! I don't know how long it had been there but assume a very long time. This fact might explain why she was a grazer because of the space that the rock occupied in her stomach, resulting in a feeling of fullness. However, after the rock had been removed and she fully recovered, I saw no change in her grazing habit.

After ten years with me, Nannett developed a visual problem. I took her again to the College of Veterinary Science, where an animal ophthalmologist offered to operate on both eyes. After the first eye hemorrhaged, he chose not to work on the other eye, lest she be worse than she was with one eye damaged. However, her vision was not sufficient for dog guide work. She had to be retired.

Edith Nedrud and family, my friends for many years, offered to adopt Nannett. They had her until two days before her fourteenth birthday. She was euthanized because of incontinence.

I recall an experience when in training with Nannett. Our trip one afternoon was to a mall. While the instructor took two teams on a tour through the mall, the rest of us sat on a marble hassock, as I called it.

A gentleman sat beside me and commented on how beautiful my dog was. He asked her name. Just the day before, my instructor had advised us not to give our dog's name to strangers, just in case the stranger might try to attract the dog away from the master. Yet I did not want rudely to tell this man that it was none of his business to know my dog's name.

Then I had a brainstorm! Although I knew how to pronounce my dog's name, I had not yet been provided with the unique spelling of it. For instance, The Seeing Eye may have several dogs with the same name, but each is spelled differently. For instance, spellings may be Vicki or Vickie or Vicky or Vickey. Thinking that her name was spelled *Nannette*, I reversed the spelling in my mind: *Ettennan*. I told the man that my dog's name was Et-ten-nan. He commented that it was a very unusual name.

I followed up with, "Oh, yes, Ettennan was an Egyptian goddess of travel." I chose Egyptian rather than Greek, because I feared he might know more about Greek mythology than I do and hoped he knew less about Egyptian mythology. He was happy to have a name; I was happy to keep secret my dog's real name.

(Later, with Waffle, when strangers asked her name, I said it was Blackie, because she was totally black. The name seemed obvious.)

Over time, I made many improvements in and out of the house. These included a new concrete driveway, a fenced backyard, a sidewalk from the back door to the trash cans beside the garage and back to the dog's "park" (relief area) behind the garage, new inside steps down to the basement, soft-water system, lawn-sprinkler system, high efficiency furnace, improvements in the apartment, ceiling fan and light in my dining room, new refrigerator, new washing machine, new floor covering in my kitchen, new water heater, siding on exterior wooden surfaces of the brick house to eliminate painting those areas, new double-paned windows for better insulation, exhaust fan on second floor—all implemented over several years.

The realtor had given me the name of a handyman, though she qualified her referral by saying she knew nothing about his workmanship. I followed through to contact Don Stanske. He worked for me for nineteen years. His primary job was mowing the back and front lawns and keeping the greenery trimmed. However, when other jobs arose, such as repairs and painting, he did those, too. He was completely honest, trustworthy, and honorable. I had no concerns when both of us were in the house or when he was alone in the house. I paid a lawn-care company to treat the lawn as needed but not to mow it.

I rented the basement apartment to university students. Some were excellent tenants, while others demonstrated that they knew nothing about housekeeping. I remember one who obviously did not know anything about trays under burners in stoves and never removed them to clean. Another had a bathroom faucet that needed repair, unknown to me. Instead of telling me about it, she let the faucet run into the sink endlessly until I discovered it after she had vacated the apartment, despite the fact that when she moved in I had emphasized that I would have repairs done immediately and wanted her to report any problems.

I recall a student who could not start the vacuum cleaner, not because it was broken but because she did not know how. Her boyfriend advised her to cut off the plug at the end of the cord. DUH! She followed his advice. Then she wanted to stick the cord, without a plug, into the wall socket! After all this had happened, she told me that the vacuum cleaner did not work! After I had the cord repaired, I demonstrated how to turn on this appliance. Problems like these and others are the bane of the landlady's existence.

I fear that some parents do not teach their sons and daughters beforehand how to do routine tasks of daily living. Then the young people go off to college and assume tenant life without knowing the basics about equipment, cooking, and cleaning. Another tenant baked a small roast overnight and was surprised that in the morning it was dry and unappetizing.

After being retired nine years and because I have no relatives in Colorado, I felt that I should be proactive in planning for my future as I grow older. Having decided to move to Bonell Good Samaritan Center, I sold my home in 1995. At Bonell I rent an apartment for independent living. It has an all-electric kitchen with a walk-in pantry, living room, two bedrooms, bathroom, and a deck outside the kitchen door. I have a front door and a back door in this brick fourplex, requiring no supervision. It is like living in any other apartment in town but with other services when needed.

Bonell is now called Bonell Good Samaritan Community, where approximately five hundred residents comprise the community. Bonell has different accommodations to fit individuals' needs: assisted living, nursing care, Alzheimer's disease section, etc. Free bus transportation is available for medical appointments. Independent residents may eat in their apartments or in the main dining room for a fee. A chapel and chaplain are available, as is a warm-water pool with or without physical therapy. Cable television is included in the rent. Even the apartments for independent living are varied with a range of rents. Management provides mowing and sprinkling of lawns, removal of snow, carpentry, electrical, and plumbing repairs free of charge.

Because Bonell is only two blocks from the house I had owned, the neighborhood is familiar to me. From here, I walk to all the places where I formerly went on foot: church, pharmacy, bank, Senior Activity Center, beauty shop, and other destinations for shopping and other errands.

In 1996, I trained with Waffle, a black Labrador retriever. She was a honey, truly a *Wunderhund*! She was the first dog guide to live in the independent living section at Bonell.

In 2005, Waffle and I and her veterinarian, Dr. Francis Freemyer, coped with malignant skin tumors caused by mast cells. We did not know what was happening inside Waffle's body relative to tumor development. The veterinarian used DERMEX to treat the tumors. The medication (in paste, capsule, or liquid form) attacks malignant tissue, converting it to liquid. Then the tumor usually dries up, shrinks, and disappears. However, as, some tumors disappear, others appear! It is a constant problem that was with us for more than two years.

Waffle's quality of life was good. She ate with gusto. She welcomed the harness and work. She enjoyed playing.

As an interesting fact to note, DERMEX has been used by human patients who have been declared terminally ill with cancer but have experienced complete recovery. Unhappily, DERMEX does not cure mast-cell malignancy.

After Waffle's death from cancer at age eleven, I waited from March to late October for my new dog, Esma, a yellow Labrador retriever. Esma is vastly qualified. I received my training with Esma here in Greeley; The Seeing Eye accommodates some veteran users of dog guides when the master has valid reasons for not traveling to New Jersey for training. The instructor, of course, gave one-on-one instruction for ten days while here.

Esma and I worked until May 3rd of 2006, when another instructor came to Greeley to take Esma back to Headquarters while I had total-knee surgery on May 4th and then recuperated for eight weeks when a third instructor returned Esma to me late in June. That instructor stayed three days to monitor how we as a team functioned. During her stay in New Jersey, Esma received maintenance training to keep her in practice. When she returned to me, her performance was as if she had never been away from me.

The Seeing Eye does not offer this at-home instruction to students receiving their first dog but only to graduates with extensive experience with dog guides.

I have been retired since 1986. I do not own a rocker and would not have much time just to rock if I had one. Instead, I keep busy with activities that interest me.

Memberships in organizations keep me involved. These groups include:

- Greeley Exchange Club

- American Business Women's Association

- Delta Kappa Gamma Society, International

- Emeritus Faculty

- County Retired School Employees' Association

- American Association of University Women's Gourmet Readers

- Christian Women's Club

- Coffee Break (a Bible study program aimed at women who don't attend church)

- GRASP (Greeley Retirees' Academic Study Program)

- Chapter EC, P .E .O.

I don't hold memberships and then not attend. I have had to drop some of the activities, however, because their meeting places had moved and were too far away with no transportation.

At church, I teach an adult Sunday school class and am a member of a circle of United Methodist Women.

Although I used to attend the conventions of the American Council of the Blind and some of its subgroups, I have discontinued those yearly events. With so many blind attendees, I have grown weary and impatient with many of them who are rude when a general session ends. As all of us were trying to exit the hall, persons behind me pushed and poked me with "Move it!" even though I could not move forward because of persons not able to move forward. Also, when some of the attendees discovered that I had a dog guide instead of a cane, many would denounce the presence of a dog guide. (It was all right that they used canes and poked people with them, but no one else was welcome to use dog guides.)

I felt that all of their behaviors were unbecoming, rude, and a hardship on my well-behaved dog. With that frustration and sympathy for my dog, I stopped attending ACB but continue to support its publications of interest to me.

During retirement, I have composed sacred music. I have done this in four different ways:

- Composing new tunes to words of old, standard hymns

- Composing music for specific Scripture

- Composing music for specific poems

- Composing songs with original music and original words

There was a time when I owned a piano, an electronic organ, and a keyboard. When I moved to Bonell, I came with only the organ because of space limitations.

Later, I wrote two novels: *Marissa: Obstacle Illusions* and *Marissa and Dan: Grace Notes* (a sequel). Both have been published by SELAH PUBLISHING GROUP in 2002 and 2003 respectively.

I've had numerous opportunities to travel during retirement. For instance, I attended my fiftieth year reunion at Douglass College in 1994. In 1996, I attended the Coffee Break convention in Vancouver, British Columbia, Canada. In 1997, a Donkersloot family reunion convened at Winter Park, Colorado, set in the Rocky Mountains, with more than one hundred attendees from the United States and Canada. In 2001, I attended the fiftieth wedding anniversary of Bud and Marinell Napier in Illinois. I was still there when terrorists flew two planes into the World Trade Center, another plane into the Pentagon, and a fourth into a field in Pennsylvania on September 11th.

In 2004, I attended the seventy-fifth anniversary of The Seeing Eye on its campus where 157 graduates and their dogs were present. The total number of attendees was 450. During that visit to New Jersey, I also visited Virginia and George Kelcec, who live quite close to The Seeing Eye. Ginny and I had been friends at Douglass College and were classmates in our eurhythmics courses.

When I went to Headquarters to train with a new dog, Ginny visited me on weekends. After I returned home after receiving Waffle, Ginny phoned to ask for specific measurements of my body. After a few months, I received a package containing a lined, white sweater jacket with a black Labrador retriever stitched into its back. I receive many compliments each time I wear it because of Ginny's mastery of needlework!

Those trips and others during my twenty years at the university when I traveled to supervise practicum students brought the total of states reached to thirty-nine. Because the university could not place all practicum students in programs located in Colorado, we had to include other programs scattered throughout the nation.

As I write this, I have had to miss the weddings of my grand-niece Michelle Joy Donkersloot and her fiancé, Christopher S. Lewis, in Sioux Falls, South Dakota, where the church is located. The reception was in Minnesota. The couple have resided in Iowa. Consult a map to see how these three states are connected. I have also had to miss weddings of Ryan and Michelle on the beach in Mexico and the wedding of Carina and Jeff in Des Moines.

To visit relatives, I have traveled to Schaumburg, Illinois; Pella, Iowa; Lafayette, Indiana; and Mt. Pleasant, Iowa. Sometime in the future, I hope to visit a nephew in Inwood, Iowa.

When I tell friends where I am going or have returned from, I am amused to hear some of them ask, "Did you take your dog with you?"

My response is, "She took me." All of my travels have been by plane.

Above, I mentioned having been in Illinois on September 11, 2001. Everyone remembers where he or she was on that day! We also recall where we were when we heard President Roosevelt announce that Pearl Harbor had been struck or when we heard that President Kennedy had been assassinated in 1963 or when the Challenger burst into flames in January 1986.

In an earlier chapter, I mentioned having nine-year-old Gary Milo Ridley visit me from Chicago for ten days while I lived in New Jersey. That boy has matured into a man in his fifties who is now director of the Oklahoma Department of Transportation (ODOT). We are very proud of his accomplishments. Gary's sister Judy and Gary's daughter, Daphne, are nurses; Daphne teaches nursing at a hospital and is working on her Ph.D. degree. Gary's mother's brother, George Napier, was second in command in the Chicago Fire Department. Several nephews have also served in that department.

Other celebrities in my family include William M. Donkersloot, my brother's son, a pastor in the Reformed Church in America. He has served in Florida, California, New Jersey, Indiana, and twice in Iowa; such is the life of a pastor. It's a moving experience. His wife, Marcia, is a high school teacher of business courses.

Their daughter, Michelle, has a master's degree in health and well-ness management and works in that field. Her employer sends her on a team to evaluate employees of businesses. Her older brother, Scott, with a degree in recreation, has worked in that field on a cruise ship. Currently, he is in training with Aaron's.

The younger brother, Jason, as a graduate from Purdue University in the field of technology education, is now a teacher in Indiana.

Bill's younger brother, Robert T. Donkersloot, is a public school teacher of art, communications, and drama. His wife, Barbara, also a teacher, has a master's degree in elementary education.

Their oldest is Carina, with a degree in accounting. She is now stationed in Des Moines as a full-time sergeant with the Iowa National Guard. Her older brother, Ryan, is also in the National Guard after having served in Iraq.

The youngest, Austin, has recently graduated from high school.

My cousin, Gertrude Donkersloot Cooper, has a son who is an attorney. Another son and son-in-law are medical doctors. A grand-daughter is in medicine also. A daughter is an artist.

My cousin, Ida Donkersloot, graduated from college, but in her middle twenties died from Hodgkin's disease.

I list these family accomplishments to note the contrast to my parents' levels of education—fifth and sixth grade. I was the first in the family on either side to attend and graduate from college. I find the achievements of relatives very gratifying when I recall the family's humble beginnings as immigrants from The Netherlands.

Only in the United States can so many college graduates stem from immigrants who entered this country in 1896. The United States encourages its citizens to strive, stretch, and achieve higher goals than their parents and grandparents in order to make greater contributions and to climb out of poverty. Education is the key that unlocks doors otherwise unavailable to them. Individuals' stations in life among the poor are no indication of their future or their children's potential to rise above humble origins.

Our country's history is replete with countless stories of impoverished immigrants who rose to positions of great responsibility and invaluable contributions to the improvement of society inside and outside our national borders. Education is the stepping-stone from lower class to middle class. Great teachers try to impart that truism to students who live in a project or ghetto.

Children need not succumb to poverty as a permanent way of life merely because they had been born into poverty. Today many financial resources encourage people to seek higher education. Scholarships and fellowships from private and public sources, federal aid in the form of grants, loans, and stipends to students to encourage recruitment into specific fields of study where shortages of professionals exist, and the G.I. Bill after military service are only a few examples.

Because some parents lack the vision that escape from poverty is possible through education, teachers must stress that fact and encourage children to be excellent students, graduate from high school, earn scholarships to attend college, and perhaps even pursue degrees beyond the bachelor's.

In some countries, a person born into poverty remains in poverty all his or her life. In such countries, if your father and grandfather were bakers, you are taught how to be a baker. This kind of mindset is difficult to accept once someone is acquainted with our country and the freedom to move up the economic ladder and horizontally across society's plethora of career choices, regardless of the jobs held by siblings parents, grandparents, uncles, etc. We do not have to stay stuck in poverty. However, just wishing to be rich or have a "nice" career will not accomplish the fact. As children, we must study well and prove ourselves to be excellent learners. As adults, we can study when not working on a menial job. Either route may lead to scholar-ships and college.

While I was on the faculty at the University of Northern Colorado, once a year for several years, a teacher from the Denver metropolitan area brought with her to Greeley a vanload of adolescents to meet with me. These students were bright intellectually but poor financially. Nor were these students blind or visually impaired. The teacher knew the story of my early life and wanted her students to hear it from me. Also, she pointed out to them that Dr. Napier had climbed out of poverty through education, even though blind.

The teacher wanted to ignite in these students the belief that they could escape poverty, crime, illegal drugs, tobacco, alcohol, pregnancy, and venereal disease, and instead realize careers as teachers, computer programmers, entrepreneurs, lawyers, medical doctors, clergy, psychologists, therapists (speech, occupational, and physical), engineers, scientists, musicians, graphic artists, etc. She named innumerable professions, hoping that one career would ignite interest of even one student.

Teachers were the only professionals or college graduates that many of them had been exposed to, so they needed to know about all the other careers open to college graduates.

That teacher is to be commended for her effort to rescue those students who might otherwise become dropouts or at best might graduate from high school but then go no further with their education, only to become discouraged and cynical about the futility of life, perhaps even to the point of becoming suicide victims.

In her own way, she was being a Katharine Taylor in her students' lives just as Katharine Taylor had blessed my life with her intervention. Miss Taylor's efforts were more genuine and loving than my mother's efforts exerted in the opposite direction. I chose to follow Miss Taylor rather than my mother. Young persons in poverty need that kind of hero to help them escape lifelong poverty.

I do not know whether any other university faculty member continued this valuable undertaking after I retired. I truly hope someone stepped forward in the effort to point the way for these youngsters and others like them in years afterward. That teacher from the Denver area also needed morale building to energize her efforts to point the way for her students. What better achievement for any teacher than to have future professionals say of her, "Miss — — saved my life by emphasizing that I have a bright mind and that my life could be changed with education. I owe her much for caring about me not only when I was in school but also when I am an adult!" Education and educators are change agents. This is a grave responsibility but a rewarding one when it occurs—to point adolescents to a fulfilling life in professional service rather than to life as victims in negative channels.

Because impoverished secondary school students probably lack understanding of what kind of service specific professions offer, students can benefit from shadowing professionals to gain understanding of how one profession differs from others.

Another role I had while on the faculty (and continued into retirement) was as speaker to student clubs and organizations as well as guest speaker in courses taught by other faculty.

I remember speaking to a sorority on campus, delving into dating, sexual purity, meeting Mr. Right with no need to hide from him ghosts in the closet.

Afterward, a young woman came to me to say, "I wish my mother had talked to me the way you did this evening."

A day or two later, a young male student fell in stride with me while crossing the campus. He explained that he had gone to the University Center to attend a different meeting. Thinking he was in the correct room, he settled into a chair and waited for the meeting to begin. When I started speaking, he knew that he was in the wrong room, but his interest had been piqued. He stayed for the entire meeting.

Students have a hunger to hear the truth. Some do not attend church or synagogue or religious education classes. On campus, they hear that "everyone is involved in alcohol, drugs, and sex." These uninitiated students may not be hearing the other side of the story. The desire to be accepted and the power of peer pressure are tremendous. Some students might not be encouraged to listen when references to morality or religion are used. Yet without labels, they were hearing from me a different rationale about how to behave as college students—hearing, in fact, that a different rationale exists. Campus life can be confusing and even dangerous without prior preparation provided by parents. New students are vulnerable when more experienced students choose to promote their lifestyle as the one all other students must adopt to be accepted as "sophisticated" and in the know.

Even as I write these lines, I am painfully reminded that in the past few weeks two students, one each at two of our state universities, have died of alcoholic poisoning in Greek houses. Having come from Douglass College, a state institution with no Greek houses, I discourage all colleges and universities from having them. I distinguish between professional organizations with Greek names for educators or journalists or scientists, etc. and Greek houses primarily for socializing with wild parties, regardless of academic major. The latter is my objection because of the lifestyle that they promote and their hazardous hazing practices. These Greek fraternities divide the student body into those students who have been accepted and those who have been rejected. Students may be rejected based on their fathers' livelihood and income and other meaningless criteria. Fraternities and sororities are undemocratic and should be banned from campuses because of their negative impact on a democratic student body.

With these speaking engagements of mine, I sensed a need of many students to hear some other credible choices, especially when presented by faculty and not by some smart-aleck student puffed up with his or her worldly experience, claiming to represent the total student body.

I encouraged students to focus on their career goals at all times. Driving drunk, acquiring AIDS or other sexually-transmitted disease, or drifting away from their goals because of drugs can wreck and even end their lives, eradicating their chances of becoming that medical doctor, engineer, or scientist that they desire to become. To them I say, "Just as when you are driving on a highway you don't want your passengers distracting you from the responsibility of driving safely, just so, as you steer your life toward your career goals, do not permit other students to mislead you into alcohol, sex, and drugs, away from your goals, perhaps never to return to your career preparation." Although my next comment is brief, it is not trivial. This is the matter of whatever happens to a student on campus is confidential and screened from parents. When parents are paying for tuition and fees, room and board, books and materials, etc., why are they prevented from knowing what parents have a right to know about their sons and daughters? Where would those students be and where would any university be when parents say, "If I have no right to know, I refuse to pay the bills?" The university must not assume the role of parent for all student. This is a role that any university will fail to meet, and in the process, students (our sons and daughters) will be irreparably damaged. As mentioned in an earlier chapter, in one of my large classes, a student asked me, "How can you be so optimistic and upbeat when you are blind?" Each faculty member must recognize the moment when he or she must shed the academic robe, as it were, and be genuine as a person, not only that person on campus but that same person at home or witnessing a ball game or that person as a member of a service club or in any of his or her roles as a human being. Share your character and basic beliefs with students, especially when they ask questions not directly associated with the content of the course you teach. You are more than the courses that you teach. Who are you, and what do you stand for? You have freedom to do what and freedom from what? We as university teachers teach not only from the textbook in our discipline but through our genuine character.

Humorous moments enter our academic lives, too, both on and off campus. Once, when in need of specific information, I phoned the university library, requesting to be connected to the periodicals room. An unprofessional male voice answered, "Hullo."

Because he had not identified the library service, I asked, "Is this the periodicals room?"

The answer was, "No. We've got only magazines here!"

While traveling from Denver to the east coast, our plane stopped in Chicago, but I did not have to change planes. Because the time in Chicago was between six and seven a.m., I decided to feed my dog. So I left the plane. Some airline employee summoned Travelers' Aid to assist me because I had said, "I need to feed my dog."

The person at Travelers' Aid said I could leave my briefcase in her office while we went to the bathroom. I insisted upon taking it with me. In the ladies' room, she steered me to a toilet stall. I protested that I needed a sink. "You need the sink?" I can imagine that she may have thought she had some freak or pervert on her hands. Then I opened my briefcase and removed a can of dog food, can opener, knife, and feed pan and proceeded to make my dog's meal ready for her. When the dog was eating, the woman said in surprise, "Oh, you really did want to feed your dog!" Apparently, she had thought "I need to feed my dog" was some code meaning, "I need to use the toilet" instead of its straightforward meaning!

Another time I was in the ladies' room in the university library building when a woman, unknown to me, asked, "How does your dog know when you have to use the bathroom?" I explained that I am the one to know that, not my dog, that I know it just the way that woman does. (My dog is my guide, not my brain, not my computer, not some body system that rings a bell when I need to urinate or eat a meal or go to bed or appear in the correct classroom at the correct time to teach.) When in the bathroom, I put the dog's leash around a faucet while I was in the toilet stall, so that the dog does not wander about in the bathroom or look under doors—which experience upsets many women. This time, my dog moved in such a way that the faucet turned on with water running until I turned it off. A woman present asked, "Do you always leave the water running so that you can find your dog?" I patiently explained that the dog had turned on the water, and let her figure that out.

When I was traveling somewhere in the U. S., I entered a ladies' room to use it myself. The room had a "hostess." When I attempted to enter the stall, the hostess tried to force herself in with me. I resisted her with force. She said, "I am the hostess. My job is to give help when needed." I assured her that I did not need help. She persisted by saying, "I don't mind helping you."

I reassured her that I needed no help and added, "I can pull it down and up again all by myself!"

While seated against a window on a plane after aloft quite a while, the woman beside me said, "Excuse me, ma'am, but your fur piece is on the floor!" Because I had no fur piece with me, I knew what she was seeing was my dog!

Another campus tidbit came in the voice of a student announcer on the university radio broadcast of classical music. He was obviously trying very hard to sound sexy and seductive. When I had my fill of that, I phoned the radio station, where the same person answered. I reminded him that the broadcast was not limited to the campus but reached many residents in the Greeley listening area. Therefore, he should not sound as if he were sitting on a sofa with his girlfriend whom he was trying to seduce or at least impress as a professional communicator. Classical music requires a straightforward presentation; it needs no such "enhancement."

A not-humorous situation was the campus newspaper, operated completely by students without supervision by a faculty member professionally qualified to oversee the publication. Some articles were libelous and irresponsible. How can writing for this paper be a profitable educational experience for students when they are not learning from professionals that specific articles are offensive and dangerous and would be seen as such in any responsible publication? How could students learn responsible reporting when an adviser was not present to pass judgment?

While I was on the faculty and during retirement, I visited many elementary classes as a guest to supplement the children's health and science studies. Many schools use a health program about the eye and vision. The children learn about the various parts of the eye and actually dissect a cow's eye. Afterward, I was invited to speak about blindness and demonstrate equipment and devices. These included a Braille book, Braille-writing equipment, talking calculator, talking clock, Braille watch, tape measure, disc and cassette as forms of recorded books, organization of paper currency and identification of coins, the long cane, dog guide, and demonstration of human guide techniques.

In these settings I begin by asking the children, "What is one problem you think of when a person is blind?" I do not know what will be the answer. Nevertheless, I use it as a jumping-off place. For instance, if a child says, "The person can't read," I then introduce Braille reading and writing. If a child says, "He bumps into things," I present the long cane and dog guide.

I encourage the children to ask many questions. Beforehand, I alert the teachers not to be embarrassed by the questions, that I will not be disturbed by them and that the teachers should not be either. Children's questions might include: How do you shop for groceries? How do you know whether it is day or night? How old are you? How do you shop for dresses? Do you live alone, or does someone take care of you?

Along the way, I ask the children, "What do you use when you eat?" They respond with "spoon," "fork," and "knife." When I push for more answers, I may hear "hand." With more pushing on my part, I may hear silence. Sometimes a more sensitive child offers "eyes" — exactly what I want. A blind individual does not have assistance from eyes in eating or in writing to sign his name. He signs his name more with muscle memory than vision.

In one school, I talked with all six grades in the building, two grades at a time: first and second grades together, third and fourth, fifth and sixth. Kindergarten was last. With each level, I changed my vocabulary to fit the children's comprehension. I explained to the kindergarten that my dog was a guide dog, why I have a guide dog, what "guide" means, how the dog helps me, etc. I thought I was communicating with these youngsters.

After the session, a girl came to share with me that she, too, had a dog. I said I was glad she had a dog friend. She went on to tell me that her dog was a girl dog, not a *guy* dog like mine!

Schools have invited me back repeatedly, indicating satisfaction with my presentations.

Referring to the talking calculator above reminds me of an experience one of my graduate students had. While enrolled in a mathematics methods course as an elective, he mentioned to the class that the blindness field has a talking calculator. The instructor protested that the student was wrong, that if such an item existed, she would know about it, because mathematics was her field of professional training.

After that class, the student came to my office to request permission to take our talking calculator to his next math class. I eagerly concurred. In class, he demonstrated the talking calculator, educating other students and especially the instructor.

One of the pleasures and luxuries of retirement is having time to remember and reflect upon past experiences, not only what we have done but more especially the impact others have had on us.

Because young persons are our country's most valuable commodity, I advocate in their behalf. This is why I have included in this last chapter memories of youth's impromptu responses that reveal their reactions to the reality of blindness and of university students' hunger to know whether campus life is truly as consumed by sex, drugs, and alcohol as some others boast.

I recall a student who on Monday said to me, "I saw you yesterday morning, all dressed up, walking on Eighth Avenue. Where on earth were you going at that time of day?"

My simple response was "to church."

That question jolted me. It would not have surprised me to hear, "I don't go to church." The question, "Where were you going on a Sunday morning?" however, stunned me, that in our country an American had to ask the question rather than assume "She is probably going to church." Even if the student's family had never attended church, the assumption that other people might go seems natural.

Another aspect of the issue might be that this student could have come from generations of university graduates who abandoned church attendance once "educated," feeling no further need for spiritual guidance. He may have assumed that I, a university faculty member, surely would have discarded such an opiate years earlier.

I am reminded of a graduate student from Taiwan. Because his advisor, Mel Weishahn, was going to be out of town when the student arrived on campus, Mel requested that I be available to assist his student in adjusting to his new environment.

After having read his first issue of the campus newspaper, the student visited me, troubled. He explained that he had just read the campus paper but could not find a section on religion.

I explained that the paper was published by students and that they included only topics of interest or importance to them.

The absence of attention to religion disturbed him. "That is sad," he said. "Then head may be full, but heart is empty!" I had to agree. After that, he accepted my invitations to accompany me to church on a regular basis.

Many Taiwanese students attended the University of Northern Colorado. A few majored in education of visually-impaired and blind children.

In 1981, Dr. Shirley M. Carriar, Professor of English, and I took a Caribbean cruise on the *Love Boat*. After flying to Puerto Rico, we boarded the ship. The first day, with rough water, we traveled without stopping until reaching Barbados where passengers went ashore. While there, I bought a sunhat that I continue to wear during Colorado's intense heat! Its five-inch brim completely around the circular hat provides adequate protection. It also rolls up conveniently, though made of straw.

Then on each of the next several days, we stopped at an island until we returned to San Juan.

When we returned to Colorado, we encountered snow after our warm experience in the Caribbean.

My first stop in Greeley was to rejoin Ruthie who had been boarded at Dr. Freemyer's Eldred Animal Hospital. She leaped to lick my cheek before I had time to bend to pat and hug her.

Later that same year, I received a telephone call from Taiwan, from Dr. Mao Lian-Wen who invited me to present a paper at an international conference on special education to be held in Taipei. Because Dr. Mao, my graduate and now my host, advised me not to bring my dog to Taiwan because some natives there eat dog meat, I planned to go alone, knowing I would have escorts once I arrived in Taipei.

On the Friday before I was scheduled to leave the U. S. on Monday, Joan Ord, one of our graduates who worked in Denver, drove to Greeley to have lunch with me. In telling her about my forthcoming trip, I piqued her interest. I related that Dr. Mao had said that I might bring a friend. If she paid her airfare, all other expenses would be borne by Taiwan. Joan excitedly expressed her desire to go with me. However, she still had to process her passport and purchase a plane ticket to match mine. Could she accomplish this by Monday evening when I would be boarding a 747 China Airline?

Joan left Denver Monday morning, hoping to achieve her goal of flying to Taiwan with me.

Literally, at the last minute, I learned that Joan Ord was going with me. I did not know this until I was already in San Francisco preparing to meet my China Airline plane at midnight. If she had not appeared, I was prepared to go alone.

The flight on the 747 was thirteen hours in darkness plus several other hours.

Announcements on board were in English and two other languages that I identified as Japanese and Chinese. Because the English announcement always ended with THANK YOU, I assumed that the other two languages also ended with equivalent words. I concentrated on the Chinese and learned *Sheh*-sheh. I decided to use it when the attendant served tea. She said in surprise, "You know Chinese!" I explained how I had learned THANK YOU by listening to the announcements.

At Taipei, Dr. Mao met us and escorted us to the Five-Star hotel where delegates were lodged.

During the conference, attendees listened with headphones on various channels to the same presentations disseminated in multilingual versions depending on which channel had been chosen. For instance, while I was reading my paper in English on the English-language channel, other readers were reading my paper in Chinese, Japanese, French, Korean, an Indian dialect, etc.

For the benefit of translators, each presenter had been requested to send the paper weeks ahead of the conference to provide translators time to translate the paper from one language into another.

My paper was about the value in special education and rehabilitation of reading biographies and autobiographies about and by writers who have experienced disabilities and applying that information to supplement textbooks about special education and rehabilitation.

At mealtime, each event was a festive banquet with perhaps fifteen courses. Each item of food, such as fish or a specific vegetable or soup or fruit or squid or shark tongue or chicken foot or rice or pork, etc. was a course, each brought separately on its respective plate, removed, and replaced by the next. Taiwanese hospitality was of very high standard of national pride. Alcoholic toasts were abundant to honor one guest or another with that guest honoring the host similarly.

After the conference which last three days, Joan and I traveled the country, visiting colleges and programs for blind children, all prearranged by Dr. Mao. Everywhere we went, I was introduced as Dr. Mao's professor. Dr. Mao's name was known throughout the island as Minister of Education. I spoke slowly in English, sentence by sentence, allowing the interpreter to insert in Chinese what I had just said.

On a train to Kaoshung, Joan was concerned that we would not understand the announcement for Kaoshung and disembark at the wrong station. When I heard Kaoshung, I urged Joan that this was our stop, but she was now apprehensive that this was not our designated station. Happily, this was Kaoshung, where someone was waiting to greet us and escort us to lunch with Harbormaster Wu, who was awaiting our arrival.

Afterward, Joan and I toured a department store. One floor was devoted to groceries. The top floor was a playground for children. Cashiers used both abacus and cash register but seemed more comfortable with the former. At this store, I bought a suitcase on wheels to accommodate gifts that Joan and I had already received and gifts that we would continue to receive as Dr. Mao's international guests.

After our more formal appointments had been met, persons in Taipei took Joan and me on sight-seeing tours, some with overnight stays in resorts. Our driver wanted to show me the statue of a lion where he guided my finger to its eye and said "Ear" and to its ear and said "Eye." At another site, he asked to be permitted to walk with the professor.

After all the sightseeing adventures, Joan and I were again in Taipei, walking a main street at noon. When Joan noticed a young man following us and coming closer, she expressed apprehension about his motives. I felt no alarm. When he came abreast of us, he asked whether we speak English. He said that he wanted to practice using his English.

Although we had stopped in Honolulu and Tokyo, we had limited time on the ground except to walk about in the terminals while our plane refueled and attendants cleaned the cabin. In Honolulu, we noticed immediately high humidity.

When I returned to Greeley, my first stop was to retrieve Ruthie. I was prepared this time for her type of greeting. Our reunion was sweet, making both of us whole again.

In retrospect, my very special, special education teacher, Katharine Taylor, reshaped my life from what it had been under Mamma's warped and stultifying influence to what it became when I was an adult. Miss Taylor not only ignited a candle in my mind but also taught me to focus on my dreams, saying, "Grace, you can become whatever you set your heart on achieving. Dare to reach and stretch beyond what is within your immediate grasp. Listen to your own heart rather than to others' lesser expectations for you." I think she was guiding me away from my mother's domineering, negative spirit without identifying her.

I want each of our graduates to be a Katharine Taylor in the lives of children whom they teach.

The subtitle of this book is *Unshackled*. I should like to elaborate on that as it applies to me. When I first met Katharine Taylor and later appreciated fully her impact in my life, Subconsciously, I knew even as a young child, that Mamma's approach to life and her influence on me was wrong. With Katharine Taylor in my life, I became unshackled from Mamma and her negative and damaging and imprisoning vise-like grip on me.

When I trained with Rachel, my first dog guide, and brought her home, I experienced the freedom in mobility possible with a dog guide. With all of my dog guides and the countless miles that we have walked and the distances that we have traveled, I have been unshackled from the fetters that blindness may have on us, if we permit blindness to limit the size of our world.

In college, I experienced firsthand social acceptance by my peers and faculty and the reality of how education is the key to doors to release us from poverty. I had witnessed my relatives employed in seasonal work, not having health insurance, never taking a real vacation, wondering when and from where the next paycheck would come, being told during the Great Depression, "You are not eligible for food stamps, because you own your house." But how could someone sell his house in the Great Depression? They had no medical insurance; without it, they could not learn about their own health problems and have them treated to prolong life. They had no Medicare coverage, no Social Security, no pension. Their savings were meager and insecure. They lacked the education to pass Civil Service examinations in order to rise to jobs with more security and steady income. My father had a three thousand dollar mortgage with which to build his home in 1925, but it took him more than twenty years to pay it off, though he scrimped and saved barely enough to pay the interest twice a year during all that time. I have been unshackled from such poverty by being employed as a teacher for forty-one years (1945-1986). I have paid Income Tax as many seeing individuals have done and are still doing. When someone received a three thousand dollar scholarship, he paid no Income Tax on it. When I earned sixteen hundred dollars from Syracuse University, I paid Income Tax on it.

As an educated person with four university degrees, I appreciate having been taught to be a critical thinker and critical reader. This does not mean finding fault but rather not making snap judgments and unfounded conclusions. For instance, I know a woman who in 2004 was slavishly for President George W. Bush but admitted that she did not read newspapers or magazines or listen to news reports on radio or television! What kind of citizen responsibility was she exhibiting as a voter except "Don't confuse me with the facts. My mind is already made up." With education, I have been unshackled from her mental blindness greater than my ocular blindness. In my own family, I have witnessed bigotry and prejudice toward individuals or groups of individuals about whom my family knew very little and did not associate with them.

By attempting to protect my health by keeping my weight down, eliminating certain foods, including nutritious foods, by much walking, especially when younger, I have attempted to prolong my life as a healthier individual, especially when knowing that cardiac conditions exist in my family history. I have outlived my father who died at 52, my mother at 65, and my brother at 72 in addition to most of my cousins, all of whom died because of heart disorders. Now at eighty-five, I have a similar health problem but have helped to postpone the impact of it until recently. I am unshackled by having helpful information received through education and reading to help prolong my life.

Recently, I have belonged to a reading group. After the book has been selected, the members of the group read it independently and then met on a designated date to discuss the book. The present book and the preceding one have much foul language, gutter words, and blasphemy in them. Two meetings ago, I mentioned my displeasure. I absented myself from the most recent meeting, explaining why. Why can authors not pen the intended emotions without resorting to vulgarity and blasphemy? Do they lack the vocabulary to achieve this goal? Is this the way such authors speak in their daily lives? My friends and relatives do not talk this way. Neither do I.

As a Christian, I am offended to read the names of Jesus and God dragged into the gutter instead of being revered and respected. If Jesus were to walk into my home and find me reading such books, I would be deeply ashamed and saddened by my un-Christian behavior. These are not great books worthy of my time, effort, and thought. Publishers do not necessarily produce books because publishers consider them great literature; rather, publishers know that many consumers will buy such books, regardless of their filthy language—but I have digressed.

Although my family received a daily newspaper, I am unsure whether anyone in the family read editorials and thought-provoking articles. I have been unshackled by being able to read via Braille books and magazines, recorded books and magazines, via the computer, digital books, even printed material through the use of Optacon and scanner, as well as through a live reader in a face-to-face situation. Who would have thought when I was a child that I would some day be reading print books?

My nine dog guides have enabled me to be a student or faculty member on several campuses, to be an itinerant teacher, to travel without requiring a human guide to accompany me to supervise students in practicum sites throughout the country. I live alone independently, without a caregiver. I exercise autonomy over my own life and project a positive image in order to encourage, by example, other blind individuals to destroy the mold that many persons—blind or sighted—expect us to fill. I have encountered some persons who prefer that I lean on them in order that they may feel needed and in charge of my life. True friendships cannot be established when one person discourages independence in another individual, merely to make the seeing person feel important and superior. I have had to break away from such individuals in order to exercise my right as an individual who is blind to assert myself rather than be a submissive, clinging vine, because someone thinks that role is appropriate for me.

I have discussed my marriage in great detail. I will not here review or summarize it. Suffice it to say when I divorced my husband, I became unshackled from an abusive, controlling, and mentally-ill man. I was confident that I could survive very well without him; I had been doing so even when married to him. I retained my married name because I felt that twenty-one years of marriage was a reality in my life. Returning to my maiden name would not erase the facts of having been married.

The foregoing paragraphs may sound like gloating and boastfullness; that is not intended. Instead, I am thinking of blind or visually-impaired children too young to read this book now and their parents. You can be a Katharine Taylor in the life of your own son or daughter by allowing your child to become the independent adult God intended him or her to be. Every parent's responsibility is to teach his or her child how to become a responsible adult rather than a needlessly prolonged child.

In 2002 and 2003, my two novels portray the main character, Marissa, as a composite of several competent blind women I know in order to convey to readers a positive image of a woman who happens to be blind. The books are intended as much to be educational as entertaining. Although my second novel contains many accounts about my dogs' amazing behaviors, I will record a few more in this volume, plus other anecdotes scattered throughout my life.

When I was commuting to visit my husband every weekend, I used a bus and train to Paoli, Pennsylvania. On our return trip to Philadelphia and back to New Jersey, my dog and I walked a certain route inside the train terminal to the outside. After doing this for several weeks, my dog changed our route to the outside. Because she did it confidently, I followed obediently, assuming that our former path was blocked for whatever reason. After that, my dog always chose her own way to an exit—a way that was shorter than the way we had been following. Apparently, she reasoned that the goal was to exit the terminal and that she knew a shorter and more direct way to the outside.

When I was a graduate student at Temple University and living near the campus, we were en route to class one stormy afternoon with a cold rain and sleet pelting us directly in the face. Although I lowered my head to avoid the full impact, my dog had the responsibility to see even though at a great disadvantage. My destination was the door at the far end of this long building and from there a flight of stairs up to our classroom.

Several times Vicki turned to the right, but I urged her forward to the far end of the building.

Finally inside the building out of the storm, we reached the classroom, and I sat beside a woman classmate. We discussed the storm outdoors. I explained how my dog tried to turn right several times. I wondered whether she was confused because of the rain in her face. The lady began to chuckle. "Grace, I think your dog is smarter than both of us. I, too, am accustomed to walking on the outside to the far end of the building, but your dog saw doors along the side of the building and was trying to use those entrances to escape the storm. Both you and I took the long way outside when we could have entered any of those doors and then walked inside the building to its far end. You and I did not have the sense to get out of the rain, but your dog tried to help you do that." Both of us enjoyed the joke on ourselves.

While living at Bonell Good Samaritan Community, I had been out for the evening to the retirement party of one of my graduates. Another graduate offered to drive me home. Although we were on the Bonell campus, the driver parked her car in a spot unfamiliar to me when I left the car. Unsure about which direction to go, I relied on Waffle's knowing where to go. I said, "Waffle, want a vitamin?" She thinks her vitamin tablets are a treat, not medicine, so she immediately swung in the right direction and unerringly led me to my front door. Yes, I did give her the vitamin tablet as her reward. She had earned it.

One year during Thanksgiving week, snow began falling on Monday and continued until Thanksgiving afternoon. Although Wednesday was a vacation day for faculty and students, the announcement on Wednesday morning's radio was, "All employees report for work." I considered myself an employee. The announcement had not used the words "buildings and grounds employees" or "civil service employees," but just said unspecified "employees."

Ruthie and I headed to the campus with no paths to ease Ruthie's work, since the blizzard had quickly obliterated them. After we reached the far side of McKee Hall, we had an open area to cross before reaching the library building where my office was located. With drifts and no paths, Ruthie had to jump over piles of snow. My only command to her was, "Where is it?" I could not direct her with "left," "right," or "forward." I felt sure that she would reach the library because of many prior trips to my office. After a most irregular "walk," she stopped at the door we usually used.

Inside, very few employees of any type were present. I busied myself in my office for an hour before a phone call from the main special education office relayed a message that the president had declared that everyone should go home.

Happily, one of my colleagues, LeAnn Olson, offered to drive me home. I gladly accepted. En route, the car became stuck in the snow several times before reaching my home. I was so proud of Ruthie's ability to work in deep snow without paths and to arrive at my destination.

When Rachel, my first dog, and I explored the neighborhood, we passed my grandfather's home on Second Street and continued through the next block where we were met by several unfriendly small dogs belonging to the last house on the block. Rachel worked very well under unnerving conditions. She had not been attacked, but the dogs were at our heels with threatening sounds.

A week or so later, I walked past my grandfather's house again and crossed the next street. On the far side, Rachel, without a command from me, turned left and proceeded along that block. I understood her behavior; she had really been intimidated by those dogs. To avoid them, we walked two sides of the block and crossed the street before Rachel was willing to turn right to reach Second Street. Rachel's behavior told me just how much she did not want to encounter those curs again.

When I was a student at Syracuse University in 1956, Beryl Nuzum and I lived in Sims Hall. The next summer, when I was faculty, I lived in Hafts Dormitory. Out for a walk one day, my dog Vicki and I meandered with no thought on my part about our location relative to Sims. When abreast of Sims Hall, Vicki turned in as if to enter that building. Only then did I realize the significance of Vicki's behavior.

She had remembered after a year where we once had lived for a summer session. Although I knew where I was in relation to other known streets and buildings, I had not specifically thought about Sims Hall, but to Vicki that building had obviously taken on a warm and friendly connotation.

While I was employed for ten summers at Syracuse University, many of us who were summer-only faculty went out to dinner together in the evening. Sometimes we numbered twelve or fourteen at one restaurant.

One man in the group drank several cocktails before the food arrived, several during dinner, and a few more after dinner. When the check arrived, he suggested self-servingly, "Let's just divide it by twelve (or fourteen); that's so much simpler." This went on each time he was with us. He liked these big groups so he could use his gesture of "Let's do it the easy way."

Several members of the group did not like his maneuver, but no one ever challenged him. Toward the end of summer session, he pulled it again. I spoke up: "No. If you want to drink several cocktails at one meal, that's your privilege. However, be a man and pay for all of your cocktails and stop expecting us to pay for your drinks." He said not a word in protest.

Afterward, several in the group said, "I'm so glad you said what you did. I wanted someone to say it, but I wasn't brave enough to say it myself."

During the summer, faculty members who lived in Syracuse entertained us by inviting us to their homes. The host approached each guest by asking, "What drink may I bring you?" I simply said, "Gingerale will be fine. Thank you." I did this all through the summer.

The wife of a faculty member said, "I have noticed that at each gathering you do not drink alcohol. Is that a matter of principle or health?"

I answered simply, "My principle is to protect my health."

Once a summer, the chancellor entertained us at his home. He mailed each of us a written invitation that included the beginning and ending times, such as from 8:00 to 9:45. Later he confided to some of us that originally some guests stayed as long as liquor was available. After that, he included the beginning and ending times in order to rid himself of those who were not savvy enough to leave at an appropriate time.

Dredging up these memories is great fun after all these years.

One summer at Syracuse, we were pleased to have Dr. Ed King from England with us. Two years later he was with us again.

When I heard his voice, I knew immediately who he was—but what is his name? I lingered to the end of the welcoming line. What is his name, I pondered. I still did not recall it when it was my turn to greet him, but aided by epiphany, I greeted him with, "How is everything in Reading?"

His response was, "You do remember me!" He was pleased, and I was greatly relieved that I had finally remembered his hometown, impressing him with that detail others might have forgotten.

When individuals comment about how well I am aging and ask my secret for maintaining youthfulness, I say, "Do as I do: Don't use a mirror! Then you can't fret about a new wrinkle or sagging skin. If you don't know about them, you have less to fuss about." On a more serious note, aging is a natural phase of life. A sense of humor and an optimistic attitude go a long way to preserve that quality of life that slows the ravages of aging whether wrinkles are present or still less evident. In truth, what I do or don't do may have nothing to do with how youthful I appear. The answer may be in my genes, and I did nothing to select them.

I recall reading a term paper from one of my international students. Suddenly, an alarm inside my head rang loudly. What I heard as my reader progressed sounded *very* familiar. *I think those are my words*, I told myself. I asked my reader whether quotation marks had been used or whether a footnote gave attribution to the author. The answer was no to both questions.

I referred to one of my publications and zeroed in on a specific chapter. Yes, word for word from an extended passage was plagiarism as bold as can be. The student must have used a copy in the university library.

However, international students from certain countries claim to have heard nothing about plagiarism. They are supposed to have been taught about plagiarism as soon as they arrive in the United States, where they have their use of listening comprehension and spoken English skills evaluated for graduate study in our country. Perhaps either some students claim ignorance, or old habits die hard.

I discussed plagiarism with this student and how it is wrong in our country and showed him how his writing should be done when he wanted to quote another person's published writing. Perhaps, he thought he was flattering me by using material that I had written earlier. Perhaps, he truly did not know how to do it our way. Copying material from his own professor would certainly not go unnoticed.

How can any published material in countries that practice plagiarism, as we know it, attribute any thought to the original author? Here is an example of how it goes: Mr. A is the original author. Mr. B copies from Mr. A with no attribution. Mr. C copies from Mr. B. Mr. D copies from C. Mr. E copies from Mr. B. Mr. F copies from Mr. A, etc.

For a memory on a lighter vein, in 1948 when I was a patient in the hospital in Passaic, New Jersey (the city adjacent to Clifton), my mother was with me. I was Mrs. Napier; Mother was Mrs. Donkersloot.

When a nurse learned Mamma's name, the nurse told her, "You can go into the kitchen to get whatever Grace needs. Just help yourself."

Because I thought this very unusual, I asked, "Why is my mother permitted to go into the kitchen with such freedom?"

"Because she is Mrs. Donkersloot," I was told.

I added, "We have several Mrs. Donkersloots in the family. Why is she an exception?"

"Isn't she *the* Mrs. Donkersloot, the nurse, who has studied the Sister Kenny practice of therapy for polio patients?" she asked.

"No. That Mrs. Donkersloot is Liza. This one here is Carrie, who is not a nurse," I supplied.

"Oh, I see my error. Thank you for clarifying that situation for me!"

I never asked Mamma to go into the kitchen to get food or drink for me.

Another recollection is of attending general faculty meetings (for all departments of the university), when certain officials or chairs of departments distributed pages of materials to all present except to me. I would have to ask for my copy after being passed by. The comment, meant in apology, was, "But you can't read it," or "Because it is not in Braille, it won't be of any use to you," etc.

I might say in rebuttal, "I am not illiterate." I might not have been able to read the material then, but I could read it in my office or at home with my variety of technology, which was unknown by the "wise one." Even though we were all on the faculty of the same university, some colleagues would place me several notches beneath them, assuming that my only access to reading is Braille. Each time they did this, it revealed their ignorance and arrogance. Even if I could not read print,someone could read it to me. Was it a waste of paper that would bankrupt the university to supply me with a copy nonetheless?

I think of another faculty member who, whenever addressing me, said, "Hello, Grace. This is Dr. − −." I was never Dr. Napier.

When I had occasion to phone his home to speak with his wife, he answered. I said, "Hello, Frank. This is Dr. Napier. May I please speak with your wife?"

On another occasion when vice presidents of the university were present at a social, someone mentioned music that I had composed. A vice-president said, "Oh, I didn't know you compose."

I refrained from saying, "How would you know? You don't really know me. When did we ever have a genuine conversation?"

When I was scheduled to speak to a group off campus, a colleague in that group said to someone, who repeated it to me, "What of value can she tell us?"

The point of including the last several examples is to illustrate that when a person of a minority group (female or other minority) is on the faculty of a university, this is no guarantee of equality with all other colleagues. The tone that permeates is, "She can't work as hard as we men do" or "She can't produce scholarly material or make a solid contribution to the university." Some of you may maintain that your contributions affect every department of the university. Has your contribution ever impacted special education and rehabilitation of the same university?

Not all faculty meetings are productive or worth the time invested in them. One faculty meeting began with the announcement that paying five cents for a cup of coffee in the office was not clearing expenses, now that the price of coffee had risen in stores. The chair should have made an administrative decision: "From now on, a cup of coffee in the office will cost a dime in order to clear expenses," and moved to the next agenda item. Instead, he spent *forty-five minutes* permitting individuals to sound off on the subject!

After my first two dogs had died, I had a dream that I, carrying my dog harness, had gone to heaven. There, I witnessed each dog's trying with eagerness to insert her head into the harness. Faced with a dilemma, I did not know which dog to harness. Whichever dog I chose, the feelings of the other dog would be injured. Then, with relief, I remembered that in Heaven I would not need a dog guide, because my blindness would be a condition of the past. Then I could love the dogs, not for how they help me, but for their own sweet loving selves, God's gift to humanity.

The previous paragraphs are a mishmash of memories, much like a photo album. As you turn pages, you see scenes unrelated to each

other except that all of them occurred in the same life of one individual. A few are sad as when my husband threw his life into the hands of
a drug dealer; others are perceived as injustices. The majority are my
Heavenly Father's goodness and greatness manifested in my life.

Because my father was my strong encourager and emotional
support, I wish that he had witnessed my professional growth and
advancement. The only teaching position that he knew about was at
Royer-Greaves School—nothing to write home about, as the expression goes. He would have been so pleased to know about the honors
bestowed on me, listed later.

In 2006, I underwent a total-knee surgery, rather common surgery
nowadays. The outcome was very successful. However, the process to
recovery was problematic. I had had several surgeries in my life with
excellent results. This last surgery, unfortunately, caused delirium for
several weeks! The surgeon and physician were extremely concerned,
I learned much later. Immediately after surgery, I remember hearing
the surgeon tell me that she had not needed my extra blood I had donated before the surgery and that she would give it back to me later
that day. That is the last that I remember for several weeks! I was unable to separate dream, hallucination, and reality. Only gradually did
my memory return. Even after I returned home after seven weeks, I
went to the telephone to call someone but had forgotten how to use
the phone! A few days later, that skill returned.

I had a shattering glimpse of what Alzheimer's disease must be
like – not to know where you are, who you are, how to do the sim-
plest of tasks, who the people are visiting you, etc. It is a horrendous
and harrowing experience from which to emerge. I am truly grateful
and amazed to have regained my memory. Some patients in similar
predicaments fail to recover their memory. I shudder at the thought!
Aside from that nightmarish experience, I consider myself richly
blessed, though with painful arthritis and with a cardiac condition,
at age eighty-five.

Someone has asked me which unfulfilled ambition I would like to experience. I would enjoy being a college or university commence-ment speaker. I feel that I have something different to offer graduates from messages by politicians, government officials, financiers, indus-trialists, scientists, general educators, or psychologists. I'm available. The honors alluded to are as follows:

1) Bryan Gerritsen of Utah, one of our earlier students, nominated me during my retirement for recognition by the Western Divi-sion of the Association for Education and Rehabilitation of the Blind and Visually Handicapped (AERBVH) for my creation in 1969 at the University of Northern Colorado of the dual pro-gram combining (A) academics and (B) orientation and mobility (O&M) in the preparation of teachers to equip them with both sets of competencies to serve especially blind children enrolled in small school districts. I attended the meeting in Estes Park, Colorado, thanks to Irene Boettcher, one of my P .E .O. sisters, who provided transportation. Besides hearing spoken com-mendation, I received a plaque. That has been my only public acknowledgement by the field of blindness of my contribution of the dual program even though many other universities have since duplicated it. Thank you, Bryan.

2) During my M.Ed. degree program in 1959, I had the highest grade point average (GPA) of all graduate women in the Col-lege of Education at Temple University. In each of Temple's colleges (Medicine, Law, Theology, Engineering, Fine Arts, Sci-ence, etc.), each dean determined which graduate woman of the college had earned the highest GPA. In 1959, women in ed-ucation were already numerous, serving in roles of instructors, supervisors, department heads, principals of schools, superin-tendents of school districts, and faculty members of post-sec-ondary institutions. On the other hand, women in engineering, medicine, theology, and pure science were less numerous and deserved public acclaim. Each of us, representing her respec-

tive college, was interviewed separately by a special committee which would present only one cash gift to a outstanding
pioneer. Readers must be reminded that this was in 1959 and
not 2005.

In 1968, in my doctoral program at Temple, I again had the
highest GPA of all graduate women in Education. The whole
process repeated itself.

3) Rutgers University's Douglass College (named for its first dean)
   created the Douglass Society to honor distinguished alumnae
   in the middle or late 1970s. I was among the first fifty or fifty-
   five of the college's alumnae to be so honored with induction in
   1979 into the Douglass Society, selected from among thousands
   of graduates before and after me since the founding of the college in 1918.

4) The Greeley chapter of the American Business Women's Association (ABWA) selected me as its Woman of the Year, eligible
   to attend the national convention in Minneapolis at the expense
   of the chapter.

5) During my M.Ed. program at Temple University, one of our
   assignments with Dr. Miriam E. Wilt was to write a research paper related to the content of the course. Because I wanted to relate reading and writing in Braille, I did a word-count study of
   first-grade basal readers to determine the most frequent words
   containing Braille contractions and of them the most frequently
   occurring Braille contractions which would then become the
   first contractions to be taught in writing.

   For instance, *ST* was one of those contractions. When a child
   knew how to write the *ST* sign, he could write a multitude of
   words, such as *stop, Steve, fast, store, stay, still, stick, most,* etc.
   I wanted to keep the first group of words limited to only one
   contraction per word. When other contractions might be included, the child has even greater independence: *(st)(and), fa(st)*

(er), si(st)(er), (st)epp(ing), etc. The writing vocabulary provided great mileage for writing independence for young children.

My paper included columns of words derived from six series of basal readers and all the numbers of words with contractions. Everything was documented. My efforts uncovered the most frequent and, therefore, useful contractions to be taught to beginning writers of Braille. My study was cited in one of our professional journals.

Dr. Wilt was duly impressed. Her commendation included, "This study would qualify as a doctoral dissertation if you were a doctoral candidate."

6) As my retirement approached, I received word from the president's office that I would be receiving a diploma designating me "Professor Emeritus of Special Education." I wrote to the president to point out that as a woman, I am not Emeritus but Emerita! At NJC we had learned that as a single graduate we are alumna; as a group of graduates we are alumnae. Alumnus and alumni pertain to males. Similarly, emeritus and emeriti are male.

The president responded that he would make the change, but at commencement I would receive the emeritus diploma but later I would receive the correct diploma. When he presented me with the diploma, he emphasized Emeri*ta.* I am uncertain whether the emphasis was in derision or whether he wanted to impress his audience with his correct usage of Latin.

Not every faculty member who is retiring is automatically declared "Emeritus." Some retire without that designation.

7) The greatest of honors for me is that God has made us His children by holy adoption! Can you imagine being the son or daughter of an earthly king? We would then be princes and princesses, be a son or daughter of God! Our Father is King of all kings, King above all other kings! When we love and follow God's Son, Jesus, God is pleased that we recognize the gift to us

that God has given us in His Son. As brother or sister of Jesus, we become members of God's family! This honor is the greatest of all of them, because I had done nothing to merit God's adoption of me, except to accept it by faith.

The Good Friday event shows three crosses, with a man on each. These crosses might be viewed as REPENTANCE, REDEMPTION, and REBELLION. Jesus, on the middle cross, is the only one who can provide redemption. Then as individuals, we are either repentant or rebellious. Which of the two we are is essential to know about ourselves. Without repentance, we cannot become a son or daughter of God and a brother or sister to Jesus.

I read or heard about a tombstone in a cemetery somewhere. It bore no name of a person or the dates of life – from and to. It had only one word inscribed on it. The word is: FORGIVEN! We do not know anything else about this deceased person. Does FORGIVEN relate to some heinous crime such as murder? We don't know. Or was this person already familiar with God and counted God's most important gift His forgiveness, even though he or she had not been a criminal in the usual sense of that word? We can only raise questions; we have no answers. However, the tombstone portrays the truth, namely, that the most important condition of life is being forgiven so long as we also supply forgiveness to others who seek it or deserve it.

The following, though historical, deliver a spiritual message. Napoleon from France and Wellington from England had their countries at war. At the end of a battle, a message about the outcome was sent via smoke signals from one hilltop to another until it reached London. However, fog intervened, making the reading of smoke signals difficult, even impossible. The message received in London was: WELLINGTON DEFEATED! The government and citizenry were devastated.

When the fog finally dissipated, the men responsible for sending smoke signals decided to send the message again because of not knowing where the fog had eradicated it. This time the entire message reached London: WELLINGTON DEFEATED NAPOLEON!

We had a similar situation on the first Good Friday when the message clearly seemed to be: JESUS DEFEATED! However, when Easter dawned and Jesus was seen alive, the correct message was: JESUS DEFEATED DEATH!

These three anecdotes summarize the gift of salvation. Are you in God's family? Do you know that you are forgiven? Are you repentant or rebellious? Do you see Jesus as defeated or as defeating death? Because we sinners fail miserably does not mean that our failures are Jesus' failures. You may know of excellent teachers whose students have not internalized what the teacher has taught. Don't blame the teacher for students who disregard the content of the teaching and stumble through life regardless of the excellent teachers they have had.

The paraphrased story of "Footprints" is worth repeating here. A man in a dream was walking along the beach and saw his life in review. When things were going well—graduation from college, excellent employment, marriage to a wonderful woman, birth of a beautiful and healthy son—he saw two sets of footprints in the sand, one pair his own and the other belonging to Jesus walking alongside him during those happy events and other joyous occasions.

When the man continued his dream along the beach, he was reminded of unhappy and tragic events when he saw only one set of footprints during the hardest times in his life, namely, when the house burned to the ground, when his wife died young from cancer, when his adult son was killed in an auto accident; however, he saw only his own footprints. Where was Jesus when he needed Him most? Why had Jesus deserted him in his most painful experiences?

In his dream, the man finally went to heaven and met Jesus face to face. The man of the story asked Jesus, "Why did you desert me when I needed you most?"

Jesus answered, "I have never deserted you. I was with you in happy times and in sad times."

The man protested, "I saw your footprints beside mine in happy times, but I saw only my footprints in sad times. Where were you, Jesus?"

Jesus responded, "When you saw only one set of footprints, those were mine, not yours. My child, I was carrying you!"

Have you ever been carried by Jesus? Are you too proud to admit that you needed carrying? Or are you consoled to have the confidence that when you cannot go on by your own strength, Jesus is there to carry you?"

I know, in fact, that Jesus has carried me when times were tough, as when my father died, when I learned that Chuck was a drug addict, when each of my dogs died, when Mamma abused me, when faculty caused stress, etc. I am grateful and appreciative that He was present to carry me. You men, especially, don't claim that you can do it all without any help, thank you. Jesus wants to help and has probably already helped you without your knowing it. It is more unmanly to claim that you don't need Jesus than it is to acknowledge Jesus in your life and what He has done for you in addition to saving your soul and providing eternity in Heaven with Jesus and God.

CPSIA information can be obtained
at www.ICGtesting.com
Printed in the USA
BVOW08s1307090617

486483BV00001B/1/P